*f*P

DRIVING
CUSTOMER
EQUITY

How Customer Lifetime Value
Is Reshaping
Corporate Strategy

Roland T. Rust

Valarie A. Zeithaml

Katherine N. Lemon

The Free Press

NEW YORK   LONDON   TORONTO   SYDNEY   SINGAPORE

THE FREE PRESS
A Division of Simon & Schuster, Inc.
1230 Avenue of the Americas
New York, NY 10020

Designed by Brady P. McNamara

Manufactured in the United States of America

1   3   5   7   9   10   8   6   4   2

Library of Congress Cataloging-in-Publication Data

Rust, Roland T.
Driving customer equity : how customer lifetime value is reshaping corporate strategy/
Roland T. Rust, Valarie A. Zeithaml, Katherine N. Lemon.
p.   cm.
Includes index.
1. Customer service. 2. Customer relations. 3. Marketing. 4. Strategic planning.
I. Zeithaml, Valarie A. II. Lemon, Katherine N. (Katherine Newell) III. Title.

HF5415.5 .R87 2000
658.8–dc21
00-026485

ISBN 0-684-86466-5

PERMISSIONS

The authors gratefully acknowledge permission from the following sources to reprint material
in their control:

Amazon.com, a registered trademark or trademark of Amazon.com, Inc. in the U.S.
and/or other countries, for the screen shot of the Amazon.com home page.
Copyright © 2000 Amazon.com. All rights reserved.

Arnold Communications, Inc. for the www3.vw.com/vwworld Web site page.

Chiharu Rust for the photograph of the Harley-Davidson rider.

Clint Clemens for the screen shot in the www3.vw.com/vwworld Web site page.

General Motors Media Archives for the 1999 Saturn Advertisement: "Saturn Homecoming."
Copyright © 1999 Saturn Corporation.

Kraft Foods, Inc. for the www.kraftfoods.com Web site page.

Mail Boxes Etc. for the www.mbe.com Web site page.
Copyright © 1997–1999, all rights reserved by Mail Box Etc.

Miele & Cie. GmbH & Co. for the www.miele.de/E/philosophie.html
Miele Company Philosophy Web site page.

To Grace Rust (1902–1999)—R.T.R.

To Pamela Kirkpatrick, for her guidance and dedication—V.A.Z.

To Loren Lemon, my best friend, for everything—K.N.L.

CONTENTS

PART IV
Managing Customer Equity

PREFACE

Companies everywhere know that they need to become more customer-focused, but many companies have no idea of how to implement this transformation. Systems, metrics, and strategies that are based on the outmoded, product-centered view of the world still dominate in most companies. The purpose of this book is to address this problem by helping companies reshape the way they approach corporate strategy. We do this by providing a conceptual framework to help companies to maximize their most important asset, the lifetime value of their customer base—their "customer equity."

The three of us converged on this book from different directions—Rust from the financial impact of service quality (Return on Quality), Zeithaml from service quality measurement and customer value, and Lemon from customer retention. Rust and Lemon began teaming up on understanding what was known about customer retention. Lemon's doctoral dissertation with Russell Winer at the University of California at Berkeley had persuaded her that customer satisfaction was not the only key driver of retention, a finding that was echoed in the managerial writings of Frederick Reichheld. At the same time, Rust, in his consulting work with a variety of companies, was hearing a need for an expanded strategic framework by which companies could trade off various corporate initiatives such as brand building and service. The work of Blattberg and Deighton on customer equity seemed to provide a promising direction. Using the concept of customer equity, we began searching for an expanded model of customer retention that could be used to drive strategy.

At the same time, Rust and Zeithaml were working on market segmentation based on customer profitability (the Customer Pyramid). Working in the banking industry, we were discovering that segmenting customers based on profitability was highly promising, and gave important managerial in-

sights. The two projects came together in our realization that customer profitability, customer lifetime value, and customer equity could be used to
drive strategy by recognizing the drivers of customer retention and brand
switching. Oddly enough, although brand switching models have been used
for many years in marketing, especially for consumer packaged goods, those
models have rarely, if ever, been used before to help understand customer
lifetime value and customer equity.

Mathematical modeling forms the foundation for much of what we describe in this book. Given the nature of this book, however, we did not dwell
on it. For those interested in the technical aspects, we provide greater detail
in an academic paper that is available from the first author. We felt that it
was important not to lose sight of the key findings by using too many equa-
tions, because there is a lot of insight to be gained without ever going near
the mathematics.

Our approach to strategy is the logical culmination of the shift from a
product economy and product-based thinking to a service economy and
customer-based thinking. We use the information and insights that can be
obtained from the profitability, behavior, and perceptions of individual customers to drive corporate strategy. In so doing, our framework clarifies the
relationship between customer value, brand equity, and relationship/reten-
tion management.

We hope that our book helps companies to complete the paradigm shift
from product focus to customer focus. To be truly customer-focused implies
organizing the company around customer equity and its drivers. Our book
is a blueprint of how to accomplish this goal. We would be most interested
to hear from you with regard to corporate applications of this framework.
We can be reached by email at roland.rust@owen.vanderbilt.edu (Rust),
ZeithamV@icarus.bschool.unc.edu (Zeithaml) or klemon@hbs.edu (Lemon).

Roland Rust
Valarie A. Zeithaml
Kay Lemon

ACKNOWLEDGMENTS

Many individuals deserve our heartfelt thanks for their professional contributions in making this book a reality. First, we are grateful to Harini Gokul, who worked many long hours to do the spreadsheet programming that formed the basis of our empirical examples. Tim Keiningham of Marketing Metrics provided invaluable direction and comments. We also thank our editor at Free Press, Robert Wallace, who not only believed in our concept, but also made a number of truly excellent suggestions that significantly improved the book. We greatly appreciate the assistance of Anne-Marie Sheedy, Editorial Assistant at Free Press. We also appreciated the many corporate executives who provided a sounding board, laboratory, and source of ideas for this book. We especially want to acknowledge Serban Teodoresco at DiverseyLever Consulting (Unilever), Jack Murph at DuPont Flooring Systems, and Fred Newell, of Seklemian/Newell, who made contributions to early drafts. Our students at Vanderbilt, North Carolina, and Harvard must also be acknowledged for stimulating many new thoughts. Last, but certainly not least, we owe a great debt to Cordy Cates, Cheryl Johnson and Natalie Zakarian, the finest administrative assistants on Earth.

Several institutions were also instrumental in allowing the book to develop. Vanderbilt's Center for Service Marketing provided research funding for the project. The Harvard Business School helped with many aspects of the production of the book, particularly the artwork. We especially thank Ele Jaynes and Peter Amirault, who were able to take our hand-written drawings and turn them into intelligible and effective figures. The Marketing Science Institute, and particularly Katherine Jocz, David Reibstein, and Rohit Deshpande, stimulated interest in the topic of customer lifetime value.

Finally, gratitude is due to our families for allowing us to focus on this project. Chiharu Rust stuck with her husband (RR) during the months when he worked so many hours that she questioned whether or not he remembered her name. Jim Palmer cooked dinners and folded wash to allow his wife (VZ) to spend extra hours in her home office writing. Loren Lemon provided the intellectual and emotional support to keep his wife (KL) going through the writing process, and Thomas Lemon handled the seemingly random contacts with his mom with great self-reliance. Thank you all.

Roland Rust
Valarie A. Zeithaml
Kay Lemon

BEYOND BRAND EQUITY

The business world is increasingly organizing itself around customers rather than products. This is an inevitable reaction to a series of historical trends. Customer focus requires a new approach: managing according to Customer Equity (the value of a firm's customers), rather than Brand Equity (the value of a firm's brands), and focusing on customer profitability instead of product profitability. In fact, as we will see in Chapter 2, a slavish devotion to product profitability can be hazardous to a company's health.

The Case for Customer Equity

From Brand Equity to Customer Equity

Our Argentinian friend Marcos was involved with launching a popular American consumer products brand in Argentina. The brand was already a top brand in the United States, Europe, and most of the world. It was number one in the market in terms of market share, although its quality was only equivalent to that of its competition, and its price was similar to most competing brands and greater than that of the discount brands. The brand was known worldwide, even in countries in which the brand was not available. By any measure this brand had outstanding Brand Equity. Everyone expected that such a powerful brand would quickly assume a dominant market position in Argentina, and subsequently in the rest of Latin America.

What actually happened came as a complete shock. When the brand was rolled out, it failed to gain much of a foothold. Its market share remained anemic, and the local brands continued their market superiority, in spite of the fact that their quality and price were no better than the American brand. How could such a thing happen to such a powerful brand, with its superior level of Brand Equity?

In retrospect, what happened was clear. The American brand had superior Brand Equity, but the domestic brands owned the customers. The American brand had more *Brand Equity,* but that was not enough. *Customer Equity,* not Brand Equity, was the key to market success.

What Is Customer Equity?

The long-term value of the company is largely determined by the value of the company's customer relationships, which we call the firm's *Customer Equity*. The term was introduced, in a somewhat different context, by Robert Blattberg and John Deighton.[1]

To clarify our use of the term, we define Customer Equity as follows:

> A firm's Customer Equity is the total of the discounted lifetime values of all of its customers.

In other words we view the value of the customer not only in terms of that customer's current profitability, but also with respect to the net discounted contribution stream that the firm will realize from the customer over time. Summing these up gives the total value of the customers of the firm, which we call Customer Equity.

Illustrating Customer Equity

For example, suppose a firm has two customers—Mr. A and Ms. B. Mr. A produces only $100 per year in contribution to profit, but is expected to remain a customer for ten years. Ms. B is expected to produce $200 in contribution to profit this year, but is not expected to remain a customer. The discounted lifetime value of Mr. A is (for the firm's current discount rate) $650. (Note that this is less than the $10 \times \$100$ total contribution for the ten years, due to discounting.) The discounted lifetime value of Ms. B is $200—the contribution received this year. Thus, the firm's total Customer Equity is $650 + $200 = $850.

It is easy to see that for most firms, Customer Equity is certain to be the most important component of the value of the firm. While the value of a firm's customers cannot be the entire value of the firm (for example, the firm's physical assets, competencies, and intellectual property also lend value), a firm's existing customers provide its surest and most reliable source of future revenues. Thus, figuring out how to drive Customer Equity is central to the decision making of any firm. Coherently formulating how to do this can give a firm an important competitive advantage.

The Inevitable Shift to Customer Equity

Several broad interrelated trends that are currently shaping economic change in every developed economy make it inevitable that management will shift its focus from Brand Equity to Customer Equity. The central implication of all of these trends is a shift from a product focus to a customer focus.

FROM GOODS TO SERVICES. The underlying basis for all of the trends is the dramatic long-term shift of every developed economy from goods to services (see figure 1-1). For example, in 1900, the percentage of workers in the United States in the service sector was approximately 30%. By 1970 that figure had risen to 64%,[2] and by 1995 that figure was about 77%.[3] Other developed economies lag behind the United States by a few years, but all show the same trend toward service, and similar percentages.[4]

FROM TRANSACTIONS TO RELATIONSHIPS. Let us consider, first, the "old" goods economy. Consider a customer of a typical consumer good—breakfast cereal. A customer might buy Kellogg's Corn Flakes this time, then switch brands the next time, and then switch the next time to something else. The goods economy tends to be relatively transaction-oriented. Management's attention is naturally drawn to the constant battle for attracting (rather than retaining) customers, and it is on that battlefield that Brand Equity reigns supreme.

Now consider the "new" service economy. Services work differently in

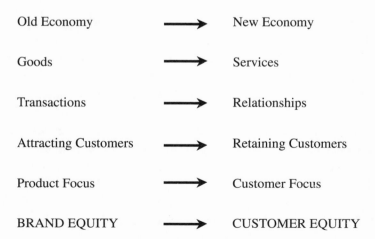

Old Economy ⟶ New Economy

Goods ⟶ Services

Transactions ⟶ Relationships

Attracting Customers ⟶ Retaining Customers

Product Focus ⟶ Customer Focus

BRAND EQUITY ⟶ CUSTOMER EQUITY

Figure 1-1. Long-Term Trends

the marketplace than goods. Think about a typical service—retail banking. A bank customer opens an account, and has dealings with the bank over time. The customer does not reconsider his/her choice of bank at every transaction, although a bad experience might trigger thoughts of switching. This has led to a shift from a focus on consumer transactions to a focus on long-term, one-to-one customer relationships, fostered by much work by Don Peppers and Martha Rogers.

FROM CUSTOMER ATTRACTION TO CUSTOMER RETENTION. For the bank, keeping or retaining customers is very important to the bank's success. Managing the relationship with the customer is very important and is central to the bank's thinking. While the bank still worries about attracting new customers, that issue must compete for management's attention with issues such as customer retention and cross-selling. On this battlefield, Customer Equity reigns, and Brand Equity plays a lesser role.

FROM PRODUCT FOCUS TO CUSTOMER FOCUS. In general the increasing emphasis on customers and relationship management coincides with a decreasing emphasis on products. It is not as though products are unimportant. It is just that they are secondary to satisfying the customer. Another way of thinking about this is that in a rapidly changing technological environment, products come and go, but customers remain. The secret to success is maintaining a profitable relationship with the customer, regardless of what products are involved, or how the products needed may change over time. Just as an automobile customer's needs and wants may shift over time from a Plymouth to a Chrysler to a Mercedes-Benz, a customer's brand preferences may change over time. The job of the modern company is to maintain the customer relationship (with DaimlerChrysler in this case) even while the individual customer's brand loyalty becomes irrelevant.

The Shift to Customer Equity. The continuing shift toward a service economy, thus, leads inexorably toward a shift in emphasis from Brand Equity to Customer Equity. However, unlike Brand Equity, which has been extensively studied by both business people and academics, little has been done at this point to understand Customer Equity. This book provides a framework for understanding Customer Equity and shows how this framework can help management focus its resources to maximize long-term profitability, through the successful cultivation of profitable customer relationships.

Where Do Profits Come From?

Almost every business carefully accounts for the profitability of its products. Detailed financial reports show the revenues and costs associated with each product, and each product's contribution to the company's bottom line. Profitable products are maintained or spun off into multiple, related products. For example, regular potato chips spin off into barbecue-flavored potato chips and low-fat potato chips. Unprofitable products are jettisoned. The seldom-questioned underlying assumption is that the product is what generates the profits. But is that true?

Consider a young retail bank customer. The customer first opens a checking account. Checking accounts are notorious money losers at retail banks, so the bank may be tempted to conclude that the checking account is an unprofitable product. However, what if the customer, having established a relationship with the bank, then opens a savings account, or takes out a car loan, or buys CDs, or takes out a home mortgage? If these events were made possible by the checking account, then the checking account would not look so bad after all. However, *product-specific accounting will never reveal this long-term view.*

Where did the bank's profits come from? It is clear that it was the long-term customer relationship that produced the profits. The profits of individual products are not separate and distinct, but rather synergize to produce a successful and profitable customer relationship.

This example shows that profitability needs to be analyzed with respect to customers. Product-specific financial accounting need not be abolished, but it should assume a lesser role. More important, detailed, customer-specific accounting is necessary to get an accurate picture of profitability and, hence, the long-term value of the firm.

Driving Customer Equity

While it is easy to see that Customer Equity is important, it is more difficult to determine exactly how to increase a firm's Customer Equity. Of all of the potential levers that a company might pull (e.g., advertising, quality, price, retention programs, etc.) which will yield the best return on investment? Where should the firm focus its efforts?

Value Equity

For all customers, choice is influenced by perceptions of value, which are formed primarily by perceptions of quality, price, and convenience. These perceptions tend to be relatively cognitive, objective, and rational (for example, there may be little argument about a product's price, or its objective attributes). We call the Customer Equity gained from customers' value perceptions the firm's Value Equity.

Brand Equity

Customers may also have perceptions of a brand that are not explained by a firm's objective attributes. (This view of Brand Equity is consistent with the definition of Brand Equity given by Wagner Kamakura and Gary Russell in their pioneering research on the topic.[5]) For example, a car may be considered sexy, or exciting, or classic. These perceptions tend to be relatively emotional, subjective, and irrational. We call the Customer Equity gained from the subjective appraisal of the brand the firm's Brand Equity.

Retention Equity

Customer Equity comes from customers choosing to do business with the company. Some of the firm's business comes from customers who chose the company in their most recent purchase occasion and this time choose it again, and some of the firm's business comes from customers who did not choose the firm last time or are new to the market. For repeat customers, retention programs and relationship-building activities can increase the odds that the customer will continue to choose the firm. We call the Customer Equity gained from retention programs and relationship building the firm's Retention Equity.

Where to Focus?

We can, thus, decompose Customer Equity into its constituent parts: Value Equity, Brand Equity, and Retention Equity. By determining which of these equities is most influential in a firm or its industry, we can then focus on the driver(s) of Customer Equity that has the greatest impact. Figure 1-2 shows a tree diagram, illustrating how a firm can think about the drivers of Customer Equity.

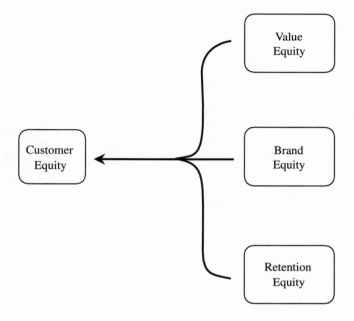

Figure 1-2. Drivers of Customer Equity

Customer Equity: The Key to Strategy

Analyzing Customer Equity and its drivers gives a company a road map for effective strategy. It identifies the strategic initiatives that will have the greatest impact on the long-term profitability of its customer base, which should be the primary concern of any business.

The rest of the book goes into considerable detail about how to use Customer Equity and its drivers as the basis for effective strategy. We also give specific examples of companies in five industries, using actual customer data. But before we get into detail, it is useful to have the big picture of how management can use these concepts to drive decision making. For this reason we first illustrate a simple, hypothetical example of how a company might proceed.

Let us consider XYZ Corporation in the widget industry. The company might first explore which of the Customer Equity drivers make the biggest difference in its industry (see figure 1-3). It is important to note that the results will not be the same in every industry. For example, in some industries (e.g., telephone service) Value Equity may be the key driver. In other, transaction-oriented industries (e.g., consumer package goods) Brand

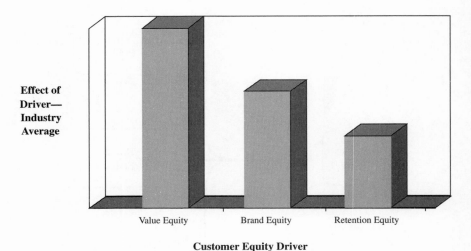

Customer Equity Driver

Figure 1-3. Relative Importance of Drivers in the Industry

Equity may be the most important. On the other hand, in some relationship-oriented industries (e.g., banking) Retention Equity may be the most important.

From figure 1-3 we can see that in the widget industry Retention Equity is the least important driver of Customer Equity (on average), and Value Equity is the most important. This is very useful information, because it tells XYZ that it should make sure that its Value Equity is very strong and maybe de-emphasize its retention initiatives.

Armed with this knowledge, XYZ can then consider its standing, relative to the best in the industry, on Customer Equity and its drivers, and compare it to the company's relative market share. We see from figure 1-4 that XYZ has a market share that is 80% as much as the leading firm in the industry, but its Customer Equity is only 60% of that of the leading firm. The fact that Customer Equity share is considerably less than the company's market share is a serious red flag, because it indicates that the long-term performance of XYZ is unlikely to be as strong as its current market share might suggest. Clearly XYZ needs to shore up its Customer Equity before its market performance deteriorates.

Figure 1-4 indicates clearly where XYZ should focus. Its Retention Equity is the best in the industry, but we already discovered (from figure 1-3) that Retention Equity was not very important in the widget industry. The key driver of Customer Equity in this industry (from figure 1-3) is Value

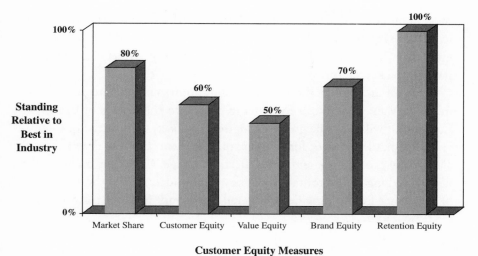

Figure 1-4. Relative Standing of the Company in Its Industry

Equity, and we see in figure 1-4 that XYZ's performance on Value Equity lags badly behind the competition. With this information, XYZ knows that it should focus its attention on Value Equity.

XYZ can then drill deeper into the drivers of Value Equity (see figure 1-5). We see that quality is the key driver of Value Equity, indicating that XYZ

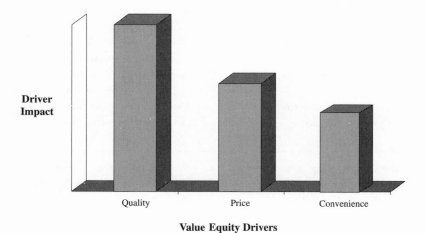

Figure 1-5. Drivers of Value Equity (Hypothetical Illustration)

must carefully examine its quality performance relative to the competition. If its perceived quality actually is worse than the competition, then the company must then drill down even deeper to identify the key drivers of quality, and perhaps the key sub-drivers of those drivers.

Such an analysis facilitates a rifle-shot approach to strategic decision making. Management can focus its resources on the drivers of Customer Equity that will have the greatest long-term impact. Customer Equity provides a broad framework for strategic management, by which executives of a company can identify and drive effective change. Customer Equity is the key to the long-term profitability of any firm, and analyzing the key drivers of Customer Equity provides an overall framework for effectively focusing strategic resources.

The remainder of the book makes the case for this customer-focused view and shows in detail how to implement a Customer Equity decision framework within an organization.

Beyond Brand Equity	
KEY INSIGHTS	ACTION STEPS
1. Brand Equity alone cannot ensure market share and market value of the firm.	• Find out what you currently use to measure your firm's performance. • Consider the history of your firm's products to identify unexplained product failures.
2. Customer Equity, the total lifetime value of the firm's customers, is the key to long-term market success.	• Find out what you know about the lifetime value of your firm's customers.
3. Profits come from customers rather than products.	• Determine whether your company is organized around products or customers.
4. The Customer Equity framework is key to developing a customer-centered corporate strategy.	• Prepare yourself for a dramatic shift in your way of thinking about your organization.

2

The Profitable Product Death Spiral

In 1997 the Opryland Hotel in Nashville, Tennessee, was a thriving convention hotel, with revenues of $231 million, and an 85% occupancy rate.[1] However, the adjoining Opryland Theme Park was far less profitable. The solution to the problem appeared clear to managers at Gaylord Entertainment, owner of the Opryland complex. The hotel was profitable, but the theme park was not. Therefore the theme park had to go.[2]

One year later, Opryland's convention room nights were down 22% from the previous year.[3] In fact, Nashville's entire tourist industry had been sent into a tailspin. It was evident that Opryland's hotel business (and the entire Nashville tourist business) had been badly hurt by the closing of Opryland Theme Park. In retrospect, what happened seems obvious. For individual customers, the presence of the theme park increased the value of the hotel. Why did Opryland's product-focused logic fail?

In chapter 1 we argued that management's thinking must shift from products and Brand Equity to customers and Customer Equity. But what happens if management does not think this way? Is any harm done? Can there be situations in which product thinking leads to disaster? As it turns out, such product thinking may lead to a disastrous outcome that we term the *Profitable Product Death Spiral.* Basing decisions on product profitability leads to predictable problems.

The Profitable Product Paradigm

Companies used to concentrating on Brand Equity find it natural to adopt a paradigm that we call the *Profitable Product Paradigm.* This seemingly reasonable viewpoint (see figure 2-1) involves the following steps:

1. Measure the profitability of the company's products.

2. Determine an acceptable level of profitability.

3. Eliminate products that do not meet the profitability threshold.

4. Go back to step one and repeat.

The Profitable Product Paradigm was made feasible in large companies by the growth of computer databases and computing technology. Consumer goods companies and retailers began to rely on product printouts that told the companies exactly which products were profitable, and which were not. Service companies, especially relationship service companies like banks and credit card companies, used their databases to figure out which services were

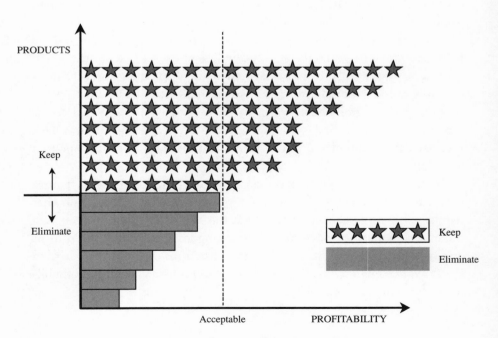

Figure 2-1. The Profitable Product Paradigm

profitable. This made the Profitable Product Paradigm feasible on a systematic basis and on a mass scale.

The logic is seemingly clear. If the unprofitable products are winnowed out, then they will cease to be a drain on the profitability of the firm. Only profitable products will remain, so the firm's resources will be focused where they yield the best return. Over time, the average profitability of the firm's products will become higher and higher, along with the overall profitability of the company. All of the major financial indicators of the firm (e.g., return on equity, return on assets, net profit, etc.) should increase as the company becomes increasingly successful.

It is hard to argue with this logic. After all, what company could succeed if it did not purge its unprofitable products? IBM would still be trying to sell adding machines, and Radio Shack would still be trying to sell eight-track tapes. It is hard to imagine how continually assessing the profitability of its products would not make a company more and more successful over time.

We will show why this seemingly unassailable logic is wrong. To do this we use examples from three different industries. In each case, the company and events described are patterned after an actual company and its experience in the market, but the situation is disguised, simplified, and dramatized to better explain the main point, and to avoid being overly critical of any particular management team.

Something's Rotten: Schmidt Groceries

We first examine the experience of Schmidt Groceries (company name changed), a major grocery chain. We consider the experience of one of Schmidt's stores over time in Music City, Tennessee. In particular we show how product thinking led the Schmidt store down the Profitable Product Death Spiral, taking it from the dominant position in the market and extremely profitable, all the way to unprofitable, and eventually out of business.

The Death Spiral

Schmidt Grocers, a leading grocery chain, was enthusiastic about the arrival of scanner technology in the late seventies. Each grocery would now have unprecedented information available about exactly which products were selling, and about the effectiveness of its sales and coupons. Store managers soon found that the balance of power had shifted from the large suppliers to the retailers, because the general sales data available to the suppliers were essentially made obsolete by the store-specific data possessed by each store manager. Why should the store manager care if Ritz crackers were selling well regionally if they were not selling in his particular store?

No longer could the supplier push unwanted products on the grocer, based on research data only partially relevant to any individual store. From now on Schmidt would fine-tune its inventory to the needs of the particular store. This would of course increase Schmidt's profits, because only profitable items would be carried, and of course those would be the same items most wanted by the store's customers. Thus, the customers would get what *they* wanted, and Schmidt would improve its profits by supplying the customers' needs. Therefore, Schmidt's management trained its personnel to regularly analyze the scanner data, and to constantly prune the less profitable items from the inventory list.

For several years this approach did very well. Schmidt's profits were up substantially. The customer service manager casually mentioned that complaints about discontinued items seemed to be more numerous than they used to be, but that seemed to be just the price of progress. There will always be a few stick-in-the-muds, set in their ways, who don't like things to change. After all, how many discontented people could there be? The only items getting discontinued were the ones that didn't sell. There was always a good retort to an unhappy customer: "I'm sorry we don't carry that anymore, but it just didn't sell. We have the numbers to prove it."

The Schmidt store in the Hillvue neighborhood of Music City, Tennessee, had always done very well. It was easily the dominant grocery in the Hillvue area. It had an upscale competitor, Andre's, but everyone knew that Andre's could never appeal to a mass market. Its inventory was too limited, and its prices were too high. Because Andre's siphoned off the high-end customers, Schmidt simply adjusted its inventory to include fewer gourmet items. Then another competitor, the Whole Health Market, entered the area. Schmidt found its sales slipping somewhat, but again Whole Health could not be taken seriously as a competitor. Its natural foods image could never attract a large customer base. Only the highly educated people and arty types shopped there. Schmidt soon found that its health foods were no longer profitable and stopped carrying most of them.

Things got a little bit more serious when Dixie Discount opened its doors nearby. Soon Schmidt's sales were seriously sagging. The low-income customers and rural customers tended to switch to Dixie. It was cheaper. Schmidt quickly found that its generic lines were no longer profitable and stopped carrying most of them.

Before long Schmidt realized that its revenues were down, but its fixed costs were essentially unchanged. This, of course, meant that more of the fixed costs had to be allocated to any one item. In other words, because demand was down, economies of scale were lost, and some items that were marginally profitable before were now unprofitable. They, of course, were eliminated. The parking lots of the other stores seemed fuller and fuller, while Schmidt's sales declined. The customer service manager mentioned with a smile that complaints seemed way down, but this did not seem to make up for the lost sales.

Eventually sales declined so far that it was no longer profitable to operate the store. Schmidt sold the store to a large competitor chain and wondered what had happened. The store manager was fired.

Profitable Products: Trouble in Paradigm

What happened to Schmidt Grocery? Why did being responsive to the customer, in the sense of stocking the most highly demanded items, not work? Let us analyze how using scanner data to weed out the less profitable items can lead to a loss of customers and a "death spiral" from which the store cannot recover (see figure 2-2).

At first Schmidt was recording good sales levels by being a general store. This was because specialized niche stores had not yet invaded the market. These sales levels were only improved (in the short run) by using scanner data to weed out the less profitable items and place more importance on the successful items. However, it was during this period that the alienation of the customer base began. Customers began complaining because items they liked were discontinued. Admittedly, relatively few customers were made unhappy by discontinuing any individual item. After all, the reason the items were discontinued was that they didn't sell well. What, then, was the problem?

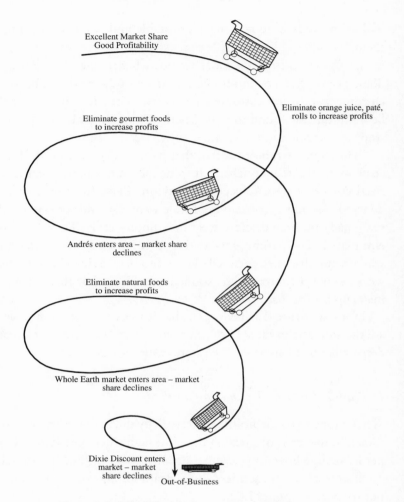

Excellent Market Share
Good Profitability

Eliminate orange juice, paté,
rolls to increase profits

Eliminate gourmet foods
to increase profits

Andrés enters area – market share
declines

Eliminate natural foods
to increase profits

Whole Earth market enters area – market
share declines

Dixie Discount enters
market – market
share declines   Out-of-Business

Figure 2-2. The Schmidt Grocery Death Spiral

SCHMIDT FORGETS ABOUT ITS CUSTOMERS.   Let us track three typical customers and see how they viewed the changes at Schmidt. The first customer, Cindy, was a successful, young, single professional. She had a taste for good cheese, pâté, and other gourmet items. At first she was relatively happy with Schmidt. Sure, they didn't carry everything she wanted, but they carried enough of her favorite foods to keep her as a customer. The second customer we will examine is Cliff. Environmentally conscious and close to the earth, Cliff and his wife lived in a restored farmhouse. They shared housework equally, and Cliff did the grocery shopping. Schmidt carried just enough bulk items to satisfy Cliff, although he wished there were more attention to natural foods. The third customer was Vicki. Vicki shopped for her husband, Joe, an auto mechanic, and their three children. At first they shopped at Schmidt because it was convenient to their Hillvue neighborhood, and because it was relatively cheap.

TROUBLE WITH THE PROFITABLE PRODUCT PARADIGM. Schmidt saw from the data that certain items could not be justified on the basis of profit. Some of the items eliminated were fresh-squeezed orange juice, fresh pâté, and bulk sandwich rolls. Cindy was very upset that the orange juice and pâté were discontinued. She complained to the customer service department. "The orange juice machine was always breaking down," rationalized the customer service manager. "Also," he confided, "we just didn't sell as much fresh-squeezed orange juice and pâté in Hillvue as we do in Emerald Heights." (Emerald Heights is the ritzy section of Music City.) Cliff also complained, because the bulk rolls were baked fresh and didn't have preservatives in them. They were also cheap. "The Health Department was always on our case about those bulk bins," explained customer service. "And, as you may have noticed, we didn't sell very many anyway." Cliff went away grumbling. Cindy began to drive to an Andre's store across town occasionally to buy gourmet items. Cliff occasionally would drive in to the health food store near the university, even though it was inconvenient, to pick up some of the bulk items he could no longer get at Schmidt's.

The Andre's store across town, noticing that its customer base was starting to include more Hillvue residents than would normally be expected, decided to open a second store in Hillvue. Cindy gleefully switched. Even though the prices were considerably higher at Andre's, she could find the gourmet foods she wanted there. Andre's was too expensive for Cliff and Vicki, who had no interest whatsoever in the expensive new store.

Having lost some of its customers, but not many, Schmidt did not notice a significant decline in its sales. Sure, sales were down some, but not enough to cause serious concern. A look at the scanner data showed that a few more items were now unprofitable. Predictably, few gourmet items did well anymore. They were discontinued. It didn't matter. All of the upscale customers were gone anyway. Also, the bulk bins, all of which had been only marginally profitable all along, were now in the red. They, too, were discontinued. Cliff knew better than to complain. That never did any good.

When the Whole Earth Market, sensing an opportunity in bulk and natural foods, opened a store in Hillvue, Schmidt's management was unconcerned. Cliff was delighted. Whole Earth had the kind of healthy food he had always wanted. Sure it was more expensive, but who can put a price on health? Whole Earth was too expensive for Vicki to consider.

By now Schmidt's sales had declined noticeably, but it was still far and away the market leader, with no direct competition. Because of its virtual monopolist standing, Schmidt's management felt that it could maintain profits at a respectable level by boosting prices some. This it did. Vicki grumbled but continued to shop at Schmidt because what was the alternative?

Then Dixie Discount, sensing that it could compete successfully on price in the Hillvue market, opened a store there. Schmidt fought back for a while with discounting, triple coupons, and other promotions, but ultimately accepted its position as a higher-priced competitor to Dixie Discount. Vicki, of course, was pleased to have a cheaper place to shop and switched to Dixie Discount. Soon Schmidt's sales were down precipitously and the entire store was running in the red. Before long the store was sold, because only a handful of the items in the store were still profitable, and they could not possibly support the entire store.

Explaining the Death Spiral

Thus, we see how the death spiral occurred (see figure 2-3). Schmidt viewed its business as being made up of products. Some products make money and some don't, so if they get rid of the ones that don't, they will make bigger profits. That strategy would work well if it were not for the existence of customers who shop for more than one item at a time. The problem is that some "unprofitable" items are considered important by some customers. Suppose, for example, that breakfast cereal was profitable but that milk wasn't. Eliminating milk would alienate cereal eaters, because they go to the store not to buy an item individually, but rather to buy an assortment of items. Discontinuing milk would probably guarantee that cereal eaters would stop buying at that store, which then would make cereal unprofitable also.

Of course, once a market segment is alienated, a market opportunity naturally arises. New entrants can enter the market successfully because the original store is vulnerable to losing the disaffected segment. Thus a large, general

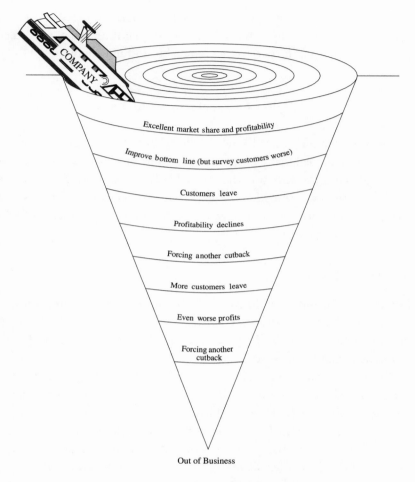

Excellent market share and profitability

Improve bottom line (but survey customers worse)

Customers leave

Profitability declines

Forcing another cutback

More customers leave

Even worse profits

Forcing another cutback

Out of Business

Figure 2-3. Understanding the Death Spiral

competitor may set itself up for attack from niche competitors. More and more niche competitors may enter the market until there is not much general market left, and the original market leader goes out of business.

There is a spiral because the more customers the store loses, the more items become unprofitable. As more items become unprofitable, more are discontinued, and, thus, more customers are alienated. The more customers are alienated, the more potential there is for niche competition, which reduces the original store's number of customers and continues the downward spiral.

All of this does not happen immediately, of course. It takes time for competitors to move through the concept stage, planning stage, and start-up stage. Nevertheless, the pattern is predictable and inexorable.

Flying Away: National Airlines

Schmidt Groceries showed how the Profitable Product Death Spiral can arise because of neglecting how customers view product assortments. However, that is not the only way the Profitable Product Death Spiral can arise. In this section we consider the experience of National Airlines (name changed) and discover another way that attention to product profitability can result in lost customers.

The Death Spiral

Let us again consider the Music City, Tennessee, air traffic market. In the mid-1980s, National Airlines was the dominant carrier in the Music City market. It flew most of the flights, occupied the most gates, and had the most passengers. Profits were good.

But profits could be even better, thought National Airlines management. A careful analysis of the Music City flights indicated that the flights connecting Music City to Charlotte and Orlando were unprofitable. In response to this, National eliminated its flights to those cities (see figure 2-4). Sensing a market opportunity, Triangle Airlines moved in to fill the gap. Soon National discovered that its market share in Music City was down somewhat, but not enough to cause real alarm.

However, continued flight profitability analysis now showed that the flights to Fort Myers and St. Louis were now unprofitable. Again National simply discontinued those flights. This time, though, a really tough competitor, Southeast Airlines, saw its opportunity and entered the Music City market. That really hurt National's market share. In addition, the flights to Chicago and New Orleans, two cities served by Southeast, were now unprofitable. They, too, were discontinued.

Every time National cut back, Southeast Airlines expanded to fill the void. Soon National Airlines found itself with badly declining market share and shrinking profit margins. Before long National could no longer support maintaining ground operations staff in Music City, so it closed up shop altogether.

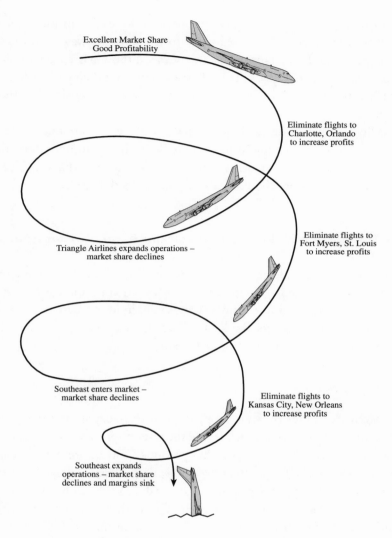

Excellent Market Share
Good Profitability

Eliminate flights to
Charlotte, Orlando
to increase profits

Eliminate flights to
Fort Myers, St. Louis
to increase profits

Triangle Airlines expands operations –
market share declines

Eliminate flights to
Kansas City, New Orleans
to increase profits

Southeast enters market –
market share declines

Southeast expands
operations – market share
declines and margins sink

Figure 2-4. The National Airlines Death Spiral

The Plane Truth

Again the problem was with customers. Passengers (customers) often fly from City A to City B to City C. It is not that they care about City B. They are just changing planes there. It is a "hub." So when the flight from B to C is discontinued, those passengers will also no longer need the flight from A to B.

For example, when the flights to Charlotte were discontinued, passengers from the Midwest who used to fly to Charlotte by way of Music City no longer could do so. This meant that some of those passengers would no longer want to fly to Music City at all, since it was not their end destination. That is why, for example, the flights from St. Louis to Music City became unprofitable.

As flights are discontinued, other flights become unprofitable, leading to them being discontinued, leading to more flights being unprofitable, and so on until the airline can no longer support its fixed costs in that city. The airline can't pull out from the Profitable Product Death Spiral.

Downsizing Right Down the Drain: Acme Corporation

A similar logic can hold for corporate downsizing. Consider Acme Corporation (name changed), which sells sophisticated communications equipment to businesses. Let us consider Acme's sales in Music City to three large business customers: Barger Book Distribution Company, Croesus College, and the Music City Manglers football team.

The Death Spiral

Management, under pressure from the top to boost short-term profits, insists on workforce reductions. In the short term, profits rise, but soon the customer side makes itself known. Barger Book Distribution now finds that its account reps take longer to answer calls. Barger starts to give some of its business to other suppliers as contracts come due. With less business but the same size workforce, Acme's productivity figures decline (see figure 2-5). In addition, its market shares start to decline, as do profits.

Given a renewed squeeze on profits, Acme again does its tried-and-true method of coping with low profits—it downsizes the workforce. This increases productivity and profits in the short run, but again service suffers. This time Croesus College finds that it is not getting the regular relationship building and hand holding that it is used to. The college is a big account, so it is used to being coddled. When the contract comes due, Croesus chooses another supplier, with better customer support.

Now things are critical for Acme. Its customers are mostly gone, and yet its office and fixed costs are still roughly constant. The only hope for

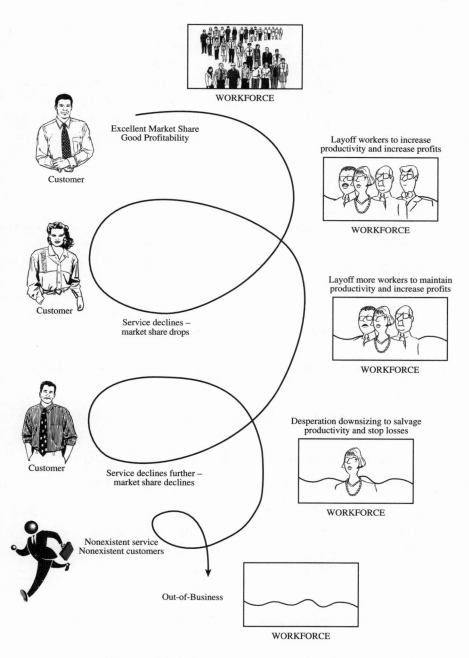

Figure 2-5. The Acme Downsizing Death Spiral

regaining profitability is to do a desperate downsizing, cutting the work-force to the absolute bare minimum. Now the Music City Manglers find that when their phone banks go down, they can no longer reach Acme by telephone, except by leaving a voice mail message. Eventually, after a day or two, Acme calls back. Meanwhile, thousands of ticket sales are lost. The next year the Manglers discontinue their contract with Acme. Now Acme can truly not afford to stay in business in Music City, so it shuts down its office.

Getting Feedback

Again the issue is whether customers are served well and whether they are retained. Again we have a feedback loop, because downsizing leads to poor service, which leads to weaker sales and profits, which leads to yet more downsizing.

Understanding the Death Spiral

Let us again consider the main steps characterizing each loop of the Prof-itable Product Death Spiral (see figure 2-3). They are:

- Company improves profitability by eliminating unprofitable prod-ucts/services
- Elimination of unprofitable products produces diminished service
- Diminished service drives customers away and lowers profits

The main reason this happens is that companies are assessing *product* profitability rather than *customer* profitability. This error, combined with the failure to consider complementary customer choices, almost inevitably leads to the Profitable Product Death Spiral.

Understanding Customer Choice Combinations

The key marketing insight is that customers do not choose products in isolation. Rather they choose *assortments* of products that fit together in a complementary manner. Consider the following complementary assortments:

- Toothbrush and toothpaste
- Flight from Madison to Chicago, and flight from Chicago to Louisville
- A textbook and the accompanying readings book
- A checking account and a savings account

But these are obvious, one might say. How could any rational businessperson make the mistake of ignoring complementarities such as these? Amazingly, they do! The textbook/readings example above was based on the personal experience of the first author (Rust), who was an author of the text and an editor of the accompanying readings book. The publisher (not The Free Press!) noted that the textbook was selling well, but the readings book was selling less well. Although many customers had gone to great trouble to structure their courses around using the textbook and readings book together, the publisher decided to increase profits by discontinuing the unprofitable readings book! A little bit of knowledge is a dangerous thing, if that knowledge is about product profitability!

Implications for Retailing

The Worst Thing to Say to a Customer

The worst thing to say to a customer is, "Product profitability is more important than your customer needs." Maybe retailers don't use those exact words, but they might instead say, "We can't stock the brand of apple juice that you want because it doesn't sell well enough." That is a product answer to a customer question. What it says to the customer is that the product is more important than the customer. In fact, it says that the retailer can only talk about products.

A customer answer to the customer question would be: "We don't currently stock the brand of apple juice that you want, but I believe Andre's down the road has it." Such an answer makes the customer's need (the brand of apple juice) the top priority and directly addresses it, even at the expense

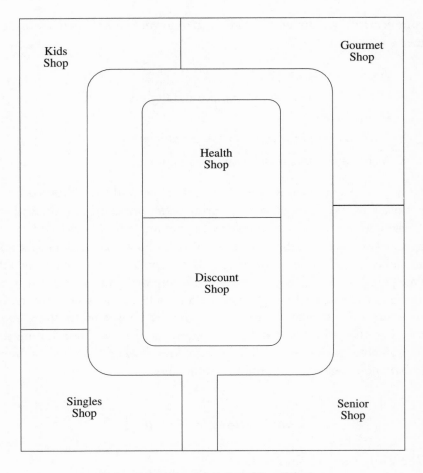

Figure 2-6. Customer-Oriented Retail Design

of short-term product profitability. That perspective serves customers better and ultimately will create more loyalty and higher profits.

Stores Within Stores

If there are customer segments who have preferences for predictable assortments of items, then the store must be sensitive to those preferences in order to be successful. The important decision unit becomes the assortment preferred by a segment, rather than the individual item. Ultimately it may

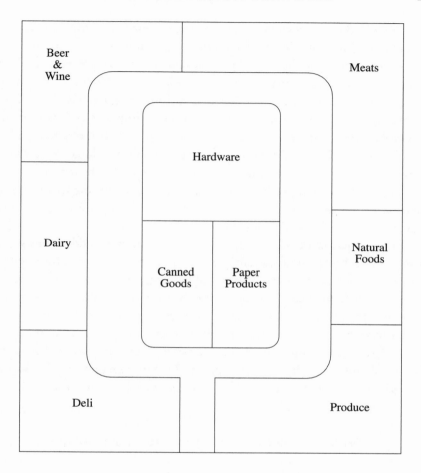

Figure 2-7. Product-Oriented Retail Design

make sense to physically design the store as a collection of departments, each of which corresponds to a major customer segment.

Scanner data can be put to use for this purpose. First, the scanner data must be analyzed by individual items. Because there is often a very large number of individual transactions, a sample must be taken, to arrive at a reasonable number. Then the customers are grouped together according to how similar their items purchased are. This produces the customer segments. Some items will be common across all segments. These are the staples. In a grocery these might be such items as toilet paper, breakfast cereal, and milk. Other items will have far greater interest to a particular segment. Examples of these are the items used in the Schmidt Groceries example.

This suggests how the store should be laid out. The staple items could be shelved in a large, common area. The specialty items could be shelved in special areas, each devoted to a particular customer segment (see figure 2-6). Some industries already implement this idea in a limited way. Groceries, for example, often feature a natural foods section, which looks like a store within a store. Note that other grocery departments may look like the same thing, but are fundamentally different (see figure 2-7). A bakery section, or a seafood section, or a produce department are not appealing to any particular customer segment. Rather they reflect an organization of the store based on product, which is not the same concept.

The physical layout also suggests how profitability should be measured. Each customer-oriented specialty section should be its own profit center. The immediate effect of this new way of looking at profitability is that some unprofitable items may be stocked, only because they make the assortment complete for the targeted segment. This is conceptually analogous to manufacturers who field a complete product line, even though some of the products offered actually lose money. The decision point comes when the section is unprofitable as a whole. At that point, the entire section may be discontinued, because the targeted customer segment itself is not profitable.

From Product Thinking to Customer Thinking

In this chapter we have seen the danger of focusing on product profitability at the expense of customer profitability. Such thinking can lead to a Profitable Product Death Spiral, in which decisions that seem to be increasing profitability alienate the customer by ignoring the effect of assortments of choices, eventually leading the firm to disaster.

The implication is clear—to truly understand how to drive long-term profitability, it is essential to understand profitability from the customer side. It is the lifetime value of the customer that produces Customer Equity, and it is Customer Equity that has the greatest impact on the value of the firm. But before exploring how the firm can drive Customer Equity, we must first get a better understanding of the lifetime value of the customer.

The Profitable Product Death Spiral	
KEY INSIGHTS	ACTION STEPS
1. Using product profitability to drive product decisions can lead to a Profitable Product Death Spiral in which more and more products become unprofitable.	• Examine your company's three most recent product retention decisions. Was the primary criterion product profitability? Was it the *sole* criterion?
2. Because profitability comes from customers, not products, product decisions should be based on the *assortment* of products a customer buys.	• Set up information systems to track the product *assortments* chosen by your company's customers.
3. Keeping some unprofitable products may be necessary to retain some profitable customers.	• Do focus-group interviews to determine the interdependencies between your company's products.
4. Product-focused strategy can lead to predictable and disastrous results.	• Make customer profitability (not product profitability) the key criterion in product retention decisions.

The *True* Lifetime Value of the Customer

We have seen how a product focus can be dangerous to the firm. But how can the firm assess its performance with respect to customers? The key to this assessment is the ability to evaluate the lifetime value of the customer.[1] We will see later that this is the key to measuring and monitoring Customer Equity.

The Continuing Customer Relationship

One of the interesting changes in the last twenty years as the developed economies became service economies is that the emphasis in marketing changed from transactions to relationships. This shift is still not fully comprehended by many business people, but it is radically reshaping the effective methods of doing business.

Transactions Versus Relationships

In the twentieth century, mass marketing took over, thanks to the existence of new mass media such as radio and television, reinforced by the mass production methods made possible by assembly-line standardization. This product-focused era, which held roughly from 1920 to 1960, resulted in a view of sales as transactions. In other words, the company advertised Brand A on a mass medium; many customers were influenced by the ad and bought Brand A. Then next week or next month a new wave of advertising would try to stimulate more sales. The focus was on the brand, and on the ad. Sales and profits were thought of as occurring in a particular time period, such as a year.

As business gradually changed, service became most of every developed economy, and the things that mattered in service were different. The relationship between the customer and the service provider became more important than any individual transaction, and customer satisfaction became more important than any ad.

This shift meant that the transaction view of revenues and profits was deficient. Who cares if profits are good for one period, at the expense of alienating the customer base? What was needed was more of a relationship view of profitability. This meant that the business needed to consider the long-term view of profitability, rather than the short-term transaction view (see figure 3-1).

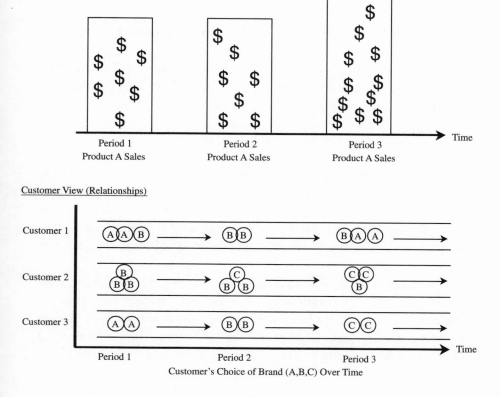

Figure 3-1. Product View vs. Customer View

Current Sales vs. Future Sales

In other words, current sales are an incomplete picture. What is more important to the modern company is the prospect for future sales. Gradually but inexorably, the things that business has traditionally concentrated on—current-period sales, profitability, and advertising effectiveness for each of its products—have been replaced. In the savvy, modern corporation, issues such as future sales and profitability, customer satisfaction and retention, and relationship effectiveness for each of its customers are now the focus.

For an accurate gauge of the health of the organization, the company must now consider not only the current performance of its products, but also the future performance of its customer relationships. Customers and customer groups must be evaluated according to their projected lifetime value to the firm.

Monitoring the Benefits from Customers

Monitoring the lifetime value of a customer requires first a definition of the benefit derived from a customer. In particular, should we be emphasizing revenues over time, profits over time, or contribution over time?

Revenue

Most early attempts to calculate the lifetime value of a customer have been based on calculating future revenues. This requires building a database that keeps track of customer transactions over time, including the revenues obtained from each transaction. Banks, credit card companies, and other financial service companies have led the way in establishing these sorts of databases.

While keeping track of revenues is a good start, it can be misleading with respect to the value of a customer. Some kinds of transactions (e.g., routine checking account activity in a bank) are inherently low-margin, or even unprofitable, while other kinds of transactions (e.g., certificates of deposit) are generally higher-margin. This means that a customer who creates large amounts of revenue through low-margin transactions may be much less valuable than a customer who creates a smaller amount of revenue from high-margin transactions.

Profit

Taking into account the idea that some kinds of revenue are more profitable than others, a more sophisticated customer database might keep track of customer profit instead. The problem with this approach is a practical one—it is very difficult for an organization to fairly allocate fixed costs. That is, centralized costs that are not directly related to any customer (e.g., management overhead, plant, and equipment, etc.) can be allocated to customers in a bewildering number of ways (e.g., according to revenue, number of transactions, direct costs, or many other possible ways). This makes it very difficult to keep track of customer profitability in practice.

Contribution

Although customer profitability is hard to obtain, a closely related measure is often practical. The contribution to profit, defined as the revenue obtained from a customer, minus the direct costs of serving the customer, is a reasonable proxy for profitability, and it is generally what companies employ.

This approach requires collecting data on customer revenues per transaction (or per time period), and also data on direct costs per transaction (or per time period). From this the contribution can be obtained.

The Nature of Repeat Purchase

Calculating the contribution to profit from an existing customer is an essential step, but it is not adequate to calculate the lifetime value of a customer. This is because of the fickle nature of customers. Customers come and go. So although a customer may be profitable now, next year (or next transaction) that customer may decide to leave. For this reason, we must have a conceptual framework for analyzing this movement.

Retention

The typical way of considering customer movement is customer retention. Widely written about both in the academic literature and by popular writers such as Frederick Reichheld,[2] the customer retention viewpoint sees customers as having some likelihood of leaving at every period (or transaction). For example, if a customer has a 90% chance of being retained from period

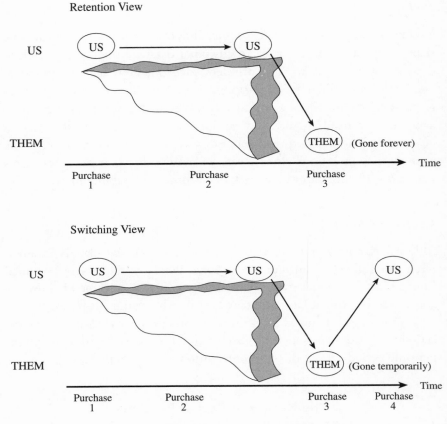

Figure 3-2. Retention View vs. Switching View

to period, then this viewpoint would say that the probability they would be retained after one period is 90%, after two periods is 90% × 90% = 81%, after three periods is 90% × 90% × 90% = 72.9%, etc.

This way of looking at retention is so well accepted now that it is not really questioned anymore. But is it right? If we look closely at this way of thinking, it reveals a central assumption. Essentially the assumption is that a customer, once gone, is always gone. We might almost say that the customer has fallen off a cliff (see figure 3-2).

Switching

Is it reasonable to assume that a customer, once gone, is gone for good? Maybe so, if the industry has very long interpurchase times, or if customers don't stay in the market long. But most industries do not seem to share these characteristics, which leads to the advisability of a different way of viewing customer retention. Professors Grahame Dowling and Mark Uncles propose that we look at customer loyalty in a different way.[3] Following the approach that researchers have used in consumer packaged goods, they posit that actually customers switch from one brand to another, and then possibly back again. They term this "polygamous loyalty." Their assumption is that the brand chosen this time is independent of the brand chosen next time, and work by academics such as Frank Bass[4] and Andrew Ehrenberg[5] have shown that this assumption works reasonably well for consumer packaged goods.

However, for service, customer retention is a little bit stickier. As has been well established by research in service marketing, a service provider that satisfies its customers has a good chance of retaining a high percentage of them. In other words, the brand chosen last time affects the brand chosen this time.

From a conceptual standpoint, the key insight from the switching viewpoint is that customers can leave and then come back (see figure 3-2). This is fairly obvious, once we look at it. For example, an MCI long-distance telephone customer may be lured away by AT&T, and then lured back again by MCI. Or a Ford owner may buy a Toyota, and then a Honda, and then a Ford again. In other words, just because a customer leaves, it does not mean that the customer is never coming back. Calculations of lifetime value of the customer that fail to factor this in will *systematically underestimate* the lifetime value of the customer.

Calculating the Lifetime Value of a Customer

Taking into account the fact that customers switch back and forth makes calculating the lifetime value of the customer somewhat more complicated, but the calculation is easily programmed into a spreadsheet model. This section discusses how best to calculate the lifetime value of the customer (the more mathematically inclined readers can find the technical details of the calculation in the appendix at the end of the book).

What Information Is Needed?

Calculation of the lifetime value of a customer requires knowledge of the following inputs:

- Time period chosen for analysis (e.g., one month, one quarter, one year)
- The company's discount rate (cost of capital)
- The company's planning horizon (how many periods?)
- The customer's frequency of purchase in each period, in the product category
- The average contribution from a purchase of this brand
- The customer's most recent brand chosen
- The customer's estimated probabilities of choosing each brand on the next purchase

Some additional explanation may be helpful. The frequency of purchase in each period, and the average contribution from a purchase of this brand each period, will generally not be known for future periods, but it can be approximated by the current frequency and contribution. This may sometimes be adjusted, if there is additional information about how customers change their expenditures over time. For example, it may be known from empirical data that the average customer in this product category increases expenditure in the product category by 2% per year. This is easily factored into the model.

The customer's average interpurchase time, in terms of time periods, is the time between purchases. It can be calculated by taking 1/(average number of purchases per period).

Projecting Share of Wallet

From the most recent brand chosen, and the estimated probabilities of choosing each brand next time, one can construct a switching matrix that incorporates this information (see figure 3-3). In this table, the top row shows what will happen to customers who currently buy Brand A. We see that 70% of them will buy Brand A next time, 20% will buy Brand B, and 10% will buy Brand C. This is a fairly typical pattern in many industries, because it shows that Brand A retains a high percentage of its customers. Likewise for Brand B's customers, 10% will switch to Brand A, 80% will stay with Brand B, and 10% will switch to Brand C.

Notice that the diagonals of this table (circled) are the customer retention probabilities that companies typically tabulate. However, this table also shows that customers can switch from one brand to another and then back.

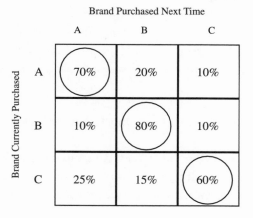

Figure 3-3. *The Customer Switching Matrix*

For example, the probability that a Brand A customer will switch to Brand B and then back in the next two purchase occasions is 20% (the likelihood of switching from A to B) times 10% (the likelihood of switching from B to A), equaling 2%.

Now suppose, for example, that on average this customer purchases twice per period. Then those two purchases may be AA, AB, AC, BA, BB, BC, CA, CB, or CC. Each possibility has a probability that may be calculated from the switching matrix, if we know what brand the customer chose last. From this we can get the expected "share of wallet," the expected percentage of business from this customer, for the three brands. (See *Enterprise One to One* by Peppers and Rogers for a more detailed discussion of share of wallet.) We can continue this process for as many purchase occasions as we need (using the customer's average interpurchase time), out to the company's planning horizon.

Obtaining the Lifetime Value

Once we have the brand's projected share of wallet for this customer, plus the inputs listed previously, it is straightforward to estimate the lifetime value of the customer. The technical details of the calculation (given in Appendix 3.1) can look somewhat forbidding, but the ideas behind the calculation are relatively easy to understand. The lifetime value of the customer is the total, across all future periods, of that customer's contribution to profit in each of those periods. Future periods are discounted, to reflect the fact that future income is worth less than current income. To be as accurate as possible, the lifetime value calculation must include the possibility that current customers might switch to a competitor, but then switch back at some future time.

Factors Influencing Lifetime Value

It is important to mention that several company-related factors have a predictable impact on the calculated lifetime value of the customer. The factors that have the most pronounced impact are the time horizon and discount rate.

Planning Horizon

A short planning horizon reduces the lifetime value of the customer. To see this, consider the extreme case of a one-period planning horizon. In such a case only current profits are considered, and the lifetime value of the customer equals the value of the customer in the current period. As the number of periods in the planning horizon increases, the lifetime value of the customer increases, because more future earnings are being factored in. Figure 3-4 shows the lifetime value of a customer, given equal contribution streams of 1.00 per period, and a discount rate of 10%. We see that a planning horizon of five periods results in a lifetime value that is more than four times as large as the planning horizon of one period.

Discount Rate

The higher the company's discount rate, the smaller the lifetime value of the customer. This can be seen very easily. Imagine a company in an extremely inflationary economy. In such an economy, sales far in the future are meaningless and the discount rate is very high. It is only today's sales that count. Therefore, only the current sales to a customer matter. In such an environment the company will not be motivated to increase service or stimulate customer retention. The lifetime value of a customer is based almost completely on current sales.

On the other hand, consider a low-inflation economy in which the discount rate is low. In such an economy, future sales still generate a meaningful net present value, which motivates the company to generate future sales

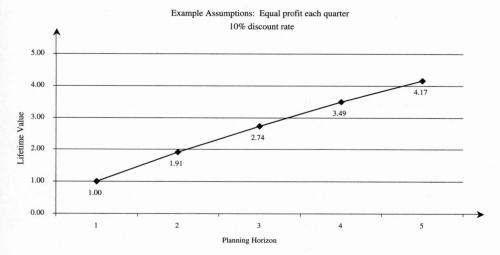

Figure 3-4. *How Time Horizon Affects Lifetime Value*

through such strategies as good service. The lifetime value of the customer is greatly influenced by the effect of future sales.

The effect of discount rate on the lifetime value of a customer is illustrated in Figure 3-5. There we consider equal contribution streams of 1.00,

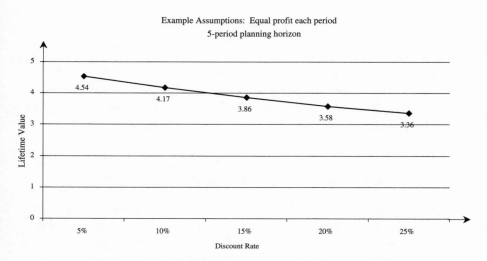

Figure 3-5. *How Discount Rate Affects Lifetime Value*

and a planning horizon of five periods. We see that a 5% discount rate results in a lifetime value that is about 30% larger than the lifetime value that results from a 25% discount rate.

Customer Lifetime Value in Business-to-Business Markets

Share of Wallet

In business-to-business markets it is not uncommon for a customer firm to use several suppliers simultaneously. Customers do this because this gives them more leverage in price negotiations and makes them generally less dependent on any particular supplier. The result is that choice of supplier at any time is a matter of "share of wallet."

We talked previously about share of market per period in the consumer context, but that share of wallet resulted from sequential choices. In other words, a consumer might choose A this time, C next time, and A again the next time, all within one period, resulting in A receiving a 67% share of wallet from the customer. In the business-to-business case, it is more like 60% from A, 30% from B, and 10% from C, simultaneously, this period. Then maybe next period, because C offers a good price, the share of wallet might shift to 40% from A, 20% from B, and 40% from C.

"Fuzzy" Brand Choice

In other words, the business-to-business customer does not choose A *or* B *or* C exclusively in any choice, but rather chooses *partially* A, *partially* B, and *partially* C (see figure 3-6). A branch of logic called "fuzzy logic" has arisen to address these sorts of cases, and fuzzy logic can be applied very naturally to the business-to-business brand choice case (see sidebar).

Share of Wallet in the Business-to-Business Case

The switching matrix (figure 3-3) can still be used, but it must be reinterpreted. Let us consider the business customer above who has chosen 60% A, 30% B, and 10% C in the most recent period. Given the switching matrix in figure 3-3, what share of wallet will these brands receive next period?

Think of it this way. The first row determines what happens to the A choice, the second row determines what happens to the B choice, and the third row determines what happens to the C choice. So the A choice becomes 60% × 70% = 42% Brand A, 60% × 20% = 12% Brand B, and 60% × 10% = 6% Brand C. We can do the same for the other two rows. Completing the calculation, we have Brand A enjoying a next-period share of wallet of 42% + 3% + 2.5% = 47.5%, Brand B has 12% + 24% + 1.5% = 37.5%, and Brand C has 6% + 3% + 6% = 15%. By applying the switching matrix again, we can estimate share of wallet in the following period, and so on.

"Crisp" Choice

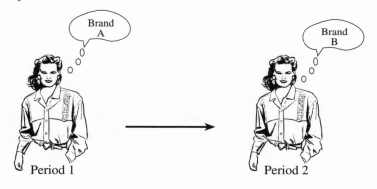

"Fuzzy" Choice (share of wallet)

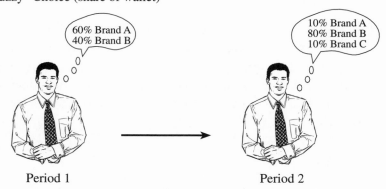

Figure 3-6. Fuzzy Choice

Calculating Lifetime Value

Once the share of wallet projections are completed, calculating lifetime value of the customer is identical to how it was calculated for consumer markets. Generally, of course, the value of a customer will be much greater in business-to-business markets.

Other Factors That Affect Lifetime Value

While the framework that we have presented captures the essence of customer lifetime value, additional factors can have a significant influence. These fall into the categories of drains on lifetime value (maintenance costs, marketing costs) and loyalty effects (increasing revenues, decreased costs, word of mouth, cross-selling, and upgrading).

Relationship Maintenance Costs

Especially in continuous services, there are customer-specific costs related to maintaining the customer relationship. These may not be direct costs associated with any particular transaction. For example, the first author's wife, Chiharu, likes to shop at an Asian market. Whenever she stops by, the storekeeper gives her some free orange juice, regardless of whether she buys anything. He knows that she is a good customer, and he wants to build goodwill. This is a relationship maintenance cost, but not a direct cost of any transaction. Customer lifetime value includes these costs.

Marketing Expenditures

While much of marketing is not targeted toward individual customers (e.g., mass advertising), other marketing efforts are more narrowly defined. Direct marketing efforts (e.g., direct mail) should definitely be factored into the lifetime value of the customer. Segment-specific marketing efforts might also be factored in, if it is possible to identify the costs attributable to specific customers.

Increasing Revenues

One of the advantages of long-term customers is that they often show an increasing revenue trend over time (see figure 3-7 for a typical pattern). For

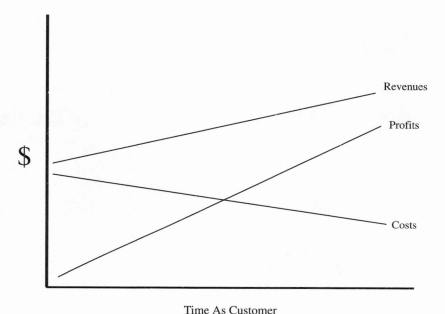

Figure 3-7. Increasing Profits for Long-Term Customers

example, a travel agency customer may travel more as he/she gets older, increasing the revenues and also the contribution to profits. If this trend is empirically verifiable across a large number of customers, then the lifetime value calculation can incorporate this effect.

Decreased Costs

Another advantage of long-term customers is that they "learn the drill." That is, they know what to do. They are experts at being the company's customer. This, in turn, leads to decreased costs, because such customers demand less attention, make fewer mistakes, and are faster (see figure 3-7). This effect is also part of the lifetime value of the customer, although estimating this effect accurately may be problematic.

Word of Mouth

Another advantage of long-term customers that is ignored in our formulation is word-of-mouth effects. That is, happy customers can influence oth-

Figure 3-8. Additional Sources of Increased Revenue

ers to buy, indirectly creating more revenues and profits (see figure 3-8). This effect is notoriously hard to measure, but it is frequently significantly large. Calculations of lifetime customer value that leave out word of mouth most likely underestimate the lifetime value.

Cross-Selling

Long-term customers can often be cross-sold on other products (see figure 3-8). For example a hotel guest might be sold a meal in the hotel restaurant, or an MBA alumnus might be sold a continuing education program. Smart companies set up their customer databases in such a way that all of the business with a customer appears on the customer's record and is summarized according to total revenue, total cost, and total contribution to profit. In that way, the lifetime value calculation will be sure to incorporate cross-selling effects.

Upgrading

Similar to cross-selling, sometimes a customer will move from an economy product to a premium product (see figure 3-8). For example, Toyota hopes that its Camry customers will eventually buy a Lexus. Again, smart companies set up their databases in such a way that these purchases are recorded together, rather than having separate databases for Camry owners and Lexus owners.

Dynamic Influences on Lifetime Customer Value

New Entrants

So far, we have presented the lifetime value of the customer as though it resulted from a static competitive environment. That is not totally unreasonable, because often the best approximation we can make is that the future will be something like the present. Nevertheless we should be aware that there are competitive events that can have an impact on the lifetime value of the customer.

One competitive event that can have a major impact is the entrance of new competitors into the market. For example, when Southwest Airlines entered the U.S. airline market, its very new approach to air service (low cost and no frills) completely changed the dynamics of the market. The existing major airlines suddenly found that the lifetime value of their customers was not nearly as great as before. A dramatically new entrant has the potential to seriously impact lifetime customer value. Conversely, a significant competitor that leaves the market can also have a large effect, but this time a positive one.

Competitive Reaction

The other competitive factor that can have a big impact is competitive reaction to strategic initiatives. We will see in subsequent chapters that it is possible to identify strategic initiatives that will significantly impact lifetime customer value. If these initiatives are both visible and effective, then it is likely that this will generate competitive response. The response might be to copy the initiative, or it might be to retaliate in other ways. Either way, the competitive reaction is likely to have an adverse impact on the lifetime customer value.

Driving Lifetime Value

Our framework enables us to identify the main ways in which a company can drive the lifetime value of its customers. The main ways are (1) increasing customer retention, (2) attracting switchers, (3) increasing customer profitability, and (4) increasing share of wallet. These basic actions form the basis for driving Customer Equity as we will see in the next chapter.

Increasing Customer Retention

A company that can keep its own customers does not lose them to competitors. That, combined with attracting competitor customers, is the recipe for market share growth. We will investigate this strategy in detail in chapter 7.

Attracting Switchers

We will see later how emphasizing Value Equity and Brand Equity can help drive this. They are investigated in detail in chapters 5 and 6.

Increasing Customer Profitability

Our customer lifetime value framework reveals clearly that increasing customer profitability through larger contribution margins is another way of building lifetime value. Another key to Customer Equity, we investigate this in chapter 11.

Increasing Share of Wallet

Especially for business-to-business customers, a key to profitability and customer lifetime value is increasing share of wallet. We have seen that this turns out to be conceptually identical to increasing market share, if we use concepts from fuzzy logic to generalize the consumer switching model.

Having established a clear framework for estimating the lifetime value of a customer, we now see how to use this information to derive effective strategies for driving Customer Equity.

The *True* Lifetime Value of the Customer	
KEY INSIGHTS	ACTION STEPS
1. Monitoring customer lifetime value is essential to accurately gauge the health of the organization.	• Set up systems to collect and store the inputs required to calculate customer lifetime value. • If yours is a transaction-oriented business in which customers are essentially anonymous, set up the lifetime value databases on a segment basis.
2. The lifetime value of a customer is usually analyzed best by considering a customer's contributions to profit over time.	• Examine your company's customer lifetime value calculations • What is the measure used—revenue, profitability, contribution, or other? • What is the time horizon employed? Why? • What discounting factor is used?
3. Calculating lifetime value based on retention probabilities systematically underestimates customer lifetime value, because it ignores the fact that customers can switch away and then switch back.	• Examine whether the calculations allow for customers switching out and then switching back.
4. Patterns of brand switching are the keys to accurately calculating customer lifetime value.	• Find out where your lost customers go. • Determine where your new customers come from.
5. Business-to-business lifetime value calculations often require the notion of share of wallet.	• Find out who else each of your customers is buying from and the percentage of their business that you currently receive.

THE CUSTOMER EQUITY
FRAMEWORK

What makes the Customer Equity engine run? It's not enough to know that Customer Equity is the key to a company's success. The company needs to know which levers to pull to foster Customer Equity. The three key drivers of Customer Equity—Value Equity, Brand Equity, and Retention Equity—must be understood and actively managed. The firm must engage in the specific actions that will strengthen each driver, ultimately driving Customer Equity.

4

A Framework for Customer Equity

A Foundation for Customer Equity

Now that we understand the true value of the customer, we can examine the key aspects of the Customer Equity Framework. In the previous chapters, we've seen examples of firms that have run into unforeseen problems because they did not understand their business from the customers' perspective. In this chapter, we explore the Customer Equity Framework in more depth, with the goal of providing a basic understanding of how it works, why it works, and why we need to measure and manage Customer Equity.

How does a company like Southwest Airlines manage to continue to grow and flourish in such a competitive marketplace? Is there a secret we all should know? What about a small, but growing chain of electronics stores in the Northeast United States, Tweeter, Etc. What is it that Tweeter does that Circuit City can't imitate? What is it about Home Depot and Lowe's, the runaway leaders in home improvement retail stores, that their competitors can't imitate? Why do so many Procter & Gamble brands lead their categories in market share and brand awareness? Companies who have truly figured out how to understand the customer have a leg up on the competition.

Understanding the customer is more than listening to the customer. It's more than creating a database to track customer purchase and service histories. It's more than conducting monthly focus groups to understand product usage and emerging customer needs. Understanding the customer requires an understanding of the factors that motivate that customer to begin doing business with a company and to continue doing business with that company long into the future. Figuring out what drives customers to a firm is what this chapter (and this book) is all about.

The Building Blocks of Customer Equity

Recall that Customer Equity is defined as *the total of the discounted lifetime value of all the firm's customers*. In other words, a firm is only as good as its customers think it will be the *next* time they do business with that firm. To truly understand Customer Equity, we need to address two key questions: (1) What leads a customer to choose to do business with the firm? (2) What leads the customer to repurchase again and again? More important, what influence can the firm have on these customer decisions? There are three specific areas in which the firm can have an impact: Value Equity, Brand Equity, and Retention Equity.

Finding the Source of Customer Equity

In order to understand these drivers of Customer Equity, let's first consider what drives a customer to buy from the firm. The mechanism is somewhat different depending upon whether or not the purchase is an initial purchase or repurchase (see figure 4-1). For an initial purchase, potential customers form value perceptions and brand perceptions prior to purchase. These perceptions influence the initial purchase and form the basis for Value Equity and Brand Equity. As the customer continues to purchase from the firm, ties or connections are established between the customer and the firm (see sidebar).

Prairie Tumbleweed Farms

Consider the example of a new Internet provider of tumbleweeds (Prairie Tumbleweed Farms, *http://www.odsgc.net/~gossamer/*). Initially just set up as a good-natured bit of fun by a Kansas family, they began receiving orders for Kansas tumbleweeds. Seizing on the potential of this new family venture (preteens Jared and Katie are listed as president and VP), the family started filling orders for the precious tumbleweeds. They now ship worldwide. So consider a potential customer who, seeing Prairie Tumbleweed Farms on the Internet, decides to order a tumbleweed as a decorative addition to a lonely corner of the house. The customer receives the tumbleweed, loves it, tells her friends, and orders more. A tie has now been created between the customer and Prairie Tumbleweed Farms. Thus far, the tie is somewhat tenuous—a few purchases, positive experiences with the product, some positive word of mouth, and several visits to the Internet site. Say the company now begins a frequent tumbleweed program. If a customer buys ten tumbleweeds he/she gets one free. Or a program in which a customer can lease a tumbleweed plant and get periodic updates or photos of the growth of the tumbleweed via e-mail. The company has now strengthened the tie between the customer and Prairie Tumbleweed Farms. If an alternate provider of Tumbleweeds tries to take away this customer's business, will she switch? Or remain loyal to PTF? Understanding the nature and strength of these ties between the firm and the customer is the basis of the Customer Equity Framework.

The customer begins to form a relationship with the firm itself, whether through formal *relationship/retention*-type programs sponsored by the firm, or through relationships with individuals with whom the customer has had interactions. These relationships form the basis for Retention Equity. The repurchase decision depends, therefore, not only on Value Equity and Brand Equity, but also on Retention Equity.

The Customer Equity Framework provides a mechanism for understanding how each of these elements contributes to an ultimate connection between the company and the customer. These three "equities" work, independently and in concert, to determine in a dynamic fashion a customer's lifetime value, or when summed over all customers, the firm's Customer Equity (see figure 4-2).

An Overview of the Customer Equity Framework

Customer Equity is based upon three actionable drivers: Value Equity, the customer's *objective* evaluation of the firm's offerings; Brand Equity, the customer's *subjective* view of the firm and its offerings; and Retention Equity, the customer's view of the strength of the *relationship* between the customer

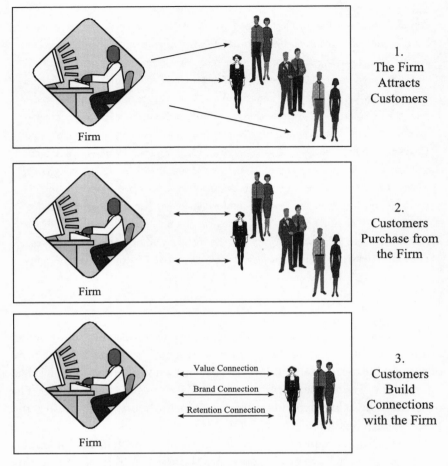

Figure 4-1. The Development of Customer Equity

and the firm. Within each of these key drivers are actions the firm can take to strengthen Value, Brand, and Retention Equity, thereby growing Customer Equity. The link between these actionable drivers and Customer Equity provides a means for firms to quickly maneuver and respond to changing customer needs—a key asset in today's fast-changing world.

- *Value Equity* is the customer's objective asessment of the utility of a brand, based on perceptions of what is given up for what is received. Value equity emphasizes the rational and objective aspects of the firm's

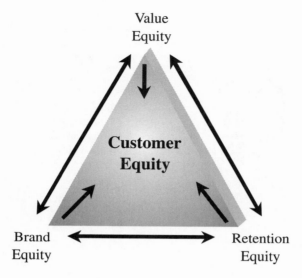

Figure 4-2. Customer Equity Defined

offerings. Value Equity considers questions such as: How does the customer evaluate the quality of the firm's offerings? How attractive is the price? How convenient is it to do business with the firm?

- *Brand Equity* is the customer's subjective and intangible assessment of the brand, above and beyond its objectively perceived value. This evaluation is shaped by the firm's marketing strategy and tactics and is influenced by the customer through life experiences and associations with the brand. Brand Equity considers questions such as: What does communication from the company about the brand evoke in the customer? Does the customer associate certain emotions, lifestyles, or experiences with the brand? Does the customer consider the brand part of himself or herself?

- *Retention Equity* is the tendency of the customer to stick with the brand, above and beyond the customer's objective and subjective assessments of the brand. It focuses on the relationship between the customer and the firm, based upon the actions taken by the firm and by the customer to establish, build, and maintain a relationship. Retention equity considers questions such as: What did the customer buy last time? Does the cus-

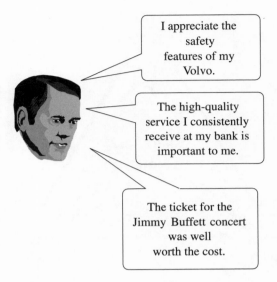

Figure 4-3. Value Connection

tomer benefit from the relationship with the firm? Does the firm benefit from its relationship with the customer? Does the customer stand to lose if the relationship is discontinued?

Why the Customer Equity Approach Works

Customer Equity represents an entirely different way of looking at the profitability of the organization, and therefore of looking at customers, marketing, information management, and strategy. It departs from the outdated view of examining only product profitability or Brand Equity, and it recognizes that customers are at the heart of any company's business.

The key reason the Customer Equity framework is effective is because it bases strategy and tactics on what is important to the customer. But the real beauty of Customer Equity goes deeper. Because Customer Equity is based upon actionable drivers—actions the firm can take to build the brand, value, and retention connections between the customer and the firm—the real relationships between the voice of the customer and the strategies of the firm can now be seen. For example, to strengthen the brand connection, building Brand Equity, a firm may find that sponsoring community events or publicizing its "good corporate citizen" activities may be the most effec-

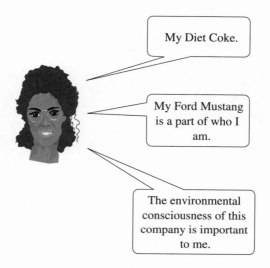

Figure 4-4. Brand Connection

tive actions. Mobil and Conoco have undertaken serious investments to enhance their brand impact by emphasizing their environmentally friendly business practices, including building double-hulled tankers.[1] Thus, these companies have been able to differentiate themselves from many other oil and gas concerns. Or to build Retention Equity, strengthening the connection between the customer and the firm, extending store hours for its best customers may be a stronger driver of Customer Equity than offering price discounts. Real actions, based on real customer input, leading to real results.

Second, the Customer Equity Framework thrives on effective customer segmentation. How do the drivers of Customer Equity differ for light users? Heavy users? Brand new customers? Regular customers? More profitable customers? Customers with a history of service failures? Customers for whom the firm's products or services have always performed well? Understanding the equity drivers of different customers will provide even stronger returns to Customer Equity. In this age of the potential of one-to-one marketing, companies can strive for an understanding of the drivers of Customer Equity for each and every customer.

Third, the Customer Equity framework is dynamic. Over time, the key drivers of Customer Equity may change for a firm, or for an entire industry.

Figure 4-5. Retention Connection

As customers experience more transactions with the firm, the brand, value, and retention connections can be strengthened (or weakened, unfortunately). Once a firm has a thorough understanding of the drivers of Customer Equity at a single point in time, the firm can begin to take advantage of the dynamic component of Customer Equity. The firm can track changes in the drivers of Customer Equity over time, and across customers. For example, understanding how to respond to customers differently depending upon their length of patronage with the firm and depending upon their future potential will become important strategic advantages in managing Customer Equity. At Bell Canada, Inc., the director of market planning and programs uses customer data to do just that. In gaining a better sense of "customer intimacy," he is able to understand, in his words, "who our customers are, what they would like, and what we deliver vs. their expectations."[2]

Fourth, the potency of the Customer Equity framework lies in its ability to direct resources where they will have the most impact. We'll see, in chapter 9, how to evaluate the return on potential investments in Value, Brand, and Retention Equity, and how to maximize return from investments in Customer Equity. By understanding what leads customers to come back to the firm and spend more money with the firm, not only is the "wasted half" drastically reduced, but scarce resources (e.g., employees, marketing dollars, information resources) are allocated more efficiently and effectively.

Finally, the Customer Equity framework provides an approach to understanding the business of the firm that is based upon the key asset that separates one firm in an industry from another—its customers. By truly defining the value created by the firm for its customers in terms of the customers' perception of the firm on key dimensions, we provide a framework that is intuitive and actionable. The Customer Equity approach focuses management on (what should be) the primary driver of stock price and valuation of a firm—the net present value of the total lifetime value of the customers of the firm, Customer Equity.

Why We Need the Customer Equity Framework Now

The old business model was based upon big ideas, big plans, and worked well for big firms with big resources. In today's world, the fast pace of change, and technological innovations, require flexible plans, actionable ideas, that allow big firms to be as maneuverable as small firms. The traditional paradigm called for the firm to be organized around products and functions. It is time for the firm to be truly centered on the customer. The Customer Equity framework is viable, and necessary, for large and small firms, from internet start-ups to old-line law firms, from mom and pop grocery stores to the Fortune 500. By redefining the firm in terms of the customer, rather than in terms of the firm's options in dealing with the customer, the voice of the customer can finally be heard. And the firm can respond to the voice of the customer with confidence and can take quick, decisive action that will *drive* Customer Equity.

We've begun to see a shift in certain forward-looking companies toward an understanding of some of these issues. In banks, we have relationship managers; in credit card companies, we are beginning to see customer relationship management emerge to a high level (see sidebar). Chase Manhattan Bank employs an integrated information network called the Relationship Management System to view customers' loan histories, deposits, investments, and other information in real time, thereby allowing the bank's relationship managers to better assist its customers and sell them additional and appropriate services.[3] In leading consumer products firms, we are seeing the advent of the role of marketing as the "steward of the brand," looking out for the effect of all company actions on the firm's brand equity.[4]

At Hewlett-Packard, marketing managers have found that almost all of their customers like to have access to all of their products. To facilitate the purchase of its merchandise, the company has even created a new position: client business manager (CBM). The CBM is focused on the customer and "blends the skills of successful salespeople with those of successful consultants and business managers." Since CBMs are rewarded on the basis of not only revenue but also customer satisfaction, their customer focus can be reinforced. "HP executives sit down with customers and ask them what criteria they think constitutes satisfaction," says Nick Earle, marketing manager for Hewlett-Packard's enterprise customer sales organization. Thus, responsibility for the company's brand lines falls on individual representatives acting in concert with current and potential customers.[5]

These changes represent only the beginning of what needs to happen. We need to see the firm organized around the customer and the drivers of Customer Equity: the Chief Value Equity Officer, the Chief Retention Equity Officer, the Chief Brand Equity Officer, reporting, of course, to the Customer Equity Officer—the CEO. We'll discuss this new organization in more depth in chapter 15.

Driving Customer Equity

How does a firm begin to get a handle on Customer Equity? Below, we outline four key elements of the Customer Equity Framework.

Step One

Understand the customers' connections to the firm. What drives Customer Equity for the firm's customers? That is, what is the *most critical* connection for the customer? If a firm seeks to maximize the total of the discounted lifetime values of all its customers, it must understand what drives customers to buy from the firm. Is it Value Equity? Brand Equity? Retention Equity? (We describe how to capture and measure these connections in chapter 8. Here, we provide the intuition behind the framework.)

Of course, the answer to this question will come from current customers, but will also depend upon current and planned company strategy. For example, if a company is in the position of *building* a customer base, it

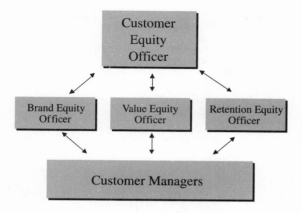

Figure 4-6. The Customer Equity Corporation

will need to focus initially on what drivers (Value, Brand, or Retention) will bring in *new* customers. In this case, the most likely candidates will be Brand Equity, followed by Value Equity, with a long-term focus on Retention Equity, leading to customers referring other customers, and the cycle continues. For companies in a more mature position in the market, with an existing customer base, it will be important to understand the impact of all three types of equity on total Customer Equity, before determining where to focus the firm's efforts and resources.

Step Two

What's most important to the customer in each of these equity areas? The next strategic step is to take a look at the factors that influence the strength of each connection (see figure 4-7). What drives Value Equity? What actions does the firm currently take (or not take) that affect the customer's perceived value of its goods and services? What actions can be taken to improve? What drives Brand Equity? What enhances the customer's associations with the brand? What drives Retention Equity? What programs are currently in place to strengthen the customers' connections to the firm? How do the firm's best customers perceive these programs? What else would deepen these customers' commitment to the firm?

In each of these areas—Value, Brand, and Retention—we identify the key drivers. Armed with an understanding of which connection is most important for the firm's customers, and which action items that influence each type

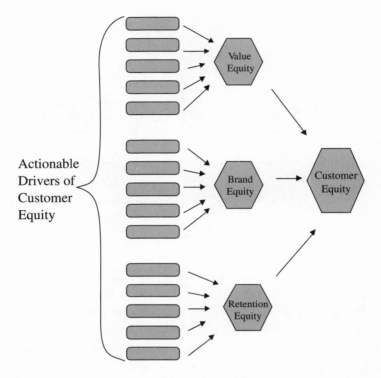

Figure 4-7. Drivers of Customer Equity

of equity have the most impact (or the least impact), the firm can develop specific strategies to strengthen brand impact, value impact, and/or retention impact. The end result: the firm develops, manages, *drives* Customer Equity.

Step Three

Benchmark the firm's position relative to key competitors. It is not sufficient merely to understand the motivations of current customers, and how the firm can strengthen the brand, value, and retention impact on Customer Equity. Except under extraordinary circumstances, a firm is usually not alone in its marketplace. Therefore, it is also critical to understand what competitors are doing, and how the firm stacks up, *in its customers' minds,* against its competitors. Think of it this way. Current customers represent a subset of all the possible customers for the firm's products or services. The firm has two goals: maximize the long-term revenue from current customers

Step 1. What's the most critical connection?
What really drives Customer Equity?
Brand? Value? Or Retention?

Step 2. What are the key drivers of Brand Equity?
Value Equity? Retention Equity?
These drivers must be Actionable.

Step 3. Benchmark against your competitors.

Step 4. Invest in the areas where the payback
to Customer Equity is highest.

Figure 4-8. Key Steps in Driving Customer Equity

and increase total number of customers. Not surprisingly, the firm's competitors share these two goals.

In determining how to drive Customer Equity, it is important to understand the strength of the competition in terms of Value Equity, Brand Equity, and Retention Equity. For example, if a firm determines that Value Equity is most important to its customers, then this aspect of Customer Equity represents the firm's most important asset and its biggest area of vulnerability. How does a firm stack up against its competitors on Value Equity? If the competition's value impact is stronger than the firm's value impact, there is some significant work to be done.

Step Four

Invest in key areas where payback (in terms of increased Customer Equity) is the highest. Determining the financial impact of investments in Customer Equity is discussed in chapter 9. The key idea is that not all investments—in the brand, in the product or service, or in the customer—are created equal. Understanding what drives customers to do business with the firm, now and in the future, should drive decisions of where to invest. By following this approach, the firm can optimally allocate strategic resources to maximize Customer Equity.

We have defined the key drivers of Customer Equity above. In the following chapters, we explore Value Equity, Brand Equity, and Retention Equity in depth. We detail what actions the firm can take to drive Customer Equity.

A Framework for Customer Equity	
KEY INSIGHTS	ACTION STEPS
1. Firms can drive Customer Equity by focusing on Value Equity, Brand Equity, and Retention Equity.	• Meet with several key customers to begin to understand their perceptions of the key attributes of Value, Brand, and Retention Equity for your firm.
2. Customer Equity is based upon actionable drivers.	• Think about actions your firm currently takes that have the potential to strengthen (or weaken) Value Equity, Brand Equity, and Retention Equity.
3. The Customer Equity Framework thrives on segmentation.	• Examine your current customer segmentation strategy. Consider how the Customer Equity Framework will allow you to serve your customer segments more effectively.
4. Customer Equity is dynamic.	• Examine your current information systems. Put systems in place to capture (1) how long each customer has been your customer and (2) how your customers' needs and purchase behavior are changing over time.
5. The Customer Equity Framework directs resources where they will have the most impact.	• Consider your company's major customer-related expenditures in the last year. Do you know which expenditures have been effective?
6. To effectively compete in the future, firms must be redefined in terms of the customer.	• Examine the current structure of your organization. Where is the customer? • Take a look at your key competitors. Are they focused on the customer?

5

Driving Value Equity

The Importance of Value Equity

Consider two restaurants, called Alpha and Beta, in a metropolitan area. Restaurant Alpha designed its meals and services with the customers' needs in mind. Before it decided upon its decor or food type—or created any of its menu items—its owners talked to potential customers and found out what they wanted in restaurants that they currently weren't finding in the area. Management asked what would be valuable to these potential customers—what features and attributes they were looking for in restaurant ambiance, how much they were willing to pay to eat certain types of food, and how willing they were to tolerate lines and waiting.

Restaurant Alpha based its service design, menu, food, and service delivery on what it found out from customers. It opened slowly, inviting a sample of customers and employees to visit and experience several of the specials and the service, just to see how they would react. Once the restaurant opened, it constantly monitored the experiences its customers had with the food and service, asking in multiple ways about how well it was meeting their requirements and needs. When the restaurant became too popular, making customers wait too long to get a table, the company expanded because it knew that its primary customers were busy and valued their free time.

Restaurant Beta, on the other hand, was designed and operated according to the beliefs and expectations of its owners. Its owners knew what kind of food they liked to cook and had what they believed was a novel environment in which to present it. The entire restaurant was created from their own ideas rather than from the preferences of any potential customers. Customers weren't consulted about the concept, the food, the decor, or the experience—either before, during, or after the restaurant opened to great fanfare.

Can you guess which restaurant closed within six months and which is still a thriving business after six years?

This chapter is about the portion of Customer Equity attributable to the firm's ability to influence the customer's value perceptions, which almost always are based on the customer's own underlying value perceptions.

Balancing the Customer's Value Equation

We all hear and use the term "value" a great deal when it comes to what we want in products and services. It is a term that is difficult—but essential—to pin down when a firm wants to understand how to obtain the first cornerstone of Customer Equity. Therefore, we will begin with a definition of value to use as a framework in this chapter.

In studying what different groups of customers mean by value, it appears that customers define value in one of four ways:

- Value is low price.
- Value is whatever I want in a product.
- Value is the quality I get for the price I pay.
- Value is what I get for what I give up, including time and effort.

As these definitions show, some customers focus on what they give up (price plus other nonmonetary costs such as time and effort) while others focus on what they receive (quality or whatever else they want in a product or service). Most customers' meanings of value fit into one or the other of these definitions, all of which could be summed up in one overall definition: perceived *value is the consumer's objective assessment of the utility of a brand based on perceptions of what is given up for what is received.* A company provides Value Equity when what it offers matches what the customer expects and perceives value to be.

The Role of Value Equity

Value is the foundation of the customer's relationship with the firm. The firm's products and services have to meet the customer's needs and expectations. If the customer does not receive value from the firm, the best brand strategy and the strongest retention strategies will have little effect.

The value connection begins with the customer's expectations of the product or service, which are formed before the first purchase. For the most part, a customer's needs and expectations already exist and a company must reveal them, as Restaurant Alpha did in the example at the beginning of this chapter. It is very difficult to create something and force or convince the customer to value it, which is the reason why many products enabled through innovative technology are unsuccessful. The customer will value them only if the customer perceives the need for them.

Value Equity is strengthened as actual goods and service-consumption experiences meet or exceed the customer's expectations. Each time the customer consumes the product or service and is satisfied, the value connection is strengthened. But the opposite is also true. Each time the product or service disappoints, there is a risk that the customer will become "dis-connected," especially if nothing is done to correct the problem.

In this chapter, we will discuss specific drivers of Value Equity, and strategies and tactics for (*a*) enhancing the value connection, and (*b*) ensuring that the value connection does not become the value dis-connection.

How Value Equity Works

We have said that value can be defined as the comparison between what a customer perceives that he gets for what he perceives that he gives. Based on this definition, there are essentially two ways that Value Equity works. First, the company can give the customer more of what he wants to get. Or the company can reduce what the customer must give for what he gets. Each of these can work in several different ways.

Giving More of What the Customer Wants

The backbone of providing value is knowing the requirements, dimensions, features, and priorities of the customer. These may seem like similar terms, and they may seem obvious; but they are not always so. For example, ask most customers what they want in most products and services and they will tell you *quality*. Later in this chapter, we will give you a framework for understanding quality in general. At this point, however, we want to show you that just knowing that the customer wants quality isn't enough to improve Value Equity. At first glance, that seems helpful because most of us know that quality means excellence or superiority—all we therefore need to know is the type of product or service and we can then define quality. However, considerable marketing research has shown us that this can result in major mistakes.

Quality in service is an ideal example. Take eating a restaurant meal as an example and ask five customers what quality means to them. One might tell you that personal attention is the most important aspect, and that a restaurant that knows him and offers him special seating and amenities is a quality restaurant. Another might tell you that getting in and out quickly is the most important thing and might offer McDonald's as an example of a quality restaurant. Still another customer might care most about the taste of the food. The fourth might mention the accuracy of the order and the cooking time, having been disappointed on many occasions. The fifth and final customer might care most about the internal setting of the restaurant—whether it is upbeat with loud music and bright colors or romantic and dark with soft music. There are two messages to learn from this example: (1) not all customers want the same thing *even if they use the same words to ask for it*; and (2) we have to get deeper than the general words like "quality" to really understand what customers value.

Besides quality, another general requirement that is often expressed by customers is *convenience*. When they use this word, sometimes they mean location or how close the firm is to their home or place of work. Sometimes they mean accessibility or how easy it is to reach a firm by mail, fax, or telephone. Sometimes they mean ease of use, as with a computer or other high-technology product. In any case, it is very important to understand the specific meaning that the customer has in mind when she says she values convenience. Great amounts of money could be expended to provide convenience that would not address the customer's requirements if the company did not listen carefully enough.

Once a company gets past the broad terms like "quality" and "convenience," it needs to identify very specific features that will provide value for the customer. Marketing research can often provide evidence of the features that can be added to a product to make it more valuable. As an example, consider Vaseline Intensive Care Cream, a product that has been available on the market for many years. In the face of maturing sales, it conducted research on baby boomer women and found that this group of consumers found existing offerings wanting in several key areas. First of all, most were getting older and felt that their hands no longer looked as young as they wanted them to. Second, no foot creams on the market truly softened foot calluses. Third, few hand creams contained protection from the sun. In response to these findings, the company came out with an entirely new line of products to directly address each of these needs. One product, called Young Hands, was extremely successful even though it is unlikely that the formula was so different from everything else on the market that it merited the market-share increase it gained. This illustrates another point about increasing Value Equity: perceptions of value are more critical than actual value.

Reducing What the Customer Has to Give Up

In addition to providing more of what the customer wants, the company can increase Value Equity by reducing what the customer has to give up. Price is most typically what is sacrificed to obtain a product or service, but what the customer gives up can also involve many other things, including time, effort, risk, search costs, and psychic costs.

There are many ways to reduce price and many other ways to reduce the perception of price, both of which will be described later in this chapter. We also want to emphasize, though, that many customers value the nonmonetary things they have to give up to get products and services.

One of the biggest nonmonetary costs of using products and services is *time*. Products and services require time to find, time to buy, and—probably most important—time to wait to receive. Consider how long customers spend waiting in lines to buy fast food, grocery products, a restaurant meal, and banking services, to name just a few time-consuming activities. Consider how long customers today wait at a pharmacy to receive their prescriptions, and how long patients wait for doctors and dentists and other professionals. One of the best ways to create Value Equity for today's time-conscious customers is to reduce the time required in using a product or service. One example of how this is being done effectively involves both restaurants and doctors' offices in malls that provide beepers so that clients don't have to wait at all and can just be beeped when their time has arrived. Another involves reducing the perceptions of waiting times in lines, a practice that has spawned many consulting firms to help service businesses keep their customers happier.

Reducing Effort

Many working women, in fact, find the act of shopping so effortful that they no longer do it. If they can't buy something through a catalog or on the Internet, they don't buy it. For this reason, virtually all companies can increase Value Equity through their distribution and availability.

Any other cost that is relevant to customers of a particular product or service—psychic costs at a dentist or risk with investment—can be a source of increased Value Equity if a firm creates ways to reduce the cost or perceptions of the cost.

In sum, Value Equity works by either giving the customer more of what she wants or reducing what she doesn't want. Either will work.

When Value Equity Matters Most

Value in some form is likely to be important to most customers most of the time, but there are certain situations when Value Equity matters most. These include the following:

- *When there are or can be differences between competing products.* When products and their competitors are virtually the same, as with most local telephone service, Value Equity is difficult to build. Part of the problem is that with competitive parity, none of the components of value can be differentially offered by one firm without other firms immediately imitating that firm's offering. This is a situation that is often said to be true of most services, where patent protection is not possible and where most offerings can be matched with little problem. When there are differences between competing products for whatever reason—patent protection, different capabilities of a company, unique resources, special labor practices, or company culture—a company can build Value Equity by influencing customer perceptions of value.

- *Purchases with complex decision processes.* When customers are making purchases that are complex, such as when they buy major durable or electronic products, companies have the potential to add Value Equity. It is in these circumstances that customers are more carefully weighing their decision and looking at the component elements of offerings, making them more aware of what elements are present. It is also under these circumstances that customers are making the highest investments in nonmonetary costs—searching, risking, and investing effort and time to make the right decision. Therefore, any company that improves the value equation by either increasing what the customer wants or reducing the costs in the selection process will increase Value Equity.

- *Business-to-business purchases.* Business-to-business purchases are purchases with complex decision processes, but they take place with different customers. Rather than occurring between the business and the end customer, they take place between the business and another business. Because these purchases are usually large and involve a great deal of money, customers consider them more carefully than individual consumers consider purchases. In fact, there is usually at least one person hired in an organization to make these purchases, whose very job is to evaluate the value (and usually to focus on the relative monetary prices) of these purchases. In these situations, Value Equity is very important.

- *Innovative products and services.* Products and services in new product categories, such as digital cameras, are also ripe for Value Equity. This is another situation where customers must carefully examine the components of the product because they are not certain what to evaluate. In many cases, they will be making one-to-one comparisons across products, and they will be trying to decide whether the new product fits their needs and wants enough that they will take the risk to purchase it. In these situations, customers are carefully looking at the give-and-get components of the product. It is worth noting that in this stage of product development, prices are usually quite high as well, so customers are closely evaluating whether to make a purchase at that point or to wait until prices go down later.

- *Firms wanting to recycle products in the maturity stage of the life cycle.* In the maturity stage of the life cycle, most customers observe product parity and sales level off. Firms that wish to recycle their products and services at this stage can use Value Equity to do so. The example given

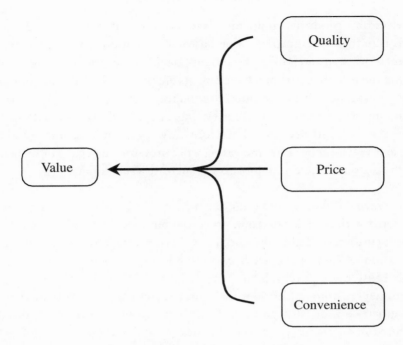

Figure 5-1. Drivers of Value Equity

earlier about Vaseline Intensive Care Lotion is one case where a firm successfully listened to customers, added to what it was currently providing in ways that were particularly meaningful to customers, and improved sales of its products.

Drivers of Value Equity

So far we have seen that Value Equity is a very important element of Customer Equity. But what can a company do to drive Value Equity? We will see that the most useful methods for driving Value Equity are improving quality, price, and convenience (see figure 5-1).

Quality

When Federal Express (now known as FedEx) entered the package mailing business in the United States, the standard for quality was the United States

Postal Service, a bureaucratic organization with rigid procedures and no real concern for the customer. FedEx saw that it could compete by creating better value for customers who appreciated quality. It delivered its packages much faster than the competition, creating an edge in quality (and permitting it to charge a higher price). FedEx became the leader in the overnight shipping market and developed such a strong reputation for quality that a 1997 novel by John Updike (*Toward the End of Time*) pictured FedEx literally taking over the world.[1]

FedEx created its quality reputation through service, and even in the goods sector, it is increasingly useful to think of quality in terms of how well the customer is served. In other words, quality is no more or less than what the customer perceives. If quality is not perceived or appreciated by the customer, then it will have no impact on the customer's behavior and can be ignored when considering Value Equity and Customer Equity.

We can visualize quality as being formed of four main components:

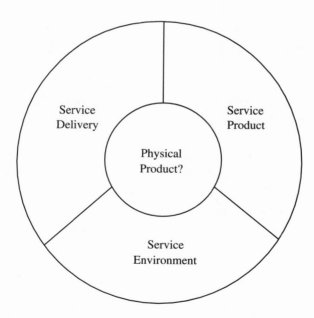

Figure 5-2. The Managerial Components of Quality

[SOURCE: ADAPTED FROM ROLAND T. RUST AND RICHARD L. OLIVER, "SERVICE QUALITY: INSIGHTS AND MANAGERIAL IMPLICATIONS FROM THE FRONTIER," IN *SERVICE QUALITY: NEW DIRECTIONS IN THEORY AND PRACTICE* (THOUSAND OAKS, CA: SAGE, 1993.)]

the physical product (when one exists), the service product, service delivery, and the service environment.[2] A company truly concerned about quality systematically investigates its performance on each of these four elements.

Companies have paid the greatest attention to the quality of the *physical product,* largely because the quality control methods of Shewhart and Deming arose in the manufacturing economy of the early to mid-twentieth century.[3] The quality revolution of the 1980s was largely manufacturing-oriented. It is well established that the quality of the physical product can drive quality perceptions, but the maturity and widespread acceptance of quality control techniques make it increasingly difficult for a company to differentiate itself on that basis. As a result, more and more goods sector companies are looking to other elements of quality to form the basis of their competitive advantage.

We are used to thinking of products being goods but it is also useful to think of the *service product,* which is the service as it is designed to be delivered. For example, insurance policies or checking accounts are service products, as is an MBA education. Both goods and services companies have service products depending upon their mix of offerings.

Service delivery, the process by which a company delivers on its promises, is also a critical element of quality. Service delivery includes many dimensions, such as responsiveness, empathy, assurance, and tangibles.[4] In service, delivery is frequently the most important competitive battleground, because it is the most difficult aspect of quality to get right consistently.

Another important component of quality is the *service environment.* This is the surroundings in which the service takes place and is especially important in retailing, and in other service scenarios in which the service takes place at facilities provided by the service provider. For example, an automobile showroom is an important component of quality for automobile dealers.

A useful way to look at service quality is to map the "moments of truth" in which the customer interacts with the company (see figure 5-3). For example, a hotel customer might first call the hotel chain's call center to make a reservation, then check in at the front desk, then go and stay in the room, then go to dinner at the hotel's restaurant, and finally check out. All

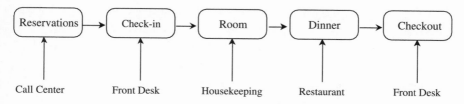

Figure 5-3. Moments of Truth at a Hotel

of these things are moments of truth for the hotel, in that they help form the customer's quality perception.

Many of the great quality gurus, most notably Kano and Juran, have looked at quality as having two basic levels—quality that merely satisfies and quality that delights.[5] These ideas have been extended and empirically investigated by the first author, along with coauthors Richard L. Oliver, Sajeev Varki, Anthony Zahorik, and Timothy Keiningham. The most important managerial conclusion from this work is that quality that merely satisfies is generally solving and avoiding problems, and quality that delights generally requires adding surprising extras.[6] This distinction is important. For example, it implies that "zero defects" will not necessarily delight the customer. Very different managerial strategies produce satisfaction as opposed to delight.

Price

When Southwest Airlines entered the U.S. airline market, it did so under a strategy of low costs, so it could offer a low price. The airline dramatically undercut the prices of its major competitors, albeit with greatly reduced service quality. This strategy produced industry-leading customer value in the price-sensitive segment and made Southwest the most profitable airline in the United States.

There are many different ways to compete on price. One is *everyday low pricing*, a strategy made popular by Wal-Mart, the hugely successful American retail company. Rather than having frequent sales to lure customers, it drives price as low as consistently possible, which it can do very well because its size and clout gives it impressive negotiating leverage with its suppliers.

The other main approach is *discounts and sales*, which draw customers by offering temporary bargains. This is a favored method of consumer packaged-goods companies, because of the transient nature of their customer base.

Payment plans are another way to compete on price. Appliance dealers are often seen to offer such inducements as "no interest until January 1" or similar payment plans that reposition the price in time.

Convenience

In Rotorua, New Zealand, in 1990, English-style "takeaways" and fish and chip restaurants dominated the fast-service restaurant market. By tradition, these restaurants made no provision for drive-through customers and tended to close at about 1:30 in the afternoon. They were sitting ducks for McDonald's, which moved into Rotorua and installed a drive-through window. At 2 P.M. on every afternoon, there were ten to fifteen cars lined up at the McDonald's drive-through. McDonald's succeeded not because it was higher quality (generally speaking it was worse), or lower price (generally comparable), but rather because it was much more convenient.

LOCATION.   This is especially relevant in retail. Convenience, just like real estate, involves "location, location, location." This is true in cyberspace, just as it is in geographical space. For example, Web sites that have entryways situated on high-traffic portals such as America Online are more convenient to users, which increases their Value Equity.

EASE OF USE.   This is especially important in products such as computer software, which is too often notoriously difficult to use. While the number of features in software may improve its quality, that can easily be outweighed by the reduced ease of use. Easy-to-use software (and easy-to-use products in general) increase Value Equity.

AVAILABILITY.   The competitive battleground for availability involves such things as hours of operation, days open, and immediate contact. Seen through a customer's eyes, the business world is fast approaching seven days a week, 365 days a year, twenty-four hours a day service, with immediate contact whenever desired by the customer.

Value Equity	
KEY INSIGHTS	ACTION STEPS
1. Value Equity represents the customer's rational and objective evaluation of your offering—the "head" part of Customer Equity.	• Ask your customers to articulate a complete list of their needs and requirements—pay attention to what they know that they know.
2. Value Equity is achieved either by increasing what customers get or reducing what they give.	• Find out through marketing research what customers want more of—and whether they are willing to pay for it. • Find out what customers give too much of (time or effort, for example) that they would like to reduce.
3. All customers do not define value in the same way.	• Engage in marketing research to understand which definitions of value are relevant to your customers. • Tailor offers to focus on different value perceptions.
4. Customers have different meanings for quality.	• Engage in marketing research to probe the specific features that signal quality to customers. • For large customers, develop individual profiles of quality perceptions and drivers.
5. A firm's Value Equity is based on the customer's appraisal of quality, price, and convenience.	• Examine your company's information systems to see if there are measures of your customers' value, quality, price, and convenience perceptions.
6. Price is not the only cost to customers, and it may not be the most important cost.	• Do not automatically assume that low price is what customers want. • Investigate what customers will pay to get time, reduce effort, and add convenience.
7. Service is one of the most important differentiators of Value Equity.	• Find out from customers what service products or outcomes will be valued. • Find out from customers what service delivery features can add to the value of your offering.

Driving Brand Equity

Of all the topics we cover in this book, the one that has been the most written about—by academics, business leaders, consultants, and even *The Wall Street Journal*—is the concept of "Brand Equity." As will become obvious as one reads this chapter, the role of Brand Equity in the Customer Equity Framework is far more focused than previously put forth. We examine the impact of the brand on the likelihood that a customer will do business with a firm. We will isolate the influence of "brand" on Customer Equity from the influence of other factors such as the objective value of the product or service or the relationship of the customer to the firm.

The Importance of Brand Equity

Firms everywhere face the common threat of commoditization, the possibility that someone else will enter the market and provide the product or service to consumers in a way that is better, faster, or cheaper, thereby stealing away the firm's hard-won base of customers. What tool have firms found to combat commoditization? The development of the brand. Brand Equity, in its broadest sense, has been defined as follows:

> Brand Equity is defined in terms of the marketing effects uniquely attributable to the brand. That is, Brand Equity relates to the fact that different outcomes result from the marketing of a product or service because of its brand name or some other brand element, as compared to outcomes if that same product or service did not have that brand identi-

fication. . . . Brand Equity represents the "added value" endowed to a product as a result of past investments in the marketing for the brand.[1]

The substantial bank of knowledge about the building and managing of brands has provided significant insights to marketers and has led to the rise of some incredibly strong brands.[2]

Brand Equity: Differentiation in the Mind of the Customer

Why does a set of consumers prefer Coke while another group prefers Pepsi? Why do consumers buy Kleenex instead of Puffs? Brand-name drinking water instead of a store brand? Why do firms invest in "image advertising"? Or sponsor community events? The answers to these questions can be found by understanding the drivers of Brand Equity, the second pillar of Customer Equity.

We offer a specific definition of Brand Equity that we will use throughout the book. Brand Equity is that portion of Customer Equity attributable to the customer's perceptions of the brand. More specifically, Brand Equity represents the *customer's subjective and intangible assessment of the brand, above and beyond its objectively perceived value.* This evaluation is shaped by the firm through its marketing strategies and tactics and influenced by the customer through life experiences and associations or connections with the brand.

The Role of Brand Equity

What does the brand do? How does a product or service's brand actually add value? First of all, the brand acts as the magnet that attracts new customers to the firm. By building brand awareness and recognition, the firm can find and attract new potential customers. Consider one of the many recent Web-based brand success stories: etoys.com. In the 1998 holiday selling season, eToys was able to build brand awareness and recognition and attract about 2 million customers per month. eToys successfully convinced customers to shift their toy-buying behavior from Toys "R" Us or Kaybee Toys to eToys.com and convinced customers new to the toy-buying market to try their site as well.[3]

Second, the brand acts as a "Hallmark card" reminder to customers. For current customers, the brand serves to remind customers about the firm's

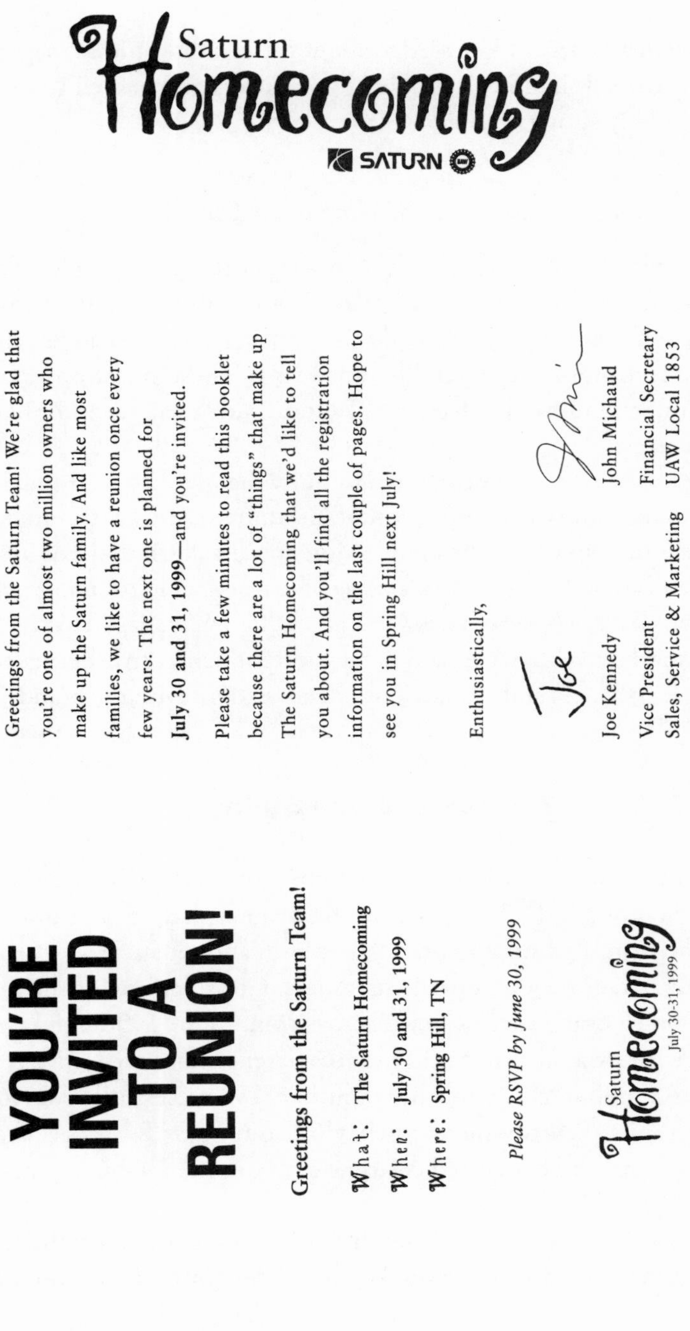

Saturn
Homecoming
SATURN

Greetings from the Saturn Team! We're glad that you're one of almost two million owners who make up the Saturn family. And like most families, we like to have a reunion once every few years. The next one is planned for **July 30 and 31, 1999**—and you're invited.

Please take a few minutes to read this booklet because there are a lot of "things" that make up The Saturn Homecoming that we'd like to tell you about. And you'll find all the registration information on the last couple of pages. Hope to see you in Spring Hill next July!

Enthusiastically,

Joe

Joe Kennedy
Vice President
Sales, Service & Marketing

John Michaud
Financial Secretary
UAW Local 1853

YOU'RE INVITED TO A REUNION!

Greetings from the Saturn Team!

What: The Saturn Homecoming

When: July 30 and 31, 1999

Where: Spring Hill, TN

Please RSVP by June 30, 1999

Saturn
Homecoming
July 30-31, 1999

Figure 6-1. Saturn Homecoming Advertisement

products and services, and to ensure that a firm's customers continue to think about the firm. As we were writing this chapter, the third author, who owns a Saturn Coupe, received a friendly postcard from Saturn (actually, her car received the postcard), inviting both car and owner to the annual Saturn Homecoming in Spring Hill, Tennessee. Although the car will not be able to attend this year, it was happy to be invited. (See figure 6-1.)

Third, the brand acts as the customer's emotional tie to the firm. Customers who have strong relationships with a brand may closely identify with the brand. Professor Susan Fournier has identified several specific forms of these customer-brand relationships (see figure 6-2).[4] For example, consumers may have a few "committed partnership" relationships with a brand—a loyal, exclusive relationship. Or consumers may have "flings"— one-shot frivolous engagements, or "childhood buddies"—brands that evoke warmly reminiscent memories of childhood. In each case, we see that the customer has developed an emotional tie with the brand in question.

- **Committed partnerships**: Loyal, exclusive relationship with Zest soap, "because it is simply the best soap you can buy and no other will suffice."
- **Flings**: A one-shot, frivolous engagement with Crest Sparkles toothpaste, "just for the sheer fun of it."
- **Secret affairs**: Occasional enjoyment of a Marlboro Light cigarette by a reformed smoker.
- **Rebound relationships**: Purchase of Honda lawnmower (out of anger at the failure of a Lawnboy servicing department).
- **Arranged marriages**: Switch to Hellmann's mayonnaise from long-standing Miracle Whip usage because the new husband insisted.
- **Marriages of convenience**: A loyalty with DeMoulas Salad Dressing is initiated by the fact that someone left it behind at a picnic.
- **Social sanctions**: Purchase of Murphy Oil Soap for hardwood floor cleaning because it is the only brand recommended by the floor installer.
- **Childhood buddies**: Warmly reminiscent memories of childhood sparked by consumption of Oreo cookies, Jell-O cooked pudding, and Hershey's Kisses.
- **Fair-weather friends**: Use of Tide…"Whenever it is on sale, and only when it is on sale."
- **Enslavements/dependencies**: Trapped and constrained in software choices by Microsoft Windows operating system preinstalled on machine.
- **Compartmentalized friendships**: Situationally restricted relationship with Avia tennis shoes worn only on the court.

Figure 6-2. Fournier's Eleven Consumer-Brand Relationship Forms

Brand Equity: Capturing the Heart of the Customer

Broadly, then, Brand Equity represents the extent to which the firm success-fully influences the customer's subjective evaluation of the firm's offerings—captures the "heart" of the customer. It is almost as though Brand Equity encompasses the customer's answer to the question: "Do I want to have this brand as a part of my life?" We see that the firm can grow Brand Equity by increasing customer awareness and recognition of the firm's products and services, by providing reminders to the customer, and by building an emo-tional tie with the customer (see figure 6-3). Pepsi has been a strong adher-ent to this concept in its constant struggle against Coca-Cola. Just in the past few years, it launched its Generation Next campaign, which was fol-lowed by its Joy of Cola effort. Both endeavored to remind the customer of Pepsi and of its association with cutting-edge or fun.[5]

How Brand Equity Works

We have said that Brand Equity can be thought of as that portion of Cus-tomer Equity attributable to the brand. There are several ways in which the customer's subjective evaluation of the brand builds Brand Equity. First, customers develop more favorable attitudes toward the brand and therefore

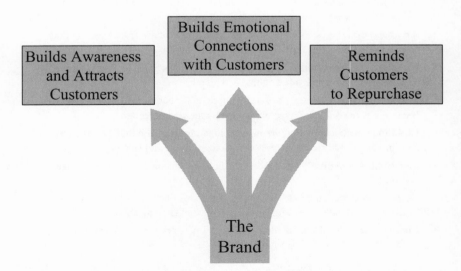

Figure 6-3. The Role of the Brand in Building Customer Equity

are more likely to purchase the brand. Second, customers have increased positive feelings for the brand and therefore are less likely to purchase a competing brand. Third, the customer's positive attitude and feelings toward the brand also increase the likelihood that the customer will recommend the brand to others, thereby increasing the probability that another customer will buy the brand.

Brand Equity is based, in part, on the notion that the firm convinced the customer that the firm's brand represents the best "fit" for the customer. This notion of fit has two dimensions: (1) this brand represents the customer's best option given the options (including competition), and (2) this brand fits well with the customer's image of self and personality.[6] For example, consider the recent plight of Levi's. In early 1999, Levi's took the decisive step to finally move its manufacturing completely offshore, laying off thousands of its U.S. workforce. Why? Sales declines of 13% in 1998, down to $6 billion worldwide, with a declining U.S. market share (now less than 15%). Although Levi's is one of the world's strongest brands, it's still in trouble. The cause? A poor fit between Levi's, the brand, and Levi's biggest set of potential customers: the teen market.[7] With Levi's, it is as though the teen market and kids (the customers) are speaking and providing opportunities for Levi's to take action. As this example illustrates, if the customer perceived a poor fit with the brand, Brand Equity can be undermined.

THE KIDS AND TEENS SAY	THE FIRM'S ACTION OPPORTUNITY
1. No, this brand doesn't fit anymore—it's my parents' brand. It doesn't fit in.	• Change brand positioning attributes • Change target market
2. The Brand doesn't fit with other aspects of my personality and the way I think about myself.	• Change communication strategy • Change creative message.
3. The brand may embarrass me where it shows up—in stores where my parents and grandparents shop.	• Change distribution strategy • Change brand name
4. And what about how it's dressed?	• Change packaging • Change pricing
5. And look who it hangs out with!	• Change merchandising

When Will Brand Equity Matter Most?

- *Low-involvement purchases with simple decision processes.* When product and service purchase decisions require high levels of involvement by the consumer, Brand Equity may be less critical than Value or Retention Equity. However, for many products, particularly frequently purchased consumer packaged goods, such decisions are low-involvement and often routinized. In this case, it is easier to build Brand Equity.

- *When the product is highly visible to others.* When customers are purchasing products or services that have the potential to be noticed by others, the firm has the opportunity to build Brand Equity. Consider Coach leather products. Coach, through a combination of exceptional quality and exceptional service (Value Equity), has built a strong brand as well. Customers appreciate carrying Coach bags, using Coach Palm Pilot cases, or even putting Coach collars on their pets (the best-selling Coach item for the 1998 holidays), in part, because of Coach's success in building Brand Equity. If other people will notice the brand of a product or service that a consumer has purchased, consumers will be more likely to consider the extent to which they believe the brand is a good fit with the consumer's sense of self.

- *When experiences associated with the product can be passed from one individual or generation to the next.* For many products and services, there are aspects of the consumption experience that involve not only the consumer, but others as well. Consider the success Procter & Gamble has had passing down loyalty to Crest toothpaste from mother or father to daughter or son. Or the comfort consumers associate with products from childhood experiences (Fournier's Childhood Buddies form of brand relationship). To the extent that a firm's products or services lend themselves to such communal or joint experiences, the firm has the opportunity to build Brand Equity.

- *When it is difficult to evaluate the quality of a product or service prior to consumption.* For many products and services, it is possible to "try before you buy" or to easily evaluate the quality attributes prior to purchase. However, for other products and services, consumers must use some type of proxy for quality when making their purchase decision. Firms that provide these types of goods or services (often called "credence goods") also have the opportunity to build Brand Equity by creating positive brand associations and brand images for such products.[8] In addition, customer knowledge or experience of high prior value associated with a product or service experience (e.g., an experience at a Marriott hotel in San Francisco, or an experience with a washing machine from Sears) can increase the Brand Equity for the product or service as customers consider purchases of the product or service in new venues or contexts (e.g., deciding on a hotel in Boston, or buying a new clothes dryer from Sears).

What Are the Key Drivers of Brand Equity?

Building upon the strong base of knowledge in this area, we have identified three specific drivers of Brand Equity. Within each driver there are sub-drivers that link to actionable firm strategies and tactics. These three Brand Equity drivers are (1) customer brand awareness, (2) customer attitude toward the brand, and (3) customer perception of brand ethics (see figure 6-4). It is important to recognize that for each driver of Brand Equity, consumers develop perceptions of the brand, even if they *never* purchase the brand. Therefore, Brand Equity involves influencing individuals who currently purchase the brand, those who have purchased the brand in the past but now purchase from a competitor, and even those who have never purchased the brand.

Customer Brand Awareness

Before a brand can successfully build Customer Equity, the customer must be aware of the brand. The strongest tool available to firms to increase brand awareness is the brand's communication to current and potential customers. We discussed the three key roles of brand equity above: building awareness, reminding the customer, and building an emotional tie with customers. Brand awareness is a necessary (but not sufficient) condition for building Brand Equity. Firms have the opportunity to deepen the emotional tie with customers and strengthen the customer's associations and attitudes toward the brand only after the initial brand awareness has been created.

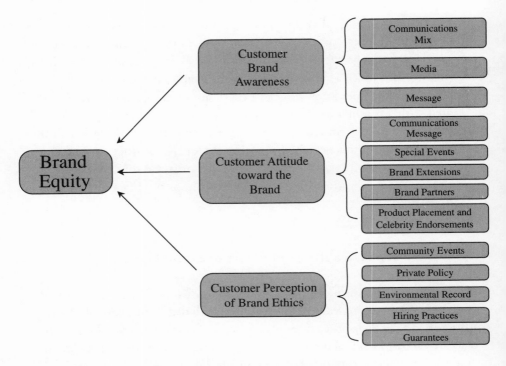

Figure 6-4. Actionable Drivers of Brand Equity

How can a firm drive brand awareness? Firms must create a seamless and consistent message to their current and potential customers. Integrated marketing communications is an approach to communicating with customers that enables a firm to engage in a synchronized, multichannel communications strategy that reaches each customer segment with a single, unified message.[9] Within this driver of Brand Equity, there are specific sub-drivers a firm should consider: the integrated marketing communication *mix,* the choice of *media,* and the *message.* In addition, firms must consider the potential efficacy of each element.

- *The communications mix as perceived by the customer* (e.g., advertising, sales promotion, publicity). For example, will current and potential customers pay attention to advertising, or would promotional events or publicity be more effective for growing brand awareness?

- *The media* (communication channels and sources, including mass media such as television, print, radio, the Web, and customized or direct media such as direct mail, e-mail, or telemarketing). When considering potential media, firms must examine the extent to which their target group of customers pays attention to mass advertising. Do they read the newspaper? Surf the Web? Watch MTV? Read their e-mail? Read their junk mail?

- *The message* (what the firm wants to convey). It is imperative that all aspects of the communications mix provide a message that is consistent with the firm's overall communication strategy. What is the single, unified message the firm wants to get across? What does the firm want the customer's initial perception of the brand to be?

Customer Attitude Toward the Brand

The second key driver of Brand Equity is the customer's attitude toward the brand. The firm can build Brand Equity by influencing the customer's emotional connections to the brand, and the customer's associations with the brand. Consider the successful communication strategy of the Gap. The Gap has successfully influenced consumers' associations of the Gap brand. Specifically, with its $20 million Khakis advertising campaign, Khakis Groove, Khakis Rock, and Khakis Swing, the Gap has shifted customer attitude toward its brand. Customers have "identified with the dressy/casual style that they [the Gap] offered and the new coolness associated with the style."[10] How does the Gap create these associations? It advertises using famous people wearing khakis; the message—khakis—everybody (who's anybody) wears them. In addition, it communicates the brand message through the stores themselves—through window displays, marketing cards, or postcards highlighting gift ideas—and everywhere its customers might go: buses, bus shelters, baseball stadiums. Its latest television ads can even be viewed on the company's Web site (*www.gap.com*).[11] Gap's goal: to bring style to everyone, and to have that style be Gap style.

So how does a firm influence brand attitude and brand associations? The firm should focus on the following specific, actionable sub-drivers: communication message, special events, brand extensions, brand partners, product placement, and celebrity endorsements. Again, it is important to remember that these distinct marketing tactics must create a cohesive message and brand portrait in the mind and heart of the consumer.

COMMUNICATION MESSAGE.   In the brand awareness driver above, we described the role of the communication message in creating an *initial* perception of the brand in the mind of the consumer. Here, we are concerned with developing an *ongoing* perception of the brand—creating a positive emotional connection with affirming associations to other aspects of the customer's daily life. In the Gap message above, the "khakis are cool" message actually *created* a style, thereby creating close, emotional connections between Gap's customers and the Gap brand.

SPECIAL EVENTS.   Firms should create opportunities for customers to develop brand associations. For example, NASCAR racing has been a strong builder of brand associations for a number of brands. Jeff Gordon, youngest NASCAR champion and driver of the DuPont car, has created strong brand associations for DuPont. Millions of consumers of all ages now know about Dupont (and have a positive association with DuPont) through Gordon's successful NASCAR racing career.

BRAND EXTENSIONS.   Firms must be careful not to dilute their customers' positive attitude toward the brand. Research suggests that failed brand extensions (extensions launched to an existing brand that were subsequently removed from the market) can have a negative impact on the customers' attitude toward the brand. In addition, brand extensions that stray too far from the core brand can also have negative consequences for the brand.[12]

BRAND PARTNERS.   It is equally important to choose brand partners carefully. For example, Coach and Lexus have teamed up to offer a Coach Edition of the Lexus luxury sedan. Clearly, this has the potential to create positive associations for both companies. Coach gains added exposure to its potential customers through the Lexus dealer network. Similarly, Lexus benefits by reaching the Coach customer list. More important, the two companies have forged a link in the mind of the consumer between Coach and Lexus. The brand association, consistent with the brand image of each firm independently, strengthens the Brand Equity for Lexus and for Coach.

PRODUCT PLACEMENT AND CELEBRITY ENDORSEMENTS.[13] Firms can create positive associations to the brand and enhance their customer's attitude toward the brand. BMW has been particularly successful by utilizing product placements in James Bond movies to create brand associations. Celebrity endorsements can also strengthen the customer's attitude toward the brand, provided the celebrity endorser is a good fit with the brand and has credibility in the eyes of the target customer (e.g., Michael Jordan and Nike).

Customer Perception of Brand Ethics

Believe it or not, in addition to creating brand awareness, and creating positive brand attitudes, the firm must also think about "brand values." The third driver of Brand Equity is the Customer Perception of Brand Ethics.[14] In considering whether to do business with a firm on a long-term basis (e.g., engage in one of Fournier's Committed Brand Relationships), customers will examine the extent to which the values of the brand or of the firm are consistent with their values. For example, customers may ask such questions as:

- Is the firm that provides this brand a good corporate citizen?
- Does this firm sponsor community events?
- Overall, is this firm ethical in its practices?
- Is this firm kind to the environment?

The strength of the ethics driver of Brand Equity will depend (as will all drivers and sub-drivers) on the firm's customer base. It is important for a firm to understand the ethics of its customers as those ethics and beliefs relate to its brand when determining how best to grow Brand Equity. The ethics driver of Brand Equity provides a good example of how firms can benefit if the driver is strengthened, but can also suffer if the key driver of Brand Equity is viewed negatively by customers. For example, following the Exxon Valdez oil spill in Alaska, U.S. customers fled to other oil providers to voice their opinion regarding Exxon's handling of the disaster.[15] Alternatively, the Tylenol brand was strengthened by Johnson & Johnson's strong stand to recall Tylenol and to take preventative action to prevent further tampering with over-the-counter medications.[16] In simpler examples, providing strong community support for causes and events that are important to a firm's customers can be an effective (and also inexpensive) means of driving Brand Equity.

The link between a company's brand and the overall organization is often overlooked and may play a strong role in a firm's development of Brand Equity, especially when considering the notion of global Brand Equity. For example, the organizational strength of Procter & Gamble is much more evident in the Japanese consumer products market (in which products are branded with an obvious link to P&G) than in the United States (where the corporate link of a consumer product to Procter & Gamble is often quite understated). In the Japanese market, it is the strength and trust of the firm that is of utmost importance and the specific brand name is of secondary importance—in essence, the company *is* the brand.

Specific actionable sub-drivers of the ethics driver of Brand Equity include the following:

- *Community event sponsorship and strong record of giving to the community.* For example, Home Depot has a strong history of giving to the local communities in which it has a retail store. Employees volunteer to build play structures in local parks or to clean up public areas to enhance the community.

- *Development and maintenance of a privacy policy for use of customer information.* American Express has a privacy policy that describes to customers exactly how it utilizes the information it receives about customers through their purchases and communications. Amex provides multiple opportunities for customers to "opt out" of the uses of the information with which they are not comfortable.

- *Clean environmental record.* A clean environmental record is expected of a firm with strong Brand Equity. Maintaining such a record will not enhance Brand Equity as much as not maintaining a clean environmental record will hurt Brand Equity. Avoid environmental mishaps or disasters.

- *Ethical hiring and work practices.* Positive publicity regarding positive treatment of employees will enhance Brand Equity. Being named to the list of the "100 Best Places to Work in America" can provide a strong boost to the ethics sub-driver of Brand Equity.

- *Strong product or service guarantees.* Standing behind a product or service sends a signal to customers about the firm's brand. L.L.Bean's unconditional guarantee, which costs the company a significant amount annually in returns of products that, by all accounts, had been worn well by their customers, strengthens Brand Equity. Customers believe in L.L.Bean products and, therefore, believe in the L.L. Bean brand.

Concluding Thoughts About Brand Equity

What is most interesting to note in looking at Brand Equity is what is not included in the Brand Equity portion of Customer Equity. Specifically, we see that nothing about the performance of the brand, or the customer experience of the brand, is included in this conception of Brand Equity. Rather, that is the scope of Value Equity. Second, nothing is included about the customer's perception of the relationship with the company, built up over time, through experiences with the company. This is the scope of Retention Equity. Brand Equity provides the means to influence the customer's overall attitude and feelings toward the brand, as well as the customer's emotional attachment to the brand. This driver revolves around customer answers to questions such as:

- How do I feel about the brand?
- Do I like it? What is my attitude toward the brand?
- Do I feel connected to the brand?
- How do I feel about recommending this brand to my friends?

Assume the customer determines that *(a)* the firm has achieved solid brand awareness, *(b)* customers have a positive attitude toward the brand, and *(c)* the brand's and firm's ethics are not out of line. The firm has now reached the stage where the brand can now have impact—where Brand Equity can drive Customer Equity.

Driving Brand Equity	
KEY INSIGHTS	ACTION STEPS
1. Building Brand Equity depends upon a successful integrated marketing communications strategy.	• Determine the right mix of communications strategies to effectively reach the firm's current and potential customers. • Utilize marketing research to determine the appropriate creative approach (the right message, communicated in the right way).
2. To build brand awareness and develop positive brand associations and attitudes, the communications strategy must not only be cohesive, it must also be effective in influencing the customer.	• Measure the extent to which your firm is attracting new customers. • Ensure that your communications strategies effectively remind existing customers to return or to tell others. • Develop communications strategies that build emotional ties with your customers. • Conduct research to examine the extent to which your communications are watched, read, listened to, experienced, and acted upon by the customer and by the firm.
3. The firm's ethical approach must be consistent with the interests of its customers.	• Determine your customers' perceptions of your firm's ethics. • Develop a data privacy policy for your organization. Communicate it to your customers, employees, and stockholders. • Examine your firm's community record, environmental record, and hiring and work practices. Improve where necessary.
4. All of the firm's strategies and tactics must work in concert to form a strong, consistent position for the brand.	• Appoint an executive to be the "Steward of the Brand." Have this individual look for conflicts within the firm's strategy.

7

Driving Retention Equity

The Importance of Retention Equity

Consider a company with the following scenario. The company has a great brand (everyone is aware of the brand and it has a strong brand image) and a great product (meets the customers' needs on each dimension). The company can draw new customers to its product with its strong brand and keep them by meeting their expectations consistently. In a world with no competition, this firm will be successful. But in today's world of heightened competition and savvy consumers, great Brand Equity and Value Equity will not be sufficient.

The firm must also find ways to build a long-term "retention connection" with its customers, to insulate its best customers from competitive offers. We call this connection Retention Equity. Through Retention Equity, the firm takes advantage of opportunities to strengthen its relationship with the customer. Once a customer has made an initial investment in a relationship with the firm—an initial purchase, a "click-through" the Web site, a phone call inquiring about the service—the firm has the opportunity to strengthen its connection with the customer.

Cementing the Relationship

We define Retention Equity as the *customer's tendency to stick with the brand, above and beyond objective and subjective assessments of the brand.* Retention impact focuses on the "experienced" relationship between the customer and the firm, based upon the actions taken by the firm and by the customer to establish, build, and maintain a high-quality relationship.[1] Specifically, it represents the influence of the company's retention programs and relationship building on the customer. How connected does the customer feel to the company? Does the customer's relationship to the firm provide a sense of community? Would the customer lose something of value if this connection were severed? The greater the retention impact—the customer's perceived cost associated with leaving the relationship—the stronger the Retention Equity.

The Role of Retention Equity

Retention Equity–building programs should be designed to respond to the specific needs of each customer. These programs should

- maximize the likelihood that the customer returns for future purchases
- maximize the size of those future purchases
- minimize the likelihood that the customer will purchase from a competitor.

In addition to the importance of Brand Equity and Value Equity, we have seen that firms that focus on building Retention Equity increase the likelihood that the best customers stick around.

The Glue That Holds the Customers

The new goal for electronic commerce is to create "sticky sites"—Web sites that encourage customers to stick around longer and to be less likely to visit someone else's site. How does a site (or a firm) create such customer loyalty? Especially in a medium that encourages "surfing," "links," and "jumping to other sites"? George Anders, a technical writer for *The Wall Street Journal*, portrays the typical Web surfer as ". . . a low-attention-span day-trading information junkie hooked on frenetic video games and the rapid-cutting pace of MTV."[2] How does a firm build a retention connection with someone like this? Some Web sites have been successful. The *www.gamesville.com* Web site offers a basketball pool; rock 'n' roll trivia; and other fun, inviting, and hopefully time-absorbing aspects. These attributes earned Gamesville.com the "stickiest site of the month" in December 1998 with an average of 246 minutes per month (compared to *www.yahoo.com* at 60 minutes/month and *www.etrade.com* at 37 minutes per month, also in the top ten). Customer stickiness is not only important in the world of e-commerce. Building retention impact—enhancing the "stickiness" of the firm's offering, in any context—is a key aspect of driving Customer Equity.

How Retention Equity Works

Building retention impact can take many forms. A firm can provide additional benefits that make it more costly for the customer to switch to a competitor. For example, e-commerce retailer Bluefly.com attracts customers by allowing them to create their own catalog from among the designer fashions on the site. Giving the customer exactly what he or she wants has the additional benefit of creating Retention Equity, since the switching costs of reentering preference data into another site can be high.[3] Through greater understanding of the customer, the firm can make it easier for the customer to do business with the firm, perhaps even customizing the purchase and consumption experience for its customers. Ultimately, through ongoing dialogue with customers, a firm takes advantage of opportunities to meet additional needs of the firm's best customers, thereby growing revenues while enhancing retention.

Second, a firm can reward behaviors that enhance the retention connection. The firm may find it most effective to reward purchase transactions (e.g., Southwest Airlines), monetary value of transactions (e.g., Neiman Marcus), or even length of consumption experience (e.g., American AAdvantage miles). These retention-impact-enhancing behaviors can be rewarded with monetary incentives, special treatment, or recognition.

Third, a firm may find that strengthening the relationship with the customer through emotional ties may be most effective in building Retention Equity. Anything that increases the sense of loss the customer will feel if he or she discontinues patronage of the firm will build Retention Equity. Typically, firms find that connecting with the customer's interests, hobbies, or personal history often provides the basis for this emotional bond. First USA's affinity credit-card programs have been very successful in creating such emotional connections with customers.[4] In addition to creating an emotional connection between the customer and the firm, firms can also create emotional ties among their customers as a means to strengthen Retention Equity.

Now let's take a look at how a firm can really take advantage of Retention Equity to drive overall Customer Equity. To maximize the return from investments in Retention Equity, it is important to understand two things: (1) When does Retention Equity matter most? (2) What are the key drivers of Retention Equity?

When Retention Equity Matters Most

- *When the benefits the customer associates with the loyalty program are significantly greater than the "actual" benefits.* The success of the world's frequent flyer programs lies, to some extent, in the difference between the "true" value of a frequent flyer mile (about $.03–$.04) and the customer perception of the value of a frequent flyer mile (I'm getting closer to my free trip to Fiji!). This "aspirational value" of a loyalty program presents a solid opportunity for firms to strengthen Retention Equity by creating a strong incentive for the customer to return. Firms that successfully create loyalty programs with high aspirational value can often build retention impact without falling into the trap of the loyalty program becoming merely one more form of price promotion. One caution here—the rewards that customers aspire to must be reachable; if customers perceive that they have little chance of achieving their reward goal, the loyalty program will not build retention impact.

- *When the community associated with the product or service is as important as the product or service.* Certain products and services have the additional benefit of building a strong community of enthusiasts. If a firm's broader "product" includes a community of individuals who consume or advocate the product or service, this can be a strong source of retention impact. For such firms, customers will continue to purchase from the firm to maintain "membership" in the community. Two examples of the strength of the community are: (1) Harley-Davidson Owners Groups and (2) a customer's "support group" of people the customer exercises with at a health club.

- *When the learning relationship created between the firm and the customer becomes as important as the provision of the product or service.* Recently, a broad set of product and service firms have begun to understand the value of making "investments" in relationships with customers, something that professionals such as lawyers, accountants, and bankers have known for years. If customers reveal significant information to a firm, they are more likely to continue doing business with that firm. Similarly, if the firm creates "structural bonds" that make it difficult for the customer to receive the same personal attention (attention based on knowledge of the customer), retention impact can be strengthened. It used to be that such "learning relationships" were restricted to business-to-business relationships and professional relationships. However, database technology has made such "learning" possible for any company or organization willing to invest the time and resources into collecting, tracking, and utilizing the information customers reveal. One expert in creating such a learning relationship is Amazon.com.

- *When customer action is required to discontinue the service.* For many services (and some product continuity programs), customers must actively decide to stop consuming the product or service (e.g., book clubs, insurance, Internet service providers, other negative-option services). For such products and services, inertia provides a certain stickiness to the relationship. Firms providing these types of products and services have a unique opportunity to build Retention Equity.

Drivers of Retention Equity

We have seen how Value Equity and Brand Equity can be used to strengthen the connection between the customer and the firm. Retention Equity provides yet another means for building Customer Equity. Research on customer retention provides some insight into actions the firm can take to increase the likelihood that the customer comes back—that is, to create "customer stickiness." Specifically, these actions fall into five distinct areas:

- Loyalty programs (frequent purchase/reward programs)
- Special recognition and treatment programs
- Affinity (emotional connection) programs
- Community programs

- Knowledge-building programs (learning relationships or structural bonds)

The extent to which each of these specific types of actions or programs will be effective for any firm will depend upon the nature of the product or service, the frequency with which the customer purchases the product or service, and the motivations of the firm's customers (see figure 7-1).

Frequency (Loyalty) Programs

It is important to understand what effects a so-called loyalty program is having or will have on current customers. For example, in the United Kingdom, supermarket chains such as Sainsbury's, Tesco, and Safeway are finding that loyalty cards are more complex than previously thought. The data are messy to analyze and utilize for targeted mailings. More important, the programs appear to be rewarding customers for their purchase

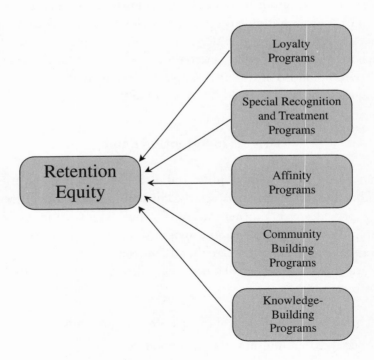

Figure 7-1. Drivers of Retention Equity

behavior (read—giving away margin through special discounts) without engendering any long-term loyalty for the store.[5]

Often, these programs were designed to provide an effective and efficient means for firms to gain access to customer purchase behavior, thereby providing an opportunity to customize offers for current customers. Instead, these programs are becoming a very expensive method for firms attempting to buy short-term market share. For example, recent estimates suggest that over 40 million loyalty cards are currently in use in the United Kingdom alone, with over 74% of the population participating in at least one program.[6]

Where have such loyalty schemes gone wrong? Such loyalty programs appear to be effective only when several key criteria are met:

- if the customer earns points frequently enough to accumulate sufficient rewards;

- if the rewards are meaningful to the customer and are worth "saving for" or receiving; and

- if the margins of the products or services offered by the firm are high enough to justify such a program.

In the case of airlines, these criteria appear to have been met. However, for supermarkets, the loyalty programs run the risk of eroding already slim margins as chains are forced to engage in loyalty wars.

FINANCIAL INSTITUTIONS: AN ALTERNATIVE MODEL. Banks have learned that customers who have multiple accounts with a financial institution tend to continue doing business with that financial institution. So the banks have started rewarding customers with multiple accounts. For example, the Loyalty Banking™ program by Harrison Company of Aurora, Colorado, rewards customers based on "number and length of relationships with the bank, loans held, credit card products used, number of referrals made and use of trust or investment services."[7] Customers are rewarded "points" based upon these relationships, and points can be redeemed for CD rate premiums, reductions in loan rates, and other benefits.

Wilmington Savings Fund Society (Wilmington, Delaware) utilizes a program created by Enamacom Data Services Inc. of Dover, New Hampshire. This program rewards points to bank customers who maintain specific balances in accounts, increase deposits, or refer customers. Rewards include coupons for merchandise and bank services. In this case, the loyalty program resulted in increased deposits (increase of $21 million) and loans from these "key" customers and provided a mechanism for the bank to maintain CD interest rates without losing good customers to competing institutions. These banks have learned that a good loyalty program can provide rewards to the bank's best customers without giving up profitability of these customers. In addition, banks are beginning to understand that such programs can be "packaged" to steer customers to lower priced transaction channels, thereby increasing profitability, through lower cost structures for serving these customers, as well as increased revenue from these customers.[8]

LOYALTY PROGRAMS: CONCLUSIONS.   Loyalty (frequent purchase) programs can be effective in some industries. However, it appears that such loyalty programs often deteriorate into a prisoner's dilemma game among competitors in an industry, as was the case in the supermarket examples above. Why do these reward programs appear to work for banks, but not for supermarkets? It may be because the customers' costs inherent in switching financial institutions are perceived by the customer as far greater than the costs of switching to a new supermarket. What, then, is a firm to do? One solution would be to find other ways to increase the customer's perceived cost of switching to a competitor. How do you increase switching costs while not alienating customers? The other drivers of Retention Equity may offer some insight.

Special Recognition and Treatment Programs

Reward programs often deteriorate into an alternative form of price discount or rebate for the customer. These programs offer rewards or compensation for customer purchase behavior, sometimes related to the products and services purchased (coupons, frequent flyer miles) and sometimes unrelated (AT&T True Rewards Program points). However, often, a firm's best customers value other types of benefits more than monetary rewards. For example, the special recognition and treatment afforded many airlines' "platinum" level members (early boarding, calling the customer by name at check-in) are valued as highly as the "reward" type benefits such as double frequent flyer miles and upgrades to first class.

A compelling example of the customer perceived value of such benefits can be found in the Sears Best Customer Program. Sears identifies "best customers" as those who have spent more than a specific dollar amount in the past year. These customers receive a special sticker to place on their Sears credit card, to identify them as a Sears Best Customer. Following the first year of the program (in which revenues from Best Customers increased substantially), Sears ran focus groups to investigate the effectiveness of its program. To its surprise, the customers reported that the nonmonetary benefits (being recognized by name as a "best customer," better treatment by salespeople because of their "best customer" status) were more valuable than the extra discounts and sales offers they received as Sears Best Customers. For Sears, the price discounts were perceived by these customers as part of the value connection, leading to Value Equity, whereas the special recognition provided additional incentive to return to Sears and increase spending levels, strengthening the retention connection.[9]

Affinity and Emotional Connection Programs

In addition to special recognition and special treatment, are there other nonmonetary approaches to increasing the retention connection? How can we increase a customer's commitment to the firm? Recent research and leading companies are beginning to understand the value of affinity groups—tapping into a customer's interests and thereby strengthening the emotional connection to the firm. Customers who share a common interest are candidates for an affinity program. The effectiveness of an affinity program or creating an emotional attachment to the product, service, or firm will most often depend upon the ability of the firm to identify and access a key customer interest or emotional link.

In a recent *Direct Marketing* article, Kurt Johnson suggests: "Affinity programs are applicable only where the brand represents a strong lifestyle. The members of an affinity program need to be acutely interested in your product and willing to invest time in learning more about it. Examples of brands that represent lifestyles include Volkswagen cars, Harley-Davidson motorcycles, North Face outdoor clothing, and Versace clothing."[10] The key aspect of affinity is that the firm, or the firm's product or service, becomes an integral part of the customer. The customer forges a link between the firm and himself or herself. In other words, through the affinity group or program, the firm has found a way to increase the customer's cost of switch-

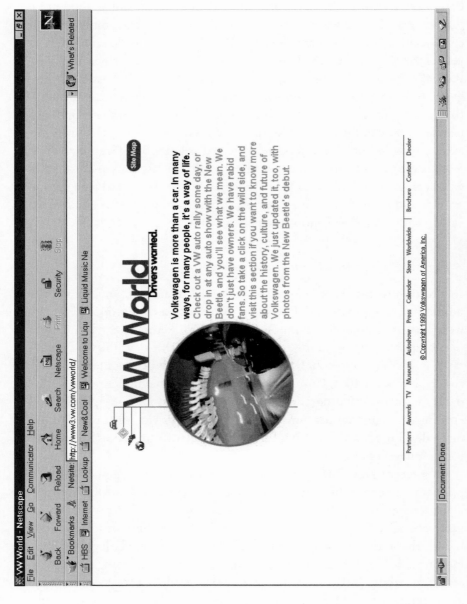

Figure 7-2. VW Creates Affinity

ing to a competitor, because such a switch would involve some type of "loss of self" (see figure 7-2).

STRENGTHENING EMOTIONAL TIES.   Affinity programs seek to imbed the firm's product or service in some strong interest or emotional link of the customer. Not all products or services are candidates for affinity programs, but some firms are finding creative ways to tap into the community and the customer's "emotional connection." First USA has successfully created several sub-brands that combine an affinity program with a rewards program. One of the authors (Lemon), an avid Duke basketball fan, has just become aware of a First USA Duke basketball Visa card, which allows customers to earn points good toward Duke basketball stuff—shirts, balls, even entry in a sweepstakes to win NCAA tickets. Given a choice between a reduction in interest rates or even cash, the card members choose the Duke memorabilia. First USA has also recently introduced a golfing Visa card, through which customers earn points good toward golfing products and vacations. Tapping into a customer's interests or emotional connection to his or her alma mater and providing rewards that forward the customer's interests are a winning combination.

Customer Community Programs

Closely related to affinity is the idea of community. For certain products and services, the firm has the opportunity to build upon the brand personality to create a customer community. The ability of a firm to create a customer community depends somewhat upon the nature of the firm's products or services, but most often upon the "personality" of the firm and the motivations of its customers. A customer community can be created when the firm can convince customers that they will benefit by being connected with other customers of the firm. In customer communities, the firm's brand often serves as the focus of the affinity group.

A great example of customer community can be found in an examination of Harley-Davidson Owners Groups (HOGS). Harley owners experience great benefits from being around other Harley owners. In fact, an entire language of customizing Harleys has developed through these HOGS. The key to a customer community is that the firm has found a way to increase the customer's perceived cost of switching to a competitor—the community that customers would lose if they stopped doing business with the firm (see sidebar).

A Demonstration of Community

Figure 7-3. Don't Mess with a Harley Owner

We encourage you to test this proposition. Find a friend who owns a Harley. Ask this person if he or she would consider buying a Honda Gold Wing. If the response doesn't leave you in the hospital, you will have probably at least lost a friend. These people are fiercely loyal to their brand and to the community created through their brand.

Will customer communities only work for very strong "brand personalities" such as Harley-Davidson? In the case of Harley, the Harley owners created the communities, not the firm. But such communities can be constructed by the firm. Consider Saturn, a division of General Motors. Saturn, through its marketing messages from inception, created a brand personality that was conducive to customer community. Saturn owners drive their Saturns "home" to Spring Hill, Tennessee, for the annual "homecoming" and routinely drop by Saturn dealerships to "visit" the latest Saturn "offspring" (Saturn dealers offer free hamburgers, hot dogs, or donuts and coffee for their effort, and in 1999, people are actually willing to *pay* for this privilege). The result: Saturn has successfully created retention impact; a large portion of Saturn customers take their cars to a Saturn dealership for routine service, and a large portion of Saturn owners repurchase Saturns.

Knowledge-Building Programs

But what if a firm doesn't have a strong "brand personality" or can't readily tap into customer interest or emotional connections, yet still doesn't want to give away margin through traditional loyalty/reward programs? What else motivates customers to continue doing business with a firm? In our discussion of Value Equity, we mentioned that consistency in performance of products and services over time can create customer trust. In considering how to build the retention connection, the firm has an opportunity to build upon that trust.

Recent advances in database technology have provided opportunities for firms to capture, for the first time since the advent of mass marketing, every transaction and interaction between the firm and the customer. As we mentioned in chapter 4, if the focus is not on the customer, such database technology is just as likely to create a customer dis-connection as it is to strengthen the connection. But how can such information be used to strengthen the retention connection?

LEARNING FROM EVERY INTERACTION. Every time a customer interacts with the firm, the firm learns something about the customer and the customer learns something about the firm. Most often, however, the firm does not use the information learned about the customer to build the relationship with the customer, or to make future transactions more effective or efficient for the customer. Consider the typical supermarket. How does the supermarket utilize the information gained about the customer to improve the shopping experience for the customer? In chapter 2, we saw that such information often results in the profitable product death spiral. But is there another way?

Consider, first of all, how the customer uses the information gained about the supermarket in future transactions. Consider one of the authors' (Lemon) first visit to Marketbasket, in Boston. Visiting the store for the first time on a Saturday afternoon, she finds the store filled with people, aisles jammed with product, and a line for checkout that winds around the frozen food aisle. The customer learns

- that there must be something good about this store because no one is grumbling about the wait in line or the cramped aisles

- that the toothpicks are located next to the candles in the paper goods aisle
- perhaps not to come to the store at 4:00 P.M. on a Saturday
- that you can't write a check without a check card
- that her weekly grocery bill was lower than usual

Most certainly, the customer will incorporate this new information on her next visit to Marketbasket.

What does the supermarket learn about the customer? To understand this side of the relationship, let's turn to another type of supermarket in the Boston area, food delivery services such as Streamline and peapod.com. Customers of Streamline and peapod.com order their groceries online (via phone, fax, or the Internet). When a household becomes a customer of Streamline, the company sends a representative out to survey the customer's current inventory of grocery products. These products represent a core shopping list. (For peapod, this essentials grocery list is built over time by the customer). The companies monitor customer purchase behavior over time, suggest products the customer might like (based upon other customers with similar preferences and purchase behavior), and even prompt the customer to check inventory if some "stock" item may be getting low.[11]

These new supermarkets are building learning relationships with their customers, increasing the structural bonds between the firm and the customer. Over time, not only are they building trust with the customer, they are also building a learning relationship with the customer. In this relationship, the customer receives greater benefits from being a customer because he or she has *revealed* preferences to the firm, and the firm has *reacted* to these revelations and found ways to *tailor* its products, services, or shopping experience to better serve the customer. Given the extra benefits a customer receives from this learning relationship, the customer finds it more and more "costly" to leave and to recreate this relationship with an alternate provider.

Another example of learning relationships can be found by looking at Amazon.com (see figure 7-4). Amazon.com uses the information it gains from customer purchases, inquiries, and click-throughs to provide possible selections (books, music, videos, etc.) to the customer that should closely

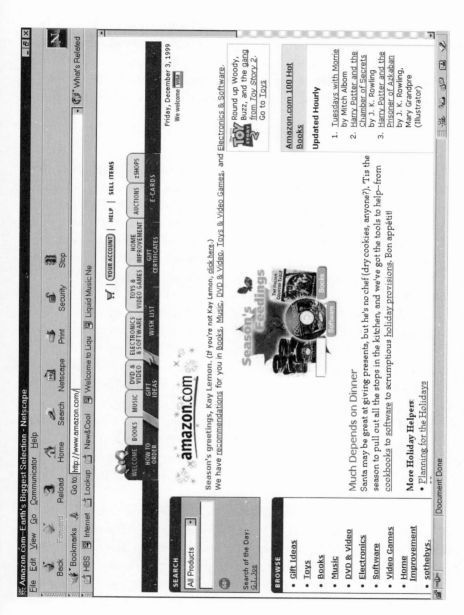

Figure 7-4. Knowledge-Building at Work

match the customer's preferences, thereby reducing the customer's search time for possible purchases and providing interesting options that the customer might not have otherwise considered. By utilizing the knowledge gained about the customer through simple interactions and purchase transactions, the firm has yet another opportunity to increase the customer's cost of switching to a competitor. The cost of starting from scratch to build such a relationship with a new provider may be much to high to pay.

Final Thoughts

Retention Equity represents the importance of the customer's relationship with the firm to the overall Customer Equity. In this chapter, we have examined the key drivers of Retention Equity and identified specific approaches to strengthening this "retention connection." Once a customer has established a relationship with a firm, the firm has the opportunity to strengthen this relationship. As we have seen, it is most important for the firm to strengthen the aspects of the relationship that are valued by the customer.

For example, consider a customer of a specialty clothing store who values special recognition and treatment, but is not at all price sensitive (one of the authors is a great example of this type of customer). Which of the following two offers will she find more compelling as a reason to keep her business at the store and potentially increase her business? *(a)* A 15% discount on all purchases made on a specific day, or *(b)* a personal shopper assigned to her who knows her size and tastes and will call her when items of interest arrive in the store? Clearly, option *(b)* will increase Retention Equity to a far greater extent than option *(a)*. However, another customer might be more motivated by the discount offer, or by a frequent purchase program that leads to free clothing with substantial purchases.

It is most important to understand that building Retention Equity is not always a matter of offering price perks or frequent flyer miles. It is a matter of understanding the customer and creating relationship-building strategies that will maximize the likelihood of that customer "sticking" to the firm, maximize the revenue from the "sticky customer," and minimize the likelihood of the customer leaving to become "stuck" to a competitor.

Driving Retention Equity	
KEY INSIGHTS	ACTION STEPS
1. The key to Retention Equity is strengthening the aspects of the relationship that are important to the customer.	• Determine the nature and extent of the relationship that your customers would like to have with your organization.
2. If customer-perceived switching costs are high, loyalty programs can increase retention likelihood and profitability.	• Examine your customers' switching costs. What do your customers have to give up to switch to a competitor? • Evaluate whether loyalty programs are important to your best customers. If so, you may need to develop such a program to reduce the vulnerability of your best customers to a competitive threat.
3. Customers want attention and recognition. Special recognition programs can grow Retention Equity.	• Determine whether your firm is up to the difficult challenge of developing and implementing a special recognition program for your best customers.
4. Affinity programs grow Retention Equity by strengthening the customer's emotional connection with the firm, and through the added benefit of strong word-of-mouth referral.	• Engage in marketing research to understand your customers' interests and emotional links. • Provide benefits to your customers that link to these emotional ties.
5. Successful community-building programs can increase switching costs—the customer perceives that the whole community must switch to maintain the benefit.	• Find out whether your customers value the idea of community prior to implementing such a program. • Determine whether your firm has a distinctive "brand personality" that may make it a candidate for community building.
6. Knowledge-building programs can often increase "customer stickiness" as the customer finds it more costly to recreate the relationship with another provider.	• Before engaging in knowledge-building programs, be sure to get customer consent and buy-in for utilizing customer information to customize the relationship. • Utilize information gained from the customer to build a learning relationship and to offer customized benefits.

CUSTOMER-CENTERED STRATEGY

The Customer Equity Framework redefines competitive strategy—laying out a truly customer-centered approach to strategy. In the customer-centered company, strategy must be based not on products or competencies, but rather on the drivers of Customer Equity. A firm's relative standing with respect to Customer Equity and its drivers is central to long-term competitive success. Successful firms will measure and monitor Customer Equity and its drivers. Strategic investments will be designed to improve Value, Brand, and Retention Equity. Improvement efforts will be financially accountable, reflecting the extent to which they support the drivers of Customer Equity.

8

Measuring Customer Equity

Getting the Job Done

In this chapter, we provide answers to questions about how to actually measure Customer Equity, and how to uncover the key drivers of Customer Equity in an organization.

Step 1. Measure Customer Equity

The most important first step is considering if you're really up to the task of committing to becoming a Customer Equity organization. As discussed in chapter 4, the commitment to Customer Equity has to come from the top. Ask yourself the following questions:

- What are the key areas of your organization that need to be onboard to truly get a commitment to Customer Equity? (Finance? Operations? Marketing? Sales? Accounting? Strategy and Top Management?)

- What is your current approach to strategic thinking? (What old ways of thinking will you be "trading in" when you begin driving Customer Equity?)

- What is the total of the discounted lifetime values of all your customers? How much is your organization worth, considering the extent to which you can count on your current customers coming back and spending what they spend now? What is the optimal allocation of resources to grow Customer Equity?

• How would growing Customer Equity benefit your organization?

Step 2. Determine Your Key Competitors (From Your Customer's Perspective)

Who do your customers consider to be your competitors? That is, if your customers stopped buying from you, what would they do instead? Would they buy the same service or product from someone else? Would they buy a similar service or product from someone else? Would they not buy the product or service at all? What would they do with the resources that they had been committing to your firm? The way your customers answer these questions helps to determine the key competitors in your marketplace (among your current customers). Competition for the spending dollars of someone who occasionally purchases *Sail* magazine, for example, may include not just other sailing-related magazines, but also producers of sailing apparel and sailing gear. In other words, a sailing enthusiast with a specific amount of money to spend may be choosing between items in different product categories that may or may not be related to each other.

Understanding your key competitors is a critical element in measuring Customer Equity. The underlying structure of the Customer Equity Framework, the customer switching matrix, requires an understanding not only of the attributes of your organization, but an understanding of your competitors as well. To whom do your customers go when they leave you? From whom do they switch when they begin buying from you?

In determining key competitors, it is important to consider *(a)* the problem(s) you solve for your customers, and *(b)* the benefits your customers receive from your organization.

• What problem do you solve for your current customers? How else could they solve this problem? Could they do it for themselves? Other solutions to the problem you solve for your current customers represent other potential competitors you must consider. Consider Streamline, a Boston company whose products and services promise to help busy consumers relieve stress in their lives. What other solutions exist for this problem? Consumers might consider: massage therapy, live-in help, or even moving to a tropical island. In determining competition, you must consider at least the close alternatives to solving the same problem you solve for your customers.

- What benefit do you provide for your customers? How else could they receive this benefit? For example, Netcentives, a company that develops customer relationship management programs and manages loyalty promotion programs for its merchant clients, provides the benefit of increasing customer acquisition for its client companies as well as increasing revenue per customer. Without Netcentives, Netcentives' customers (merchants) could utilize other promotion strategies to increase purchase likelihood and increase revenue per customer, although these other promotion strategies would most likely be less efficient and effective.[1]

Step 3. Customize the Potential Drivers of Value, Brand, and Retention Equity

Once you have identified the key competitors *from your customer's perspective,* the next step is to identify potential drivers of Value Equity, Brand Equity, and Retention Equity for your organization. In chapters 5, 6, and 7, we outline the key drivers of Value, Brand, and Retention Equity. But to apply the Customer Equity Framework to your business or organization, you need to determine the potential sub-drivers of each Equity driver, determining specifically how the drivers of Value, Brand, and Retention Equity apply to your business. This can be done in several ways.

The most logical choice is to ask. Ask customers. Ask employees. Ask experts. Look at existing data and research (see sidebar). It is important to uncover the potential sub-drivers at this point, but not to attach any importance to any driver or sub-driver. For example, a company that provides day care for young children may conduct a set of focus groups in which it becomes apparent that mothers and fathers who choose day care for their young children see safety, attention, and convenient hours as aspects of a "quality day-care setting." An organization can ask employees in key areas to brainstorm a set of key sub-drivers for each equity. For example, key operations managers could be brought into the Customer Equity process by developing a list of potential drivers of Value Equity.

Finding Potential Drivers of Value, Brand, and Retention Equity

- *Focus Groups.* Bringing together seven to ten individuals in a group format can provide a good starting point for uncovering potential drivers of each equity. It is important to collect data from groups of customers and noncustomers when using this method. Usually, a professional moderator leads the focus groups, following a "script" developed in concert with the firm. In the focus group, individuals build upon one another's ideas, often leading to insights for the firm. *Key advantage:* relatively efficient method for uncovering large numbers of potential drivers and sub-drivers. *Key disadvantage:* much chaff is collected along with the wheat; further analysis will be needed to determine the most plausible potential drivers.

- *Delphi Method.* The Delphi Method involves asking "experts" a set of questions to determine the potential key drivers of each equity. A set of experts (current customers, current noncustomers, key individuals in the industry, key individuals in the firm) are queried to determine their perceptions of key potential drivers. The set of responses (from all respondents) is then returned to each of the Delphi members, who reduce the list to a manageable number of potential drivers for each equity. *Key advantage:* excellent method for refining the list of potential drivers prior to developing the survey. *Key disadvantages:* may be inefficient, should not be used as the sole source for potential drivers, and may upset key customers if their "drivers" do not end up in final survey.

- *Brainstorming.* Brainstorming involves bringing together key internal members (operations, finance, marketing, sales, customer service, product development) to develop a list of key drivers for each equity. *Key advantage:* efficient way to get individuals from multiple functions motivated to measure and grow Customer Equity. *Key disadvantage:* individuals inside the firm may not be the best source of potential drivers of each equity (do not use as sole source).

- *Laddering.* This technique involves in-depth interviewing of existing customers and noncustomers to determine "deeper" potential drivers of each equity. Simplifying the technique, the idea is to ask these individuals why they currently purchase (or don't purchase) the firm's products or services. This question is followed by a series of "why" or "why is that important to you" questions, to determine what is driving the customer's decision. *Key advantage:* when laddering works well, it can uncover deeper motivations of customers, e.g., "It makes me feel safe," "It is important to my career growth." *Key disadvantage:* should not be the sole source of key drivers; can lead to a tunnel-vision view of potential drivers of each equity.

- *Zaltman Metaphor Elicitation Technique (ZMET).* ZMET is a relatively new approach to uncovering the mental models that drive consumer thinking and decision making. The basic idea behind ZMET is a set of techniques that serves to elicit these metaphors and mental models, that is, the consumer's interrelated ideas about a market or consumption experience. The results of this technique reveal the underlying connections consumers make between products, between products and experience, or between products and people. *Key advantage:* ZMET is a powerful method for understanding consumers' images of brands, and the powerful ways consumers often connect brands to other facets of their lives. *Key disadvantages:* it can be time consuming to collect and analyze data; should not be the sole source of potential drivers.[2]

The goal of this step is to identify potential aspects of each driver, rather than attempt to prioritize them. A secondary goal of this step is to involve any aspect of the organization that may ultimately be asked to implement changes based upon the Customer Equity Framework. For example, the individuals in an organization responsible for managing the brand (usually marketing) must be involved in determining the key drivers of Brand Equity for the organization. If they are not involved, they will not believe the results.

Whenever possible, these sub-drivers should represent something that the firm can take an action to change (convenient hours, brand perceptions, durability of product, aspects of the loyalty program, etc.). It is important to make sure that you have at least one (preferably more than one) sub-driver for each of the key drivers of Value Equity, Brand Equity, and Retention Equity, that were described in chapters 5 through 7.

Step 4. Choose the Population of Interest

In applying the Customer Equity Framework and determining the drivers of Customer Equity for your business, it is important to determine who you want to study first. Which aspect of your customer base should be your primary focus will depend upon key issues facing your firm, "the state of the company" and "the state of the market." For example, if your firm relies on a few key customers for most of its business (the 80/20 rule, see chapters 11 and 12), you will want to understand the key drivers of your most important customers first, the customers who generate most of your current revenue and profitability. However, if your firm is having a difficult time penetrating a specific segment of customers, it may be more useful to focus initial Customer Equity efforts on that segment of customers, to understand what your competitors are doing right that you are doing wrong. Black & Decker, for example, divided its power tool customer base into three categories: professional/industrial, professional/tradesmen, and consumer. Noting that the middle category was doing poorly in comparison to its competitors, the company decided to focus its attention on that segment of customers with its DeWalt line.

Alternatively, examining the drivers of Customer Equity for a cross section of the current market may provide a good baseline view of the drivers of Customer Equity, upon which the more targeted analyses can build. If you're not sure where to start, we recommend the following:

- If a few customers generate most of your business, first determine who these best customers are. Sample a cross section of your best customers to determine the drivers of Customer Equity for these customers. It is important not to make radical changes in your organization without first understanding the factors that influence Customer Equity for your best customers.

- Sample a cross section of "the market," that is, both customers and non-customers. This sample will provide a solid baseline and a good comparison for your best customers as well.

- After completing these two analyses, you can then examine any sub-segments of particular interest.

Step 5. Develop the Survey

After you have decided upon which aspect of your customer base to focus, the next step is developing the survey instrument. (Some sample survey questions are shown in Appendix 8.1, as a guide.) It is critical in developing a survey to conduct a pretest on a small convenience sample to ensure that the questions are straightforward and unambiguous to the casual reader. You may think that you are the most important thing in your customers' lives (after all, they're the most important thing in yours), but often if your organization is doing its job particularly well, your best customers may not pay much attention to you at all.

An important note from our experience in measuring Customer Equity: when designing the survey, we have found that it is most useful not to provide customers with the option of saying "don't know" if they are not familiar with a competitor's product or service. Rather, you want to encourage respondents to indicate the extent to which they believe statements are true about you and your competitors, even if they do not have perfect information. It is their *perceptions* of your organization and your competitors that are of interest, not the facts. At the end of the survey, you can ask the respondents how familiar they are with each of the companies in the survey, and thereby get a sense of whether their answers for a particular firm were based upon perceptions from experience or perceptions based upon little information.

Step 6. Collect the Data

The collection of the data is quite straightforward and need not take up significant time or resources. In our experience, we have found that a sample size of 100–1000 in a metropolitan area should be large enough for most companies to get a good sense of the drivers of Customer Equity while minimizing possibility for error.

Step 7. Analyze the Data: Determine Key Equities and Drivers of Each Equity

The analysis of the data is the key element in measuring the drivers of Customer Equity. The model is quite straightforward. The goal is to get a sense of how likely your customers are to come back, and how likely your competitors' customers are to switch to your firm. These probabilities can be aggregated to determine next period's "market share," which is then compared to this period's "market share." This is then projected to compute the lifetime value of the customer base—Customer Equity. The purchase probabilities are influenced by Brand, Value, and Retention Equity, specifically:

- Where they bought last (Retention Equity gauge)

- Quality and price (Value Equity gauge)

- Individual preferences (Brand Equity gauge)

We then determine the key sub-drivers of Value, Brand, and Retention Equity:

- Value Equity is a function of *quality* (the physical product, when one exists; the service product; service delivery; and the service environment), *price* (everyday price, discounts and sales, payment plans), and *convenience* (location, ease of use, availability).

- Brand Equity is a function of *fit* (relative to competition, and to self), *communications* (attention to mass media and direct media, efficacy of customer communication to firm), *ethics* (corporate citizenship, community events, ethical dealings), and *attitude* (feelings, overall perceptions, recommendations).

- Retention Equity is a function of *loyalty programs* (frequent buyer programs, special tangible benefits), *special recognition* (special treatment, best customer status) *affinity* (tapping into emotional connections, affinity programs) *community* (connections with other customers), *trust and dependence* (learning relationships).

These sub-drivers represent actionable items that the firm has the opportunity to change or influence based upon decision variables under the firm's control. The analysis provides the key insights, in which we begin to see what really drives customers' decisions to continue (or not to continue) to do business with a firm in the future.[3]

Step 8. Benchmark Against Competitors

It is not sufficient to understand what drives customers to do business with your firm. It is also important to understand where you stand relative to your key competitors on each of the key drivers and sub-drivers. For example, if you determine that Retention Equity is the key driver for Customer Equity, and your competitors are doing a better job of building Retention Equity than you are, then in the long run, your organization can plan to lose a significant share of its current customers.

Step 9. Determine Key Areas for Improvement

Based upon the insights from the above analyses, the firm can then begin to decide which areas require the most improvement, or which areas will lead to the greatest improvement in Customer Equity. Traditionally, firms have focused most often on areas requiring the most improvement, believing that all weak areas need to be improved. This logic may be flawed. Consider the

Table 8-1 Steps in Measuring Customer Equity

Make sure your company is up to the task.

- What are the key areas of your organization that need to be onboard to truly get a commitment to Customer Equity?
- What is your current approach to strategic thinking?
- What is the total of the discounted lifetime values of all your customers? What is the optimal allocation of resources to grow Customer Equity?
- How would growing Customer Equity benefit your organization?

Determine your key competitors (from your customer's perspective).

- What problem do you solve for your current customers? How else could they solve this problem?
- What benefit do you provide for your customers? How else could they receive this benefit?

Customize the potential drivers of Value, Brand, and Retention Equity for your business.

- Determine the potential sub-drivers of each Equity driver, determining specifically how the drivers of Value, Brand, and Retention Equity apply to your business.

Choose the population of interest.

- Determine whom you want to study first.
- If a few customers generate most of your business, first determine who these best customers are.
- Sample a cross section of "the market," that is, both customers and noncustomers. This sample will provide a solid baseline and a good comparison for your best customers as well.
- After completing these two analyses, you can then examine any sub-segments of particular interest.

Develop the survey, collect the data, and determine the key drivers of each component of Customer Equity.

- Develop the survey instrument.
- Collect the data.
- Analyze the data.
- Compute the lifetime value of the customer base—Customer Equity. The purchase probabilities are influenced by Value, Brand, and Retention Equity.

Benchmark against competitors.

- Determine key areas for improvement.
- Determine return on equity for each improvement and invest in the drivers that will provide maximum return in terms of Customer Equity.

following: suppose your firm is weak relative to your competitors on the sub-driver of *price discounts*. However, if your customers don't happen to care about price discounts, and price discounts do not drive Customer Equity, then an investment in improving your price discounting policies may not be warranted.

Key areas of improvement will be determined by two things: (1) understanding what drivers will have the most impact on Customer Equity for your organization, and (2) understanding where you stand relative to your competitors on each of those "most important" drivers of Customer Equity.

Step 10. Determine Return on Equity for Each Improvement, and Invest in Drivers That Provide Maximum Return on Customer Equity

As we discuss in chapter 9, once these analyses are complete, you can determine the best way to focus your resources to maximize Customer Equity.

Focusing Resources for Growing Value Equity

Let us consider a company that we will call Acme Corporation. Acme realizes that Customer Equity is the key to its long-term success, and also that Value Equity is a major element of Customer Equity. Acme also realizes that quality, price, and convenience are the keys to Value Equity and has analyzed the drivers of Value Equity enough to realize that, for that particular company, quality is the key to Value Equity. Once Acme knows that, what should it do now? How should it determine which quality elements to focus on?

The Process Tree

Fortunately, Acme has some good examples to emulate. Work by Bradley Gale at General Electric and Ray Kordupleski at AT&T in the late 1980s and early 1990s showed how to identify the processes on which to focus.[4] Given an identification of the key drivers of quality, the firm could then put its resources where they would have the most good. Our framework for Customer Equity is an extension and expansion of these basic ideas.

Let us consider the construction of a process tree that shows how to analyze the key drivers of quality. Figure 8-1, based on work by Ray Kordupleski, Anthony Zahorik, and the first author (Rust), shows the process tree used by a division of AT&T that sold equipment to business customers.[5]

We see that overall quality is seen as driven by the quality perceptions of the various business processes that touch the customer. For this example, the processes are product, sales, installation, repair, and billing.

The company surveys its customers, asking them about overall quality, as well as their quality ratings on each of the processes (alternatively they could be asked for satisfaction ratings or comparison with expectations). Based on the surveys, statistical analysis can reveal the processes that are the key drivers of overall quality.

The same approach can also be used to determine the relative importance of sub-processes. For example, suppose it is found that "billing" is the most important driver of overall quality. In that case a sub-process analysis might then reveal that "easy to understand" was the most important sub-process. The two analyses together provide a very specific road map of where the company should focus its attention. It should try to make its bills

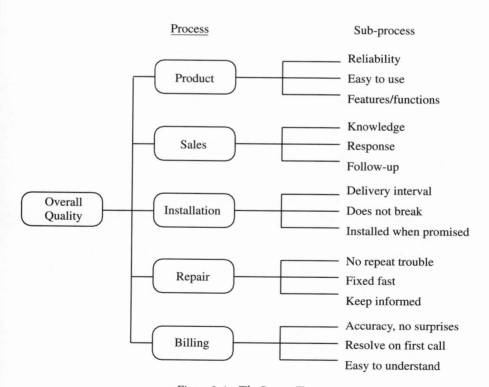

Figure 8-1. The Process Tree

[SOURCE: ADAPTED FROM RAYMOND E. KORDUPLESKI, ROLAND T. RUST, AND ANTHONY J. ZAHORIK, "WHY IMPROVING QUALITY DOESN'T IMPROVE QUALITY," *CALIFORNIA MANAGEMENT REVIEW*, 35 (SPRING 1993), 82–95.]

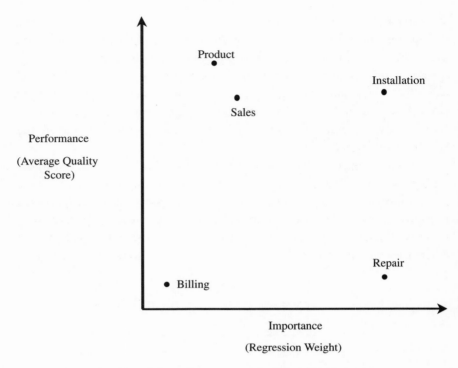

Figure 8-2. The Performance-Importance Chart

easier to understand. That is the quickest path to improving overall quality. Of course, every company is different, and the key drivers for one company may be very different from the key drivers for another company.

For both processes and sub-processes, it is useful to consider the importance (regression weight) and performance (average quality rating) together (see figure 8-2). This chart, based on the process analysis in figure 8-1, indicates the processes that demand the most attention. Based on the performance-importance chart (figure 8-2) we see that "repair" has both high importance and poor performance, indicating that it is a strong candidate for improvement.

The Bridge of Actionability

The process tree in figure 8-1 is a subtle improvement over what many companies currently do. Let us consider an actual company example (company name withheld) that did the analysis another way and ran into trouble.

Dixie Bank (name changed) wanted to figure out how to improve its customers' satisfaction levels. To find this out, it did focus groups of customers and identified the twenty-five to thirty most frequent customer satisfaction issues. Dixie Bank (DB) then surveyed its customers. Examining the surveys, it grouped together questions that tended to be answered similarly and then figured out which group was most important by conducting regression analyses that predicted overall quality.

One group of questions came out clearly most important. The underlying theme behind all of those questions seemed to be "warmth." The customers wanted their bank to be warm and friendly. That was all well and good, but what was DB supposed to do with the information? Turn up the heat? The problem was that the result of the analysis was too vague. It was not clear exactly what process to improve.

The subtle difference between the process tree shown in the previous section and the analysis described above is that the process tree (figure 8-1) lets management identify the key processes that touch the customer. This is because the results of the analysis need to be understandable by management and translatable into action.

The "bridge of actionability" (see figure 8-3) is between the management-identified processes and the customer-identified sub-processes (specific needs). Connecting the voice of the customer to a process framework that describes how management provides service to the customer provides the bridge needed to make the customer needs relevant to management action.

Competitive Comparisons

Sometimes just being good is not enough. In the 1970s General Motors and Ford enjoyed huge market shares in the U.S. automobile market, and their customer satisfaction ratings were good. Almost overnight, though, they received a competitive shock for which they were unprepared. Japanese brands like Datsun (Nissan), Toyota, and Honda made a big push for U.S. market share with cars that were of higher quality than their American competitors. They were very successful and seriously damaged GM and Ford. The problem was that while Ford and GM were still good (by early 1970s standards) their competitors were better.

Figure 8-4 shows another example (disguised) from another industry. The first author was acting as a consultant to Excelsior Corporation. Mapping relative quality against relative price, we see that Excelsior was clearly

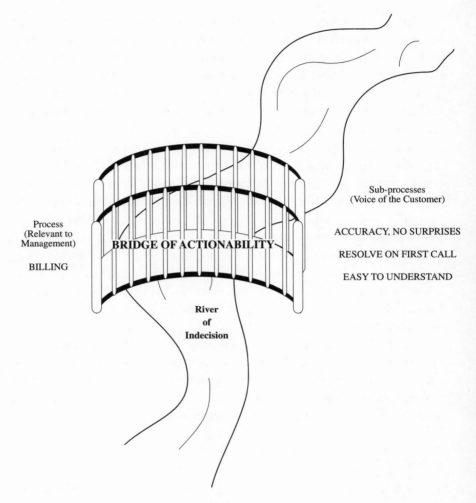

Process
(Relevant to
Management)

BRIDGE OF ACTIONABILITY

BILLING

Sub-processes
(Voice of the Customer)

ACCURACY, NO SURPRISES

RESOLVE ON FIRST CALL

EASY TO UNDERSTAND

River
of
Indecision

Figure 8-3. The Bridge of Actionability

an inferior value to its competitor, Black Knight, because it has worse quality and a higher price. Amazingly, Excelsior still enjoyed a strong market
share, and this caused the company to question whether the value map was
useful.

The answer is, yes the value map was useful, but Value Equity was not
the only driver of Customer Equity. In this case Excelsior enjoyed a large
market share because of its superior Brand Equity (see chapter 6). However,

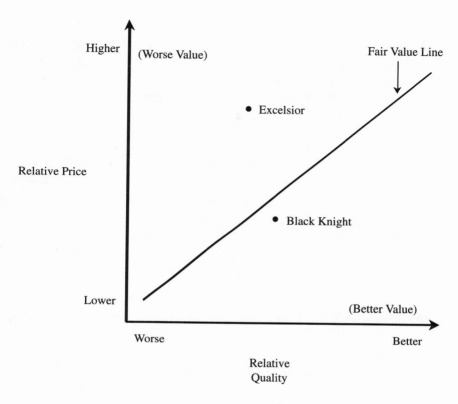

Figure 8-4. The Value Map

there was evidence that Black Knight's superior Value Equity was increasing its Brand Equity over time. This would result in disaster for Excelsior, because given parity in Brand Equity, its inferior Value Equity would cause serious damage to its market share. Therefore, Excelsior's task was to make sure that it could improve its position on the value map, preferably by improving quality.

An important technology for doing this is known as CVA analysis.[6] Devised by Bradley Gale and implemented extensively by AT&T's Ray Kordupleski, CVA analysis compares value, quality, and price against that of the competition. The quality comparison can be done at both the process and sub-process levels. This helps indicate processes and sub-processes where the company is furthest behind its competitors.

Recent research by the first author (Rust), Peter Danaher, and Sajeev

Varki indicates that comparative value changes do a better job of predicting market share change than does value change without considering competition.[7] The implication is that quality, price, and value all need to be considered in comparison to competition.

Implementation Issues

A good marketing research firm or an in-house research department should be able to implement the ideas outlined in this chapter in less than sixty days. The data collection resources required are similar to a typical customer satisfaction survey. The strategic analysis resources required are similar to a strategic consulting project. A company can be on its way to becoming a Customer Equity corporation in less than a quarter by implementing the Customer Equity Framework. Let's take a look at how a company could apply the framework by examining a short case study example.

Mega Health Club Corporation Embraces Customer Equity

Paul Price took a deep breath and looked again at the huge pile of paper in his in-box, and the long list of unread e-mails. At the top of the e-mail list was a note from his boss, Marjorie Smith, CEO of Mega Health Club Corporation (a fictional national chain of health clubs). Marjorie had spent the weekend on the Cape, reading a new book *Driving Customer Equity*. She was eager to implement the framework and ideas described by the authors. In her note, Marjorie wrote that Paul, as the director of strategic initiatives for the company, was just the person for the job and should consider this his top priority. Not surprisingly, he found a copy of the book on the top of the paper pile. He could always count on Marjorie to cover all bases when assigning a new project. What did she mean, measure "Customer Equity" for Mega? With a shrug, Paul picked up the book and his coat and headed for the closest Starbucks for a latte grande to tide him over for the next couple of hours as he read about Customer Equity.

Getting the Organization Aligned

The next morning, Paul arrived at work eager to jump right in to his new project. After a short one-on-one with Marjorie, Paul had a good idea of what the CEO had in mind. But where to begin? He first considered Marjorie's goals for the project: to get a handle on Mega's current Customer Equity, to determine the key drivers of Customer Equity for the company, and to decide how to invest resources to grow Mega's Customer Equity. Putting their heads together, they had come up with a list of key individuals—and areas of the company—who would need to be involved for this new orientation to work; his first task would be to get these people onboard. The finance folks shouldn't be too difficult; they'll be eager to finally have some numbers to make those marketing types accountable. He wasn't sure how the marketing crew would react; on the one hand, the whole focus of this new approach was "the customer," something marketing and sales were always talking about. On the other hand, the approach really forces marketing to provide a solid link between investments in advertising, promotion, and brand development and increases in Customer Equity. It would be interesting to see their excitement *and* objections to the project. The service operations gang might be an easier sell; they'd really like the "Value Equity" stuff, but might have to be convinced of the importance of Brand and Retention Equity.

The Kickoff

Paul and Marjorie had discussed alternative ways of kicking off the new project. They decided it would be necessary to bring in the key players early to help determine Mega's key competitors and to determine the potential drivers of Brand, Value, and Retention Equity. Recalling previous efforts to implement change in the company, they knew all too well the downside of trying to foist research results onto an organization that did not have a hand in the project from the beginning. Five years before, a much needed quality improvement project had almost failed because the service operations folks had not been included in the determination of the key drivers of quality for Mega. This time, Paul vowed that the key areas of the company would be involved right from the start. Marjorie sent nudging e-mails to key players in marketing, sales, service operations, and finance, suggesting that they be ready to discuss the project in about a week.

Identifying Key Competitors

Meanwhile, Paul began the task of determining Mega's key competitors. He had a pretty good idea, but decided it would be important to ask a broad cross section of current customers and noncustomers to make sure he wasn't missing an emerging giant. He first sent e-mail to Mega's Customer Advisory Board (CAB), a diverse group of customers who voluntarily serve as an advisory body to the company. The CAB members had proven to be a great asset to Mega, and to Paul in particular. They provided valuable insight on a whole host of topics, from changes in strategic direction of the firm to specific tactical changes being contemplated by the firm. They were even part of the interviewing process when Paul joined Mega! The list of competitors generated by responses to Paul's e-mail contained a few surprises; it appeared that local competition (in a variety of markets) was on the rise, but that big chain competition was relatively stable. He forwarded the list of competitors to the key area heads of marketing, sales, service operations, and finance, asking for their reactions; including additions or deletions they would suggest. The combination of input from customers and functional areas within the company would provide a pretty good set of competitors from which to begin.

The Meeting

They were now ready to get the team together to get the project off the ground. Paul scheduled a meeting with Marjorie and the directors of marketing, sales, service operations, and finance. He invited the head of marketing research as well, hoping to get a sense of how long it would take to get the data collected and analyzed. The agenda for the meeting was tight; they needed to get answers and closure on three key questions:

- Who are Mega's key competitors? (He knew they needed to narrow the list to five or six.)
- What is the population of interest?
- How will Mega determine the potential drivers of Brand, Value, and Retention Equity?

The meeting was much longer and rambling than Paul had initially intended, but he recognized the need to have this diverse group come to an understanding of Customer Equity before the project could move forward. At the conclusion of the meeting, the group had identified Mega's five most critical competitors and had decided to examine the drivers of Customer Equity for two key metropolitan markets (Boston and the Research Triangle), focusing on the "consumer" customer rather than the "corporate" customer.

The Marketing Research Director recommended conducting focus groups with current customers, competitor customers, and non-health-club users in each market to provide the basis for the determination of potential drivers of Brand, Value, and Retention Equity. In addition, each director agreed to develop a potential list of drivers independently that could be compared to the outcome of the focus groups. Finally, a set of questions was developed and e-mailed to the CAB, to get their ideas of the key drivers of the three equities as well.

Determining the Set of Potential Drivers of Equity

The marketing research group compiled ideas from the focus groups, functional areas, and the CAB responses into a list of potential drivers of Brand, Value, and Retention Equity, using the broader definitions of the drivers provided in *Driving Customer Equity* as an organizing framework. The Customer Equity Coalition (as the group of directors from marketing, sales, service operations, and finance had come to call themselves) was able to agree on a set of potential drivers for each equity. This list of drivers provided the basis for the development of the survey instrument (see table 8-2). Interestingly, the CE Coalition was surprised at the small degree of disagreement among the group in determining the potential drivers. Time spent early on in understanding one another's points of view appeared to be paying off.

Taking Action

The marketing research group developed an initial draft of the survey and then contacted its regular research company to refine the survey and administer it in the two chosen markets. The market research firm sampled two hundred random consumers (who were currently members of a health club) in each market. Because Mega's marketing research group had statistical expertise in-house, they decided to do the analysis themselves, rather than have the research firm analyze the data.

Table 8-2 List of Potential Drivers and Sub-Drivers of Customer Equity for Mega Corporation

Potential Drivers of Value Equity
   Overall quality
   Certainty and consistency of quality
   Club staff
   Classes and programs
   Equipment and facilities
   Variety of equipment
   Physical surroundings
   Hours of operation
   Accessibility
   Facilities, equipment, and/or programs available when wanted
   "Everyday" or regular prices
   "Special sale" prices
   Prices relative to other health clubs
   Membership prices
   Health club store and café prices
   Quality relative to price paid

Potential Drivers of Brand Equity
   Television advertising
   Radio advertising
   Print advertising
   Web site
   Direct mail advertising
   Direct mail communications (e.g., newsletter)
   Good corporate citizen
   Active sponsor of community events
   High ethical standards with customers and employees
   Likelihood of recommending to others
   Mega's image
   Positive feelings and attitude toward club

Potential Drivers of Retention Equity
   Big investment in membership (loyalty) program
   Special treatment and recognition
   Understanding of procedures and processes of health club
   High commitment
   Health club knows a lot about me
   Customized programs or treatment based upon past experiences
   Emotional attachment
   Sense of community with other members
   High level of trust
   Length of membership

Knowing the Drivers: Moving Forward

The results from the initial model of Customer Equity suggested that Retention Equity and Value Equity were stronger drivers of Customer Equity than Brand Equity. As they looked at the drivers of Value and Retention Equity in more depth, some interesting things emerged. It appeared that convenience and quality of equipment (condition, variety) were the most important drivers of Value Equity. Price did not appear to affect Value Equity for Mega Health Club customers. Retention Equity was most strongly influenced by the customer's perception of community and the customer's emotional connection. The loyalty program, though important, did not have as strong an effect.

Paul was eager to report the results to the coalition, but was concerned about its need to take immediate action. Would finance recommend raising price immediately? Would service operations want to invest millions in new equipment and additional employees to increase hours and class availability? Would marketing want to spend megabucks on neighborhood parties and community-building events? How should these results be interpreted? Where should they invest? How will any of these changes affect Mega's ability to attract new customers, in addition to building the Customer Equity of its current customer base?

Paul had taken the first steps in implementing the Customer Equity Framework. He'd measured Customer Equity. Now what?

Implementing the Customer Equity Framework

KEY INSIGHTS	ACTION STEPS
1. Customer Equity requires a commitment of the entire organization.	• Get key people onboard early in the process. • This is a long-term strategy, not a quick fix. • Make sure the project is a cross-functional effort.
2. Identifying the key drivers appropriately is critical to the success of using the framework.	• Don't evaluate potential drivers and sub-drivers and toss them out prematurely. • Don't confuse sub-drivers of Brand, Value, and Retention Equity.
3. It is important to choose the population of interest carefully.	• Include your competitors' customers in your sample.
4. Careful assessment of the competitive set is essential.	• Avoid including too many competitors in your sample (choose five to six key competitors). • Be sure not to miss a key competitor.

9

Evaluating Financial Impact

Customer Equity is not just a customer-centered viewpoint. It is, by its very nature, financial. Strategic decisions involving the drivers of Customer Equity require knowledge of the financial impact of improving those drivers.[1]

The Importance of Financial Accountability

Who can argue with offering customers better value, or retaining them more effectively, or building stronger Brand Equity? But we will find that not all efforts to improve Value Equity, Retention Equity, or Brand Equity are profitable. For best performance, the company must differentiate between improvement efforts that are profitable, and those that are not.

Modern thinking in finance dictates that improvement expenditures should be viewed as capital investments, with the improvement effort being viewed as profitable only if the return on investment exceeds the cost of capital. Management methods based on this principle are known by such names as EVA (Economic Value Added)[2] or Value-Based Management.[3] Our approach is entirely consistent with this economic value perspective. A failure to hold improvement expenditures to such prudent financial standards can have serious consequences, as the following section makes clear.

Spending to Oblivion

Spending without regard to financial consequence can be disastrous. We can see this quite clearly from the experiences of some of the quality champions of the 1980s. For example, the Wallace Co., Inc., a Houston pipe and valve distributor, spent large amounts to improve its delivery, invoicing, computer system, and quality organization in general.[4] It was rewarded by becoming the first small business to win the Malcolm Baldrige National Quality Award in 1990. Unfortunately, the revenue increases resulting from its improvements in quality were overwhelmed by the increased spending, and by 1992 the company was in Chapter 11 bankruptcy.[5]

Another example is Florida Power & Light. The company spent massively to install an elaborate quality program, which was impressive enough to result in both the Edison Prize in 1986 and Japan's Deming Prize in 1989 (the first U.S. company to win that prize).[6] But the company could not defend its spending to the ratepayers;[7] FP&L's chairman, John Hudiberg, was forced out,[8] and his quality program was dismantled.

The lesson in both cases is that it is not enough to spend on Customer Equity. The firm must be financially accountable with respect to its improvement efforts.

Impatient Shareholders

Even if the firm's spending is not enough to put the company out of business, the pressures of financial accountability can still be severe. An example is Centennial Medical Center, which was the flagship hospital of Hospital Corporation of America (HCA). In 1989 HCA brought in quality zealot William Arnold to run Centennial. His management style involved "person-centered leadership," a Deming-style management approach that he documented in his book *The Human Touch*.[9] Unfortunately, the improvement efforts that Arnold implemented were met with a negative bottom line. The shareholders would not tolerate this, and they fired Arnold in 1993.[10] He had failed to demonstrate financial results, and the shareholders made him accountable for it.

The Role of Information Technology

One of the less-recognized reasons for the increasing importance of financial accountability is that advances in information technology are making it easier to collect, maintain, and analyze the information required to evaluate financial accountability. Computers have dramatically increased the organization's ability to store large amounts of information, and capacity is increasing dramatically every year. This is combined with impressive improvements in computation time, resulting in an environment in which companies have an unprecedented ability to collect and analyze profitability data, often at the individual customer level. Companies that can use this information most effectively gain a competitive advantage.

Maximizing Performance

Because business is a Darwinian competition in which the fittest competitors survive, ultimately the ability to make the firm's improvement efforts financially accountable becomes a requirement for survival, because the fittest companies will be those that spend their resources the most efficiently. As we will see in the next chapter, this involves making trade-offs that reserve strategic resources for the areas in which expenditures will generate the greatest impact on Customer Equity.

Investments vs. Costs

Service quality improvements, retention programs, and advertising expenditures have two important characteristics in common. All enhance Customer Equity, and all are difficult to make accountable financially. We argue in this section that it is essential to consider these, and all other expenditures on Customer Equity, as investments rather than costs, and that it is also essential to measure the return from those investments.

Target of the Cost Cutters

If expenditures are not viewed as investments, then they become easy prey for cost cutters when times get bad. This is seen in a quote from a McKinsey consultant in a Council on Financial Competition report: "Anytime we did a cost reduction study, we went straight after the quality department. They could never justify their programs on economic terms."[11]

This is not just true for quality expenditures. For example, there is considerable pressure on promotional expenditures, such as advertising. As Andrew Parsons, director of McKinsey's, New York, said, "The Golden Age of Marketing . . . is over," and advertising and sales promotion are "the last frontier of cost cutting."[12] Analysts note that cutting advertising spending may be damaging to a company, but if there is no way to justify a spending level, that level is sure to be cut.

Advertising As a Cost

Let us consider the typical advertising scenario. Except for direct mail advertising, there is typically no direct connection between expenditures and sales. In fact, because advertising's effect is fairly subtle and long-term, even some direct measurement approaches, such as scanner panel data, routinely turn up no detectable advertising effect. Companies are reduced to collecting many periods of advertising and sales data (not practical for a company needing to make decisions now), trying to control all of the other variables that might result in a sales effect (generally a fairly hopeless task), and assuming that the environment has stayed the same over the term of the study (a bad assumption in today's rapidly changing world).

The result is that, using conventional techniques, it is almost impossible to analyze advertising as an investment.[13] The inevitable result is that advertising is viewed as a current-period cost. Various bad methods are used for setting the level of advertising expenditure. These include spending the same percent of sales as last year (how do we know we were right last year?), matching competitors' percent of sales (how do we know they are right?), setting share of voice equal to targeted share of market (again, without knowing whether any advertising is effective), or other ad hoc methods.[14] The company is left with little confidence that the level of advertising spending is correct.

Long-Term vs. Short-Term

Common sense in accounting and finance suggests that short-term benefits demand short-term investments, and long-term benefits demand long-term investments. For example, it is inappropriate to incur long-term debt to pay for short-term, current obligations. However, it is entirely appropriate to make long-term investments that will generate a long-term return.

Because Customer Equity is a long-term financial concept, it may be appropriate to consider the role of long-term investments versus short-term

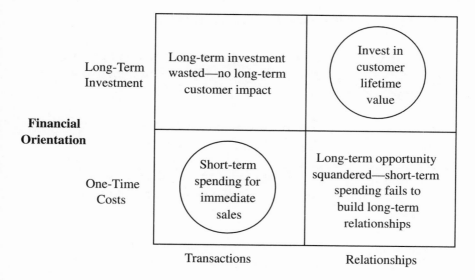

Figure 9-1. Matching Financial Orientation to Customer Relationship Orientation

spending. Figure 9-1 illustrates how we can make this determination intelligently. In essence, it is important to match the customer relationship orientation to the financial orientation. (Swedish relationship management guru Evert Gummeson has referred to the concept of "Return on Relationships," implying the necessity of considering the financial return from relationship management).[15] If the customer relationship orientation is short-term and transaction-oriented, then long-term investments in Customer Equity are wasted. For example, when the University of Tennessee became the national football champion, marketers hurried to offer commemorative memorabilia. In such a circumstance, there is virtually no continuing opportunity, so only short-term spending is warranted.

On the other hand, if the customer-relationship orientation is relationship-based, then long-term investments can be the right thing. For example, a credit card company typically wishes to maintain long-term relationships with its customers. In this situation, it may be entirely appropriate to make long-term investments in Value Equity, Retention Equity, and Brand Equity.

Pathways to Financial Impact

Investing in Customer Equity can take place through three main pathways: improving Value Equity, improving Brand Equity, and improving Retention Equity (see figure 9-2).

- *Improving Value Equity* involves investing in the more objective, rational, cognitive drivers, such as quality, price, and convenience.

- *Improving Brand Equity* involves investing in the more subjective, irrational, emotional drivers, such as advertising and the rest of the promotion mix.

- *Improving Retention Equity* involves investing in programs that make repurchase more "sticky," such as frequent buyer programs and relationship management initiatives.

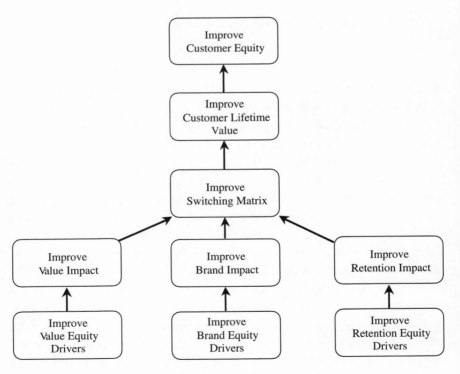

Figure 9-2. Pathways to Financial Impact

These improvements are integrated through a statistical model (details can be found in a Working Paper, available from the Marketing Science Institute). Essentially the model enables us to disentangle the relative impact of Value Equity, Brand Equity, and Retention Equity, so that we can make trade-offs between them. We will investigate each of these pathways to financial impact, in turn.

Return on Quality

The primary pathways to improving Value Equity are (1) quality, (2) convenience, and (3) price (see figure 9-3). Investigating each pathway is done in a similar manner, so we show in greater detail how to investigate quality.

The general approach to investigating the financial impact of drivers of Customer Equity has been most fully developed in the area of quality. The Return on Quality (ROQ) approach was devised in the mid-1990s by the first author (Rust), along with Anthony Zahorik and Timothy Keiningham, as a way to project and estimate the financial return that would result from an improvement in service quality.[16] The main idea behind ROQ is to project the return from the improvement effort, discounted by the cost of capital, consistent with the principles of Economic Value Added (EVA). This return could then be further evaluated against a risk hurdle, depending upon the riskiness of the improvement effort. The approach in this book is an extension of the ROQ approach to the broader managerial framework of Customer Equity.

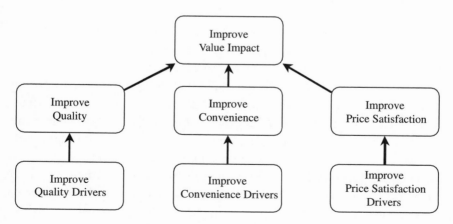

Figure 9-3. Pathways to Improving Value

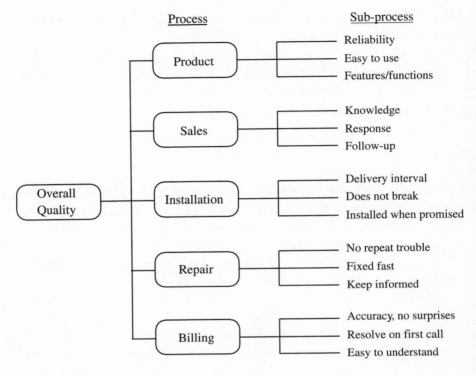

Figure 9-4. The Process Tree

[SOURCE: ADAPTED FROM RAYMOND E. KORDUPLESKI, ROLAND T. RUST, AND ANTHONY J. ZAHORIK, "WHY IMPROVING QUALITY DOESN'T IMPROVE QUALITY," *CALIFORNIA MANAGEMENT REVIEW*, 35 (SPRING 1993), 82–95.]

The Chain of Effects

The ROQ approach views a service quality (or customer satisfaction) improvement as triggering a chain of effects, from service improvement to perceived service quality to customer retention to market share to financial impact.[17] The framework in this book extends the traditional ROQ framework by noting that service quality affects not only customer retention, but customer attraction as well. In terms of the switching matrix, the off-diagonal probabilities are improved, as well as the diagonals. In most respects, though, our framework follows the conceptual approach pioneered in the ROQ method.

The ROQ approach relies upon the process framework first shown in chapter 8 (see figure 9-4). A robust regression analysis is used to quantify the relationships between the process quality levels and the overall quality, and the relationships between each process quality level and its corresponding sub-processes.[18] These statistical relationships enable us to project the impact of a shift in the quality of a sub-process, a process, or overall quality.

The Test Market Approach

Addressing the financial impact of a quality improvement effort requires that the shift in perceived quality be known. Given a known quality shift, the statistical models then project the impact on overall quality, overall value, the switching matrix, aggregated choice probabilities, market share over time, and Customer Equity. But the estimated effect on Customer Equity is only as good as the estimated shift in perceived quality.

At the outset, the shift in perceived quality can be estimated based on historical experience, or based on managerial judgment. But to get a better idea, it is often necessary to run a market test.

While most such tests are proprietary and cannot be communicated here, we can discuss two such tests that are in the public domain. For example, the first author (Rust), along with Anthony Zahorik, Timothy Keiningham, and Stephen Clemens, conducted such a test at Chase Manhattan Bank.[19] Chase was interested in the financial return from initiating a new training program that was designed to improve customers' satisfaction with their bank tellers. They designated a limited number of "test" branches, in which the improvement effort was implemented, and "control" branches where the improvement effort was not implemented. By analyzing the shift in satisfaction in the test branches versus the control branches, the shift in satisfaction due to the improvement program could be estimated:

Shift due to improvement program = Shift in test branches - Shift in control branches

By analyzing the above shifts, Chase was able to conclude that the improvement program was, in fact, profitable and resulted in a 44% return on investment.

Another test market application was conducted in a business-to-business setting by the first author (Rust), along with MIT's Duncan Simester, John Hauser, and Birger Wernerfelt.[20] That study was conducted in both the United States and Spain. That test revealed that without the careful controls, both experimental and statistical, that were employed in the study, the effect of the improvement effort would have been obscured. The financial return obtained is proprietary, but we can say that the improvement program produced a measurable increase in customer satisfaction.

In summary, the use of test markets can help produce more accurate estimates of financial impact, by using real data to calibrate the extent of improvement in perceived quality (or customer satisfaction).

Examples

Let us take a closer look at two examples of Return on Quality analyses, using the Customer Equity Framework. Consider first the question of whether Delta Airlines should spend $60 million on a quality improvement project in the United States to obtain a .1 average shift in overall quality, from 3.48 to 3.58. (We could just as easily evaluate an improvement in one of the drivers of overall quality, or one of that driver's sub-drivers.) Projecting from a survey sample (our sample, drawn from the Cambridge area, is used for illustrative purposes only—Delta would actually employ a national sample for such an analysis), we first estimate the model described in the Appendix. Using a spreadsheet model, it is then straightforward to project the percent improvement in Value Equity (see table 9-1). This improvement is seen to be 2.68%. Adding this improvement in Value Equity to all customers in the sample, we can then estimate the revised lifetime value of the customer for each customer, and the average lifetime value across all customers. This equates to a 0.15% increase in Customer Equity for Delta, corresponding to a dollar improvement in Customer Equity of $91.8 million. From this, the Return on Quality (the return on investment from the quality improvement) can be calculated, according to the simple formula:

% Return on Quality = [(Improvement in $ Customer Equity - Improvement Expenditure) / (Improvement Expenditure)] × 100

In this case the calculated Return on Quality is 53.1%, indicating that the improvement expenditure is profitable.

A second example illustrates that the result is not always positive. Consider the Best Buy company, with respect to its Cambridge, Massachusetts, operations. Let us consider whether a $1.5 million investment in service quality that would produce an overall improvement in service quality of .1, from 3.74 to 3.84, would be justified. We see that the percent increase in Value Equity (see table 9-2) would be 1.16%, which produces a 0.69% increase in Customer Equity, for a dollar improvement in Customer Equity

Discounted Improvement Expenditure	$60 million
Improvement in Overall Quality	.1
% Improvement in Value Equity	2.68%
% Improvement in Customer Equity	0.15%
$ Improvement in Customer Equity	$91.8 million
Return on Quality	53.1%

Table 9-1. Projected Return on Quality—Delta Airlines

of $1.43 million. Calculating the Return on Quality, this results in a return of -4.6%, which is not profitable. We see that the Return on Quality approach is capable of distinguishing between profitable and unprofitable quality improvements.

Discounted Improvement Expenditure	$1.5 million
Improvement in Overall Quality	.1
% Improvement in Value Equity	1.16%
% Improvement in Customer Equity	0.69%
$ Improvement in Customer Equity	$1.43 million
Return on Quality	-4.6%

Table 9-2. Projected Return on Quality—Best Buy

Return on Price

Pricing is a topic in which there has been considerable prior development, with the result that there already exist well-developed models that have a high degree of sophistication. We do not mean to suggest that these models should necessarily be replaced. Nevertheless it is useful to point out that pricing can also be addressed in our framework.

Comparison with Traditional Approaches

Traditional pricing models are based on microeconomics, with a demand curve indicating the revenues that will result from a particular price. It is worth pointing out that this approach, at its most basic, is fundamentally static, in that it considers demand at one point in time and does not consider future periods. Most important, this approach ignores the nature of customer relationships. That is, the fact that attracting a particular customer in this time period has an effect on the ability to retain that customer in the next period is not captured. By contrast, our approach considers the dynamic effect of a price change on particular customers, with respect to both current and future sales.

Increases and Cuts

There are two ways to make money from price changes. Either the company can generate more revenue per customer by raising prices, or it can lure more customers by lowering prices. Just as in Return on Quality, the benefit from a price cut (or damage from a price increase) results from a chain of effects, in this case from price change to change in price satisfaction, to change in Value Equity, to change in switching probabilities, and so on. In this case, though, price also enters into the lifetime value calculation by changing the revenue per purchase. The investment required to change a price is minimal and is limited to such low-budget items as reprinting price lists and changing prices in advertising. The Return on Price can be calculated as:

$$\% \text{ Return on Price} = [(\text{Improvement in Customer Equity} - \text{Investment}) / \text{Investment}] \times 100$$

Because the investment is generally very small, for all practical purposes the price change is profitable whenever it results in an improvement in Customer Equity.

Sub-Drivers of Price Satisfaction

It is worth mentioning that Customer Equity improvements from pricing strategy are not necessarily the result of price changes. Recall from chapter 5 that price satisfaction can be broken down into satisfaction with everyday prices, and satisfaction with discounts and promotions. While conventional price changes operate through the everyday prices sub-driver, other factors may influence satisfaction with discounts and promotions. For example customers may want different *frequency* of promotions, rather than different *depth* of promotions. Changing the frequency of promotions may often be accomplished without changing the average price at which the good or service is offered, or even without changing the average price at which the good or service is sold.

Competitive Reaction

We talk more about competitive reaction later in the chapter, but it is important to note that price changes are among the most visible competitive moves. They are much more visible than, let's say, an improvement in a sub-driver of service quality. Price also tends to have a fairly immediate impact on sales. The result of these factors is that changes in price are highly likely to attract a great deal of attention from competitors, with the result that some sort of competitive reaction is inevitable. All other things being equal, this makes price somewhat less attractive as a potential driver of Value Equity and Customer Equity.

Return on Convenience

The third driver of Value Equity is convenience. There are many ways in which a company can affect the perception of convenience, but two of the most prominent are expanding the number of locations (especially in retail), and expanding distribution (especially in consumer goods).

Return on Expansion

The effect of convenience follows a chain of effects that is essentially equivalent to what we saw in the Return on Quality section. That is, the improvement effort leads to an improvement in perceived convenience, which leads

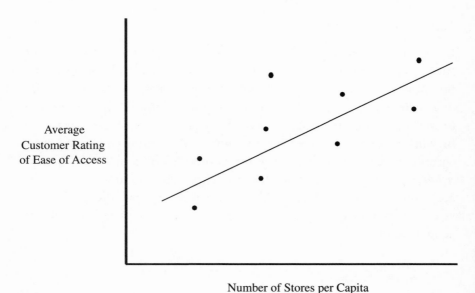

Average
Customer Rating
of Ease of Access

Number of Stores per Capita

Figure 9-5. Calibrating the Effect of Number of Stores on Ease of Access

to an improvement in Value Impact, switching probabilities, and so on. Convenience can be defined in a way that suits the product category. Especially in retail chains, a major element of convenience is the ease of getting to one of the chain's sites. This is driven by the number of sites. The more sites there are, the easier it is for the average customer to get to one of them.

If a retail chain is in a number of cities (or other geographic areas), then the relationship between number of sites and ease of access can be calibrated statistically. Figure 9-5 shows how. By plotting number of stores per capita against the average customer rating on ease of access, and fitting a regression line, we can estimate the impact that increasing (or decreasing) the number of stores will have on ease of access (convenience), and hence on the rest of the chain of effects. From this, using the dollar investment required to add a store, the return on investment can be computed, based on the effect on Customer Equity of adding a store.

Return on Distribution

A similar approach can be employed to evaluate the projected financial return from increasing distribution, an issue especially relevant to consumer

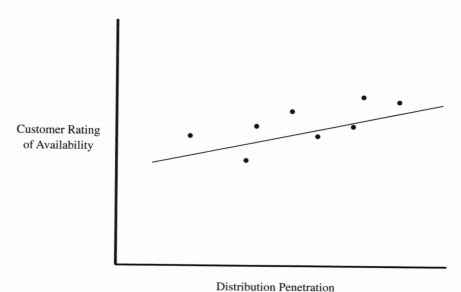

Figure 9-6.   Calibrating the Effect of Distribution on Perceived Availability

goods companies. Noting that greater retail penetration results in greater availability, we can calibrate the relationship and fit a regression line, as in figure 9-6. The slope of the regression line tells us the effect, in terms of availability, of increasing distribution penetration. This, in turn, results in greater Value Equity, improved switching probabilities, and higher Customer Equity, using the familiar chain of effects. Taking into account the dollar investment required to attain a particular level of distribution penetration, we can then calculate the projected return on investment, giving us an objective basis by which to evaluate the investment in increasing distribution.

Example

Let us consider Puffs facial tissues. In that company's product category, the most prominent element of convenience is distribution, whether or not the customer can find the product on the shelves. Let us suppose that the company can increase the average customer rating for ease of finding the brand in the store by .1, from 3.92 to 4.02, across the U.S. market, with an expenditure of $150 million. Using customer data from a sample, extrapolated to the U.S. market (again, we use a Cambridge sample for purposes of illustra-

Discounted Improvement Expenditure	$150 million
% Improvement in Convenience Impact	.1
% Improvement in Value Equity	2.05%
% Improvement in Customer Equity	2.75%
$ Improvement in Customer Equity	$210.8 million
Return on Convenience	40.5%

Table 9-3. Projected Return on Distribution—Puffs Facial Tissue

tion, with full knowledge that a national sample would be used in an actual application), we can project the return on investment from that expenditure. We see from table 9-3 that the improvement in convenience would result in a 2.05% improvement in Value Equity, and a 2.75% improvement in Customer Equity, which amounts to over $210 million. This yields a Return on Convenience of 40.5%.

Return on Advertising

Promotion is the most important driver of the emotional, subjective, irrational part of Customer Equity, the part we call Brand Equity. Advertising (and to a lesser extent other promotion elements, such as public relations) is important for establishing brand image in the customer's mind. Unfortunately advertising's accountability has long been derided. "I know that half of my advertising is wasted. I just don't know which half," as the old joke puts it. One of the most exciting things about the Customer Equity framework is that it gives us a method for estimating Return on Advertising, thus making advertising expenditures financially accountable.

Impact on Brand Equity

Advertising's effect on the customer has been measured in many ways. Using a cross-sectional data collection approach, as we do, limits us to measures such as awareness and recall. Depending upon the situation, different measures (or a combination of measures) may be called for. However, the measure chosen (awareness, recall, etc.) is not the objective. The important thing is to increase Customer Equity, by increasing Brand Equity. The chain of effects is this—the advertising expenditure and campaign increase ad awareness (or recall, or other measures), which in turn increases Brand Equity, which increases Customer Equity. Our framework facilitates the modeling of the entire chain, resulting in a Return on Advertising calculation:

% Return on Advertising = [(Improvement in Customer Equity - Change in Advertising Expenditures) / (Change in Advertising Expenditures)] × 100

Calibrating Advertising Awareness

Again, some calibration is required, to enable advertising expenditure to be related to Customer Equity. Based on data from different cities, regions, or time periods, we can plot the advertising expenditure per capita versus the advertising awareness (see figure 9-7). The regression line tells us how much improvement in advertising awareness we can expect from an increase in advertising expenditure. (It also tells us what would happen if we *decreased* advertising expenditures.)

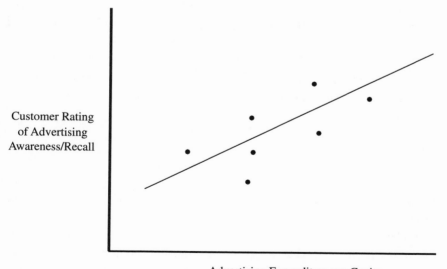

Figure 9-7. Calibrating the Effect of Advertising Expenditure on Advertising Awareness/Recall

Discounted Advertising Expenditure	$200,000
Improvement in Advertising Awareness	.1%
% Improvement in Brand Impact	16.0%
% Improvement in Customer Equity	5.72%
$ Improvement in Customer Equity	$256,389
Return on Advertising	28.2%

Table 9-4. Projected Return on Advertising—Bread & Circus

Example

Using customer data from the Cambridge, Massachusetts, market, for the Bread & Circus grocery, let us consider the Return on Advertising that we would project from a $200,000 expenditure for an advertising campaign that would result in a .1 point shift in advertising awareness. Is that expenditure likely to be profitable? Following the usual chain of effects we find the answer in table 9-4. The advertising awareness increase results in a 16.0% improvement in Brand Equity, which results in a 5.72% increase in Customer Equity, which equals $256,389 in dollar terms. The Return on Advertising is projected to be 28.2%. The increase in advertising is, in fact, justified.

Return on Retention

Retention programs have been made popular by Frederick Reichheld[21] and others, but there has been an insufficient attempt to justify such programs financially. In fact an article by Grahame Dowling and Mark Uncles in the *Sloan Management Review* suggests that retention programs may not be all that they are cracked up to be.[22] Who is right? And how can we tell whether a retention program will pay off?

Why the Usual Calculations Are Wrong

Consultants selling retention programs often fall prey to three erroneous ways of explaining those programs' financial impact. Although they generally make a case based on the lifetime value of the customer, that analysis is often flawed in the following ways:

- *Failure to discount future time periods.* This overstates the lifetime value.

- *Consideration of revenues rather than contribution to profit.* This also overstates.

- *Failure to consider the effect of switching out, and then back in.* This understates lifetime value.

To properly consider the effect of a retention program, it is necessary to consider the change in Customer Equity that results from such a program, in relation to the costs of the program.

How Retention Programs Result in Financial Impact

Retention programs result in financial impact by increasing the repurchase rate. Viewed in terms of the switching matrix, retention programs increase the diagonal element associated with the firm, but have no effect on the other elements. Improving the switching matrix results in increased Customer Equity. The expenditure associated with the retention program is the net present value of the current and future expenditures. The Return on Retention calculation is, thus:

% Return on Retention = [(Improvement in Customer Equity - Expenditure on Retention Program) / (Expenditure on Retention Program)] × 100

Example

Let us consider an example prospective retention program. Using actual customer data, we consider the prospective expenditure of $60,000 for a direct mail program in the Cambridge area to increase Retention Equity by 10%. As seen in table 9-5, this equates to a retention rate improvement of 2.91%, from 50.81% to 52.29%. Our spreadsheet model then shows that this implies a 2.07% increase in Customer Equity, equivalent to $78,282.

Discounted Improvement Expenditure	$60,000
Improvement in Retention Impact	10%
% Improvement in Retention Rate	2.91%
% Improvement in Customer Equity	2.07%
$ Improvement in Customer Equity	$78,282
Return on Retention	30.5%

Table 9-5. Projected Return on Retention—Alamo Car Rental

The Return on Retention from the program is 30.5%, indicating that the program is profitable.

Return on Ethics

Although it is customary to consider ethics as involving altruistic behavior, one may also consider the dollar impact of a company's ethical progress, by employing the Customer Equity framework. Whether a company is a good corporate citizen, or has high ethical standards toward its customers and employees, can have an important impact on a firm's Brand Equity, because they affect how the customer *feels* about the company. If the firm systematically measures the customers' perceptions of the ethical nature of the company, then those measures can be treated as drivers of Brand Equity, just as any other driver, such as advertising, brand attitude, or community involvement. (See Appendix 8.1 for examples of some ethics measures used as drivers of Brand Equity.)

Extreme cases of ethical wrongdoing are virtually certain to damage Brand Equity and Customer Equity. But even within the normal range of ethical behavior, changes in customers' perceptions of a company's ethical standing may have a measurable impact. Whether ethics have an impact on

Brand Equity will vary by company. For example, our study of the rental car industry shows that for Hertz, the driver "The company is well known as a good corporate citizen" has a positive, statistically significant impact on that firm's Brand Equity. Hence, efforts to improve Hertz's corporate citizenship would be likely to produce positive financial results.

Competitive Reaction

So far we have been assuming no competitive response. To what extent is this assumption likely to be correct? Under what circumstances will competitors be more likely to retaliate?

Generally speaking, competitors are more likely to retaliate when (1) the change in strategy is highly visible, and (2) the change in strategy has a large immediate effect. The most visible changes are changes in price and in advertising. Price is doubly threatening, because it is both visible and immediately effective. Changes in quality (especially service quality) are more subtle and may not stimulate an immediate response. Retention programs, in general, are less threatening than price, because their effects are long-term, but more threatening than quality, because they are more visible.

Improvement Initiatives as Investments

Management initiatives that improve Customer Equity are best viewed as investments, because of the long-term nature of Customer Equity. Viewing improvement efforts as investments means that those initiatives need to be financially accountable and yield an acceptable financial return.

The pathways to financial impact through Customer Equity are (1) Value Equity, (2) Retention Equity, and (3) Brand Equity. Value Equity is driven by quality, price, and convenience. This chain of effects permits us to evaluate the Return on Quality (the return on investment from improvements in quality or customer satisfaction), Return on Price (considering the long-term impact on Customer Equity), and the Return on Convenience (including such elements as adding new retail locations or increasing distribution).

The Customer Equity Framework permits objective, quantifiable evaluation of the profitability of improvement programs. As an example, firms have long believed that Brand Equity is increased by advertising. By employing the Customer Equity chain of effects, the Return on Advertising can now be quantified and evaluated. Similarly, the Return on Retention (loyalty) programs used to drive Retention Equity can be quantified as well.

All of these initiatives (e.g., quality initiatives, customer satisfaction programs, distribution efforts, retention/loyalty programs, advertising expenditures) can be objectively and quantifiably evaluated within the same framework, and by the same criterion—return on investment. This enables management to make intelligent determinations as to the effectiveness of various alternative change strategies.

In the next chapter we take this one step further, considering how top management can view a company's position in the market strategically, according to its standing with respect to the drivers of Customer Equity. We will see how this facilitates trade-offs with respect to alternative strategies and initiatives.

Evaluating Financial Impact	
KEY INSIGHTS	ACTION STEPS
1. The firm must differentiate between Customer Equity improvement efforts that are profitable and those that are not.	• Examine your company's three most recent improvement decisions, with respect to quality, price, convenience, advertising, or retention programs.
2. Information technology now makes profitability assessment more doable than ever before.	• Create customer-level databases that allow for financial evaluation of improvement programs.
3. Customer Equity improvement efforts should be seen as investments rather than costs.	• Was an ROI projected for each improvement effort, before proceeding? Was an ROI calculated after implementation? Was the cost of implementation adequately documented? • Set company ROI hurdle rates for improvement programs.
4. Return on Quality, Return on Convenience, Return on Advertising, Return on Retention programs, and return on any other Customer Equity driver can all be evaluated quantitatively using the Customer Equity Framework.	• Develop a uniform evaluation procedure for all improvement programs for increasing Customer Equity.

10

Strategic Analysis

A customer-centered viewpoint requires that competitive strategy should also be recast as customer-centered. This means that strategy should no longer be seen in terms of attributes of the brand (or the firm), but rather as benefits to the customer. We show how the brand/firm can position itself with respect to the drivers of Customer Equity and use that positioning as the basis for strategic planning and business decision making.

From Product Strategy to Customer Strategy

The most important implication of the Customer Equity Framework is that strategy should be based on customer needs rather than brands or products or capabilities. This requires a modernizing of some of the more accepted strategic approaches.

Product-Based Strategy

Let us consider a mainstream strategic approach—that of C. K. Prahalad and Gary Hamel.[1] They refer to the core competence of the corporation, meaning its specific ability to produce goods and service. This is inherently an inside-out view of strategy, because the firm's core competence determines the customers to be sought, and the customer needs that will be met.

A similar approach is espoused by Michael Porter,[2] who refers to differentiation as one of the two sources of competitive advantage. Differentiation is a product/firm concept that involves becoming different internally. Like Prahalad and Hamel, Porter views strategy in terms of the goods and services that the firm produces.

Why Product-Based Strategy Fails

The problem with product/firm-based strategy is that it is not focused on the needs of the customer. What if the firm's core competence has no relevance to those needs? What if the firm's differentiation is not understood or appreciated by the customers? In those cases the firm will not succeed in its primary goal, which is to become profitable by attracting and retaining customers.

Of course, an internally based strategy can still be relevant, especially Porter's low-cost strategy, because cost is, along with revenue, a fundamental determinant of profitability. But the demand side of strategy is more appropriately tied to the customer.

Customer-Based Strategy

Strategic thinkers have increasingly recognized the importance of customer needs and perceived value in determining strategy. For example, as Japanese strategic guru Kenichi Ohmae puts it:

> Of course, it is important to take competition into account, but in making strategy that should not come first. It cannot come first—*First comes painstaking attention to the needs of customers.*"[3] (italics added)

To Ohmae, strategy starts from the customer, and this determines what the products need to be. Successful strategy finds new, more effective ways to satisfy customer needs and desires.

A similar view is espoused by Adrian Slywotzky,[4] who notes that value migrates from providers who produce less value to those providers who produce more value. The essence of strategy therefore becomes providing value to the customer. Slywotzky notes that even competitors who are not in the same market may become competitors if they begin to satisfy the same needs and provide better value to the customers.

The lessons from Ohmae and Slywotzky are clear: it is providing utility to customers that should drive strategy. The key is to figure out the ways (with respect to Value Equity, Brand Equity, and Retention Equity) that the firm can position itself uniquely in the marketplace, in such a way that it produces current and future profits (Customer Equity) from its customers.

Customer Equity Share and Market Share

Customer Equity Share: The True Competitive Measure

It is traditional to use market share to keep score on how the firm is doing in attracting and retaining customers, but we argue that this is an incomplete measure. The problem is that a firm may have high market share, but customers are leaving. Or a firm may have a low market share, but customers are loyal. The true competitive measure is Customer Equity share. This incorporates not only current sales, but future sales as well (properly discounted). The share of the total lifetime value of the customers in the market is a true picture of how a firm is doing competitively. Two firms may have equal market share, but of the two, the firm that is doing a better job of attracting and retaining customers will be the market winner.

The Future Quotient

By comparing a firm's market share against its Customer Equity share, we can get a sense of the future prospects of the firm (see figure 10-1). For example, a firm with low market share and low Customer Equity share is clearly sick. However, a firm with low market share but high Customer Equity share is sure to grow. By contrast, a firm with a high market share but low Customer Equity share is sure to decline. The goal for any firm is to achieve the enviable situation in which both the market share and Customer Equity share are high.

A firm can quantify its future prospects by constructing a "Future Quotient" that compares the market share to the Customer Equity share:

Future Quotient = Customer Equity Share / Market Share

A Future Quotient over 1.0 indicates that the firm is going to grow its market share, and a Future Quotient less than 1.0 indicates that the firm's market share is going to shrink. For example, in the airline industry, in the Boston/Cambridge market area, United has an estimated 20.3% market

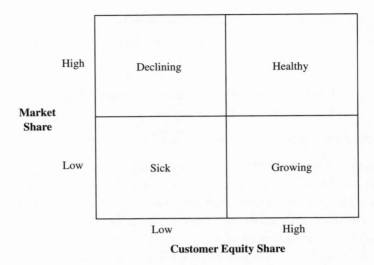

Figure 10-1. Customer Equity Share and the Future Prospects of the Firm

share, and a 24.0% Customer Equity share, giving a Future Quotient of 1.18. This shows that United will be growing its market share in Cambridge. On the other hand, Delta has a 37.9% market share, a 27.3% Customer Equity share, and a Future Quotient of .72, indicating that it is due to decline in that market, unless countermeasures are taken.

Performance Measurement

Realizing that Customer Equity is important is one thing, but knowing what to do about it is another. The first step in figuring out what to do is measuring how well the firm is doing with respect to Customer Equity, Value Equity, Retention Equity, and Brand Equity versus the competition.

Measuring Performance

We have previously shown how to measure the firm's Customer Equity. But what is the effect of Value Equity, Brand Equity, and Retention Equity on Customer Equity? One way to investigate this is to see how close the firm is to realizing its potential, based on the best Value Equity, Brand Equity, and Retention Equity that had been achieved by any firm in the industry. If it hasn't fully then the firm can achieve a higher Customer Equity by attaining industry-leading standards of Value Equity. We calculate the firm's Value Equity, relative to the rest of the firms in the industry, as:

Relative Value Equity = (Current Customer Equity) / (Customer Equity given the best Value Equity in the industry)

For example, if the firm has the best Value Equity in the industry, then the firm's relative Value Equity would be 100%. Otherwise the firm's Value Equity would be lower. We do a similar calculation for Customer Equity, Retention Equity, and Brand Equity.

Financial Benefits from Improvement

The financial benefit from improving Value Equity to the industry-best level is:

Financial Benefit = Customer Equity given the best Value Equity in the industry - Current Customer Equity

This gives the company, in dollar terms, the cost of not being at the industry-best standard.

The Performance Profile

Arraying all of these measures together (see figure 10-2) provides a performance profile of how the firm is doing with its customers, based on the components of Customer Equity. For example, figure 10-2 shows the performance profile for Delta Airlines. We see that Delta is doing fairly well with respect to Retention Equity, perhaps because of its frequent flyer program, but lags somewhat with respect to Brand Equity and Value Equity. We can calculate the financial loss (in Customer Equity) that Delta incurs by not being at the industry-leading levels of each component of Customer Equity. For example, we calculate (based on our illustrative Cambridge sample) that the cost to Customer Equity of Delta not being at industry-best level for Value Equity is calculated to be over $200 million.

Figure 10-3 shows the performance profile for United Airlines. United is doing poorly with respect to Brand Equity, but is better at Value Equity. We can see that the performance profiles can differ markedly across companies,

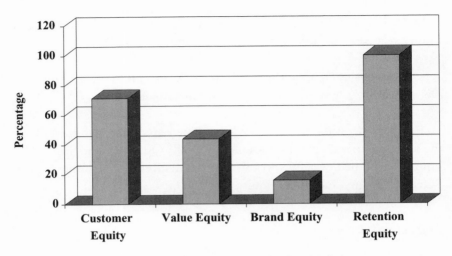

Figure 10-2. The Performance Profile: Delta Airlines

even in the same industry. Again the financial cost of not being at industry-best level can be striking. United incurs a cost in Customer Equity of about $1.6 *billion* for not being at industry-best level on Retention Equity (again projected from our illustrative Cambridge sample). In essence, if the Cambridge market is representative, it may be well worth an expenditure of

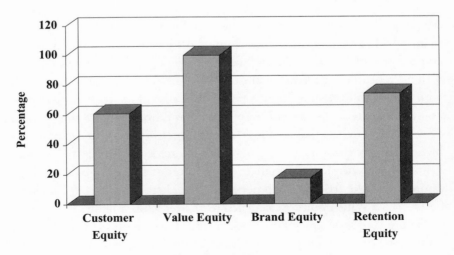

Figure 10-3. The Performance Profile: United Airlines

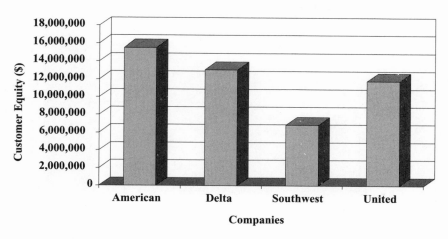

Figure 10-4. Comparative Customer Equity: Airlines

many millions of dollars to United if it were able to boost its retention programs to industry-leading levels.

Performance on Customer Equity

To get a sense of the firm's comparative position in an industry, the first measure to examine is Customer Equity. All other things being equal, the firm with the best Customer Equity will be the firm that should perform the best in the coming years. Figure 10-4 shows the Customer Equity measured from four firms in the airline industry, based on their Customer Equity in the Cambridge market. Here we see that American has the best Customer Equity standing, and Southwest the worst (due, we will soon see, to its poor Value Equity in the Cambridge market).

Performance on Value Equity

The best way to compare the companies' performance on Value Equity is to compare the companies' extent to which the customer utility is increased by the firm's value. Figure 10-5 shows an example comparison across customers in the airline industry, in the Cambridge market. We can see that in this industry, United has the dominant Value Equity, and Southwest does much poorer. Southwest's poor performance is due mostly to convenience, since the closest airport (Providence, Rhode Island) is not

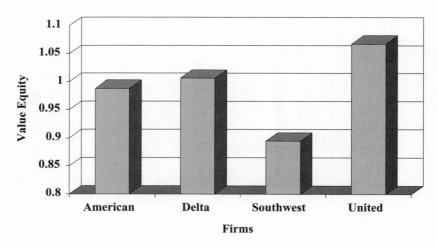

Figure 10-5. Comparative Value Equity

very convenient to Cambridge. In terms of just price and quality, South-west is competitive, due to its low prices.

Performance on Brand Equity

We see from figure 10-6 that, in the Cambridge grocery market, Stop and Shop has the best Brand Equity, and Nature's Heartland has the worst. To a

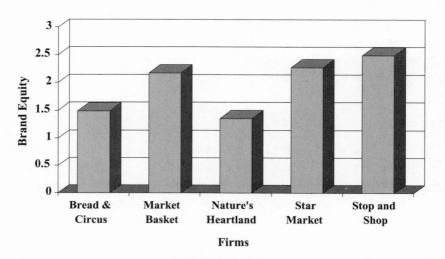

Figure 10-6. Comparative Brand Equity

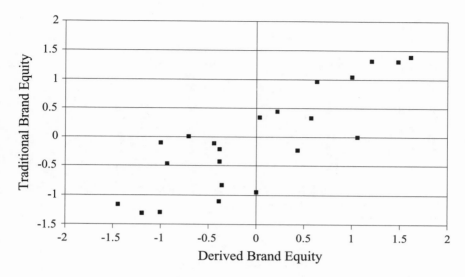

Figure 10-7. Derived Brand Equity vs. Traditional "Brand Equity"

great extent, this is due to Stop and Shop's communications (i.e., advertising) efforts over time.

It is worth noting that our Brand Equity ratings, as derived from our statistical model, correlate very well (correlation = .87) with the Brand Equity ratings derived from a more traditional approach (using items derived from Aaker and Keller and others). Figure 10-7 demonstrates the close relationship between the two measures.

Performance on Retention Equity

A similar analysis is possible with Retention Equity (see figure 10-8). Again, the statistically derived Retention Equity is used to compare the companies. Here we see that in the Cambridge grocery market, Market Basket has the best Retention Equity, and Star Market has the worst.

Importance of Customer Equity Drivers

It is interesting to note that different Customer Equity drivers are important, depending upon the industry. It is very important for firms to realize that the success factors in their industry may be different from those in other industries. The Customer Equity Framework facilitates the recogni-

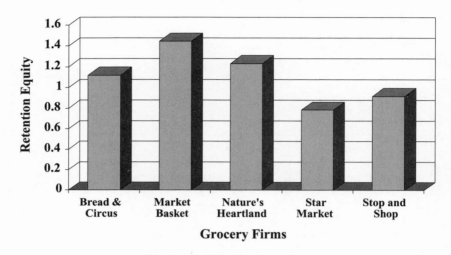

Figure 10-8. Comparative Retention Equity

tion of which factors (Value Equity, Brand Equity, or Retention Equity) are most important within an industry.

Importance of Customer Equity Drivers in Industry

Customer Equity drivers are more important in an industry where changes in those drivers will produce big shifts in Customer Equity. By estimating the average shift that would be obtained across the firms in an industry, a measure of the importance of a Customer Equity driver can be obtained (see Appendix 10.1 for details).

The results are very different across industries. Figure 10-9 shows the relative importance of Value Equity, Brand Equity, and Retention Equity across six industries. From this figure we can see clearly that different industries have different emphases. For example, in the rental car industry, the most important Customer Equity driver is Retention Equity, followed by Value Equity, with Brand Equity being least important. In the facial tissue industry, Retention Equity is much less important, and the most important by far is Brand Equity.

Importance of Value Equity

Assembling the importance of Value Equity across the various industries (see figure 10-10), we see that Value Equity's importance varies consider-

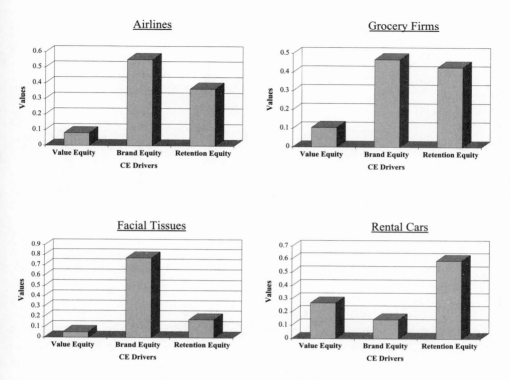

Figure 10-9. Importance of Customer Equity Drivers

ably across industry. For example, in the rental car industry, Value Equity is very important, but in the facial tissue industry, Value Equity is much less important. Because most people rent cars while on business, the objective/rational issues (Value Equity) tend to receive more weight than the subjective/emotional issues (Brand Equity). A similar pattern would be expected in any typical business-to-business environment. Thus, we expect to find Value Equity more important in business-to-business contexts.

Importance of Brand Equity

Likewise, we find that Brand Equity is important in some industries, but not all (see figure 10-11). In the facial tissue industry, Brand Equity is very important, but in the rental car industry, Brand Equity is much less important. Again much of this pattern is based on the extent to which an industry is transaction-oriented versus relationship-oriented. If the sale has to be made anew, time after time, as in the facial tissue industry, then Brand

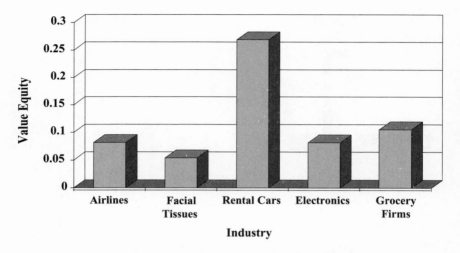

Figure 10-10. Importance of Value Equity by Industry

Equity becomes very important. In this low-involvement, frequently purchased consumer good category, subjective issues (Brand Equity) hold sway, which is why advertising tends to have a disproportionate representation by consumer packaged goods companies. Brand Equity is less important when the key to long-term sales is the continuing relationship, as in the rental car industry, with its strong loyalty programs.

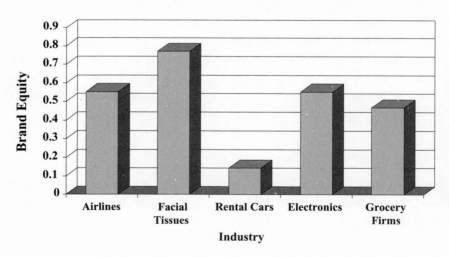

Figure 10-11. Importance of Brand Equity by Industry

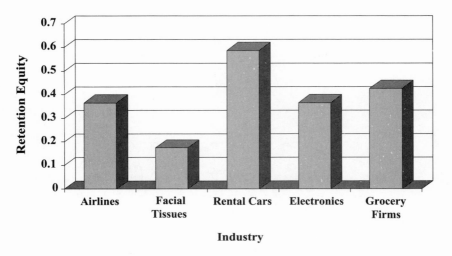

Figure 10-12. Importance of Retention Equity by Industry

Importance of Retention Equity

We see a similar story with Retention Equity (see figure 10-12). In the rental car industry, Retention Equity is very important, but in the facial tissue industry, it is not very important at all. This should not be very surprising, when we realize that in the rental car industry, continuing relationships with customers drive profitability, and the facial tissue industry is much more transaction-oriented.

The Strategy Triangle

The firm, having limited resources to allocate, must trade off its efforts between Value Equity, Retention Equity, and Brand Equity. Depending upon the importance of these Customer Equity drivers in the industry, different strategies are suggested. Figure 10-13 illustrates some of the strategic positionings the firm can employ.

Value Strategies

If Value Equity is the dominant Customer Equity driver, then the firm's emphasis should be on the drivers of value. The firm should consider efforts

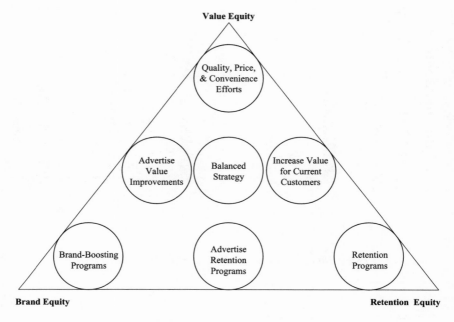

Figure 10-13. The Strategy Triangle

that focus on quality, price, and convenience, with the exact allocation of effort dependent upon the relative impact of each on value. This strategy is depicted at the top of the Strategy Triangle.

Brand Strategies

When Brand Equity is dominant, then the focus of the firm should be on brand-boosting activities, such as advertising and other methods of marketing communication. This strategy is seen in the lower left corner of the Strategy Triangle (figure 10-13).

Retention Strategies

Likewise, if Retention Equity is dominant, then the firm's strong focus should be on retention programs, loyalty programs, and relationship management. This strategy is seen at the lower right corner of the Strategy Triangle.

Value-Brand Strategies

However, it is possible that two Customer Equity drivers are important, rather than just one. If both Value Equity and Brand Equity are important, but Retention Equity is less important, then the firm might focus on connecting its advertising (and other brand-boosting activities) to specific aspects of value, such as quality, price, and convenience. In other words, in this case the firm's advertising should be less for image and emotional connection, and more to communicate objective benefits.

Value-Retention Strategies

Alternatively, if Value Equity and Retention Equity are important, but Brand Equity is less important, then the firm's focus might center on retaining current customers by increasing value to them, perhaps by adding service, providing special convenience, or giving them price breaks.

Retention-Brand Strategies

Likewise, it is possible that Retention Equity and Brand Equity are important, and Value Equity is less important. In such a case it may be useful to focus on connecting the firm's advertising to the benefits provided by the retention program or loyalty program. One way of thinking about this is that the primary target of the firm's advertising becomes existing customers rather than new customers.

Mixed Strategies

If no Customer Equity driver, or pair of drivers, dominates, then the firm should implement a balanced strategy, with Value Equity, Retention Equity, and Brand Equity all receiving attention.

Setting Priorities

In the preceding sections we explored which Customer Equity drivers made the most difference in an industry. However, for some firms the most important drivers in the industry are not the best opportunity. This is

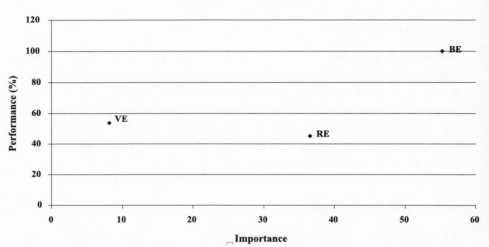

Figure 10-14. Importance-Performance Map: American Airlines

because the firm may already perform well on some drivers, and therefore might wish to instead focus on drivers that are problem areas. One useful approach to investigating fruitful areas in which to focus is importance-performance analysis. Already widely applied in the customer satisfaction area, this approach can easily be extended to Customer Equity analysis.

The Importance-Performance Map

Figure 10-14 shows the performance-importance map for American Airlines. The X axis is importance. This should be the industry importance level as explained earlier. The Y axis is relative performance, scaled between the best in the industry (100%) and the worst in the industry (0%). We see that in this case Brand Equity is the most important Customer Equity driver, but American already performs well in that area.

Identifying Problems and Opportunities

To identify problems/opportunities, it is important to search for drivers that are important, and in which the firm's performance is subpar. We see in figure 10-14 that a good candidate for improvement for American would be Retention Equity. It is moderately important, and the company's performance is not as strong as it could be, relative to the competition (even

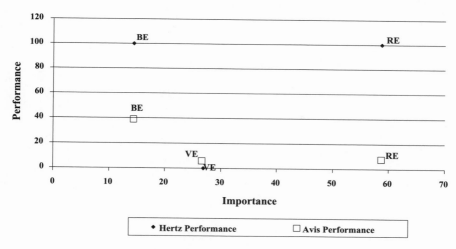

Figure 10-15. Competitive Importance-Performance Map

though American invented the frequent flyer program). The firm should strongly consider fresh initiatives in that area.

The Competitive Importance-Performance Map

An alternative map to consider is the competitive importance-performance map (figure 10-15). This is the same as the importance-performance map in the previous sections, except that it also shows the competition. If a particular competitor is targeted, then this map can show where the firm is vulnerable with respect to that competitor. For example, consider the rental car market, where Hertz and Avis go head-to-head. Avis, looking at the competitive importance-performance map, would likely conclude that the biggest gap between Hertz and them on an important Customer Equity driver is Retention Equity, and this should be the focus of their competitive efforts.

Analysis of Sub-drivers

A similar analysis can be done at the sub-driver level. For example, a company that determines that Value Equity needs to be improved may wish to investigate Value Equity's sub-drivers. Because the impact of sub-drivers is more likely to be idiosyncratic to the firm, we calculate the importance of

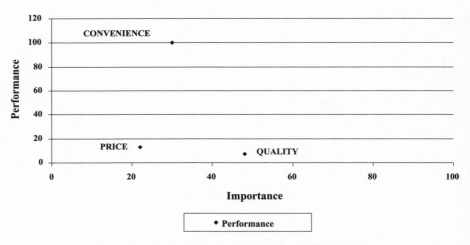

Figure 10-16. Sub-drivers of Value Equity: Delta Airlines

the sub-drivers based on a regression analysis in which we predict Value Equity from its drivers—quality, price, and convenience. We calculate relative performance as before. Figure 10-16 shows the result of this analysis for Delta Airlines. The resulting map could not be more clear. We see unambiguously from this map that the high importance of quality, combined with Delta's very poor performance on that sub-driver, makes it an excellent candidate for improvement.

Another example of this analysis is shown in figure 10-17, which shows the analysis of Southwest's drivers of Value Impact. This map is very different from Delta's. From this map, we can see that Southwest is positioned effectively as a low-price carrier, but that is not the key to future expansion in the Cambridge market. Convenience is by far the most important issue for Southwest, which makes sense, given that Cambridge residents must currently drive to Providence in order to fly Southwest.

Similar analyses can be carried out for Brand Equity and Retention Equity. Drivers of Brand Equity could include such things as the elements of the communications mix, as well as community events, corporate citizenship, and other drivers of brand image. Company initiatives can make some drivers more salient. For example, our analysis of the Cambridge electronics store market shows that for Tweeter, community event sponsorship is more important than advertising. This is not surprising, once we

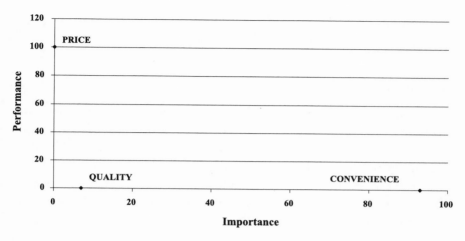

Figure 10-17. Sub-drivers of Value Equity: Southwest Airlines

realize that Tweeter has assumed sponsorship of the Tweeter Center for the Performing Arts, an outdoor concert venue halfway between Boston and Providence.

Drivers of Retention Equity could include such things as the effectiveness of the company's loyalty program and relationship-building activities. For example, our analysis of the Cambridge grocery industry indicates that for Bread & Circus the strongest driver of Retention Equity (the thing that makes the relationship the most "sticky") is that customers would lose the benefit of the knowledge that they have about the store. It is apparently the case that useful learning takes place that makes switching more difficult.

Benchmarking

The importance-performance analysis shows whom to benchmark within the firm's industry, and which drivers and sub-drivers should be given more benchmarking attention. For example, consider Avis from figure 10-15. Based on this analysis, it is appropriate to benchmark Hertz on both Brand Equity and Retention Equity, because Hertz's advantage is discovered to result from those components of Customer Equity. Hertz, on the other hand, will be well advised to benchmark companies outside its own industry for both Brand Equity and Retention Equity, because Hertz leads its own industry with respect to those Customer Equity drivers.

Considering Financial Return

It is important to note that the final decision about what improvement effort to make should come down to a careful financial analysis of the anticipated outcome, using the methods that we outlined in chapter 9. The ideal improvement opportunity is (1) related to a Customer Equity driver that is important in the industry, (2) related to a driver (and sub-driver) in which the firm's performance is subpar, and (3) projects to a good rate of financial return if accomplished.

Monitoring Customer Equity over Time

For three main reasons, it is important for a firm to monitor its Customer Equity performance over time:

- Monitoring improvements over time makes improvement efforts accountable.
- Competitor moves change the strategic landscape over time.
- Customer needs and expectations change over time, leading to changes in the importance of Customer Equity drivers, and leading to changes in how performance is evaluated.

For these reasons the smart company should maintain longitudinal data on its Customer Equity performance, and also that of its competitors.

Trends in Customer Equity Share and Market Share

Figure 10-18 shows a typical summary analysis of how a firm's market share is trending over time, along with how its Customer Equity share is trending. In this case we see that the market share is dropping, and the Customer Equity share is also dropping, albeit at a slower rate. This tells us that the company is slipping relative to its competitors, both in current sales and the value of its customer base. This profile is a very serious one that bodes poorly for the company's future, unless immediate measures are undertaken to shore up the company's Customer Equity.

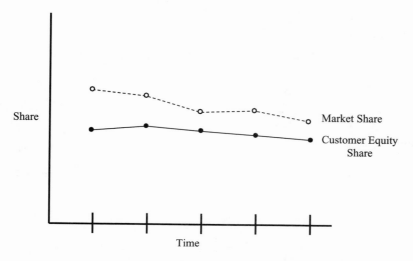

Figure 10-18. Trends in Customer Equity Share and Market Share

Trends in Customer Equity and the Value of the Firm

Another way to summarize the company's Customer Equity performance is to map its Customer Equity over time, along with its market value (see figure 10-19). The figure shows the typically expected pattern, which is Cus-

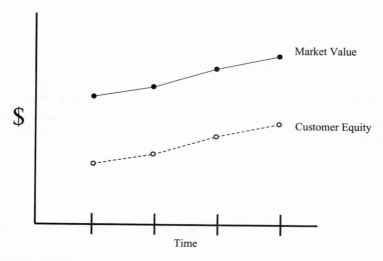

Figure 10-19. Trends in Customer Equity and Market Value of the Firm

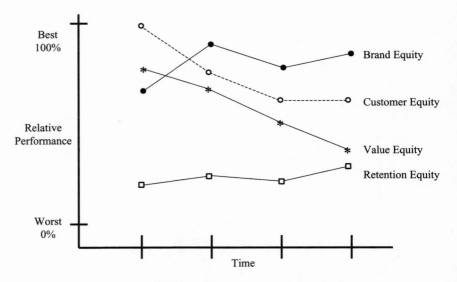

Figure 10-20. Trends in Customer Equity Driver Performance

tomer Equity tracking the company's market value closely, but at a lower level. This is because Customer Equity is not all of the company's value. To the extent that these variables can be correlated, this gives a predictive equation for how changes in Customer Equity translate to changes in the market value of the firm.

Trends in Customer Equity Driver Performance

Monitoring is also useful at the driver and sub-driver level. For example, Figure 10-20 shows a graph of trends in Value Equity, Retention Equity, and Brand Equity (along with Customer Equity) over time. Based on this figure, we see that the firm's Customer Equity is declining over time, perhaps because the firm's Value Equity is also declining over the same time period.

Trends in Customer Equity Driver Importance

It is also important to monitor the changes in Customer Equity driver performance over time. Figure 10-21 shows a graph of an industry's trends in Value Equity, Brand Equity, and Retention Equity. We can see that in this

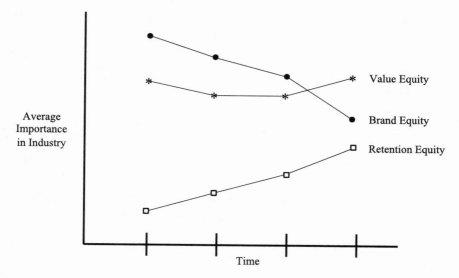

Figure 10-21. Trends in Customer Equity Driver Importance

industry, the importance of Retention Equity is increasing, perhaps because of frequent buyer programs becoming more common in the industry. We also see that over the same time period, the importance of Brand Equity is decreasing, perhaps because advertising is becoming less effective because of media fragmentation or regulatory changes.

Analysis by Segment

So far we have presented all of the Customer Equity analyses based on the entire customer base. But it will generally be useful to augment these analyses with analyses within market segment. In some cases, different segments may have very different perceptions, and very different importance weights. We briefly explore some of the differences that might reasonably be anticipated.

Segment Differences on Value Equity

Value is driven by quality, price, and convenience, and segments may vary in the importance they place on these sub-drivers. High-income customers may be very sensitive to quality, whereas low-income customers may be very sensitive to price. Two-career families may be very sensitive to convenience. A careful analysis of Customer Equity drivers by segment will reveal patterns like these that can have a huge impact on how the firm does business with those segments.

Segment Differences on Retention Equity

One may anticipate that people with more transient lifestyles (e.g., students) may be more resistant to attempts to build retention and relationships. Likewise, heavy users should be a much better target than light users for this sort of program. Analysis by segment will reveal this sort of pattern.

Segment Differences on Brand Equity

Media usage patterns will have a big impact on the effectiveness of brand-boosting programs. Heavy users of advertising media should be easier to communicate with. Another, more positive, way to think about this is that Brand Equity problems within a specific segment can be addressed by highly targeted segment-specific advertising/communications programs, or even by one-to-one communications.

A Modern Approach to Strategy

What we have outlined in this chapter is a modern approach to strategy, replacing product-based strategy with a competitive strategy approach based on how the firm addresses the specific drivers and sub-drivers of Customer Equity. Such an approach to strategy is the natural implication of the economy's shift from a goods economy to a service economy, combined with modern database and information system technology.

We have proposed that the business pay less attention to market share, which reflects only current performance, and more attention to Customer Equity share, which reflects both current and future business. Customer Equity share can be thought of as being the best leading indicator of future market share, because it compares against competition the firm's total customer lifetime values, across all of its customers.

Driving Customer Equity share is the firm's relative standing on the drivers of Customer Equity—Value Equity, Retention Equity, and Brand Equity. This Performance Profile is the firm's report card of how it stacks up against its competitors on the elements that translate to future profits.

The importance of Customer Equity drivers varies across industry. It is essential that the firm identify its industry's success factors, paying more attention to the Customer Equity drivers that drive customer choice, and perhaps paying less attention to the ones that don't.

By identifying drivers (and sub-drivers) for which there is great importance, and on which the firm is performing relatively poorly, the firm can isolate the areas in which improvement resources are likely to have the greatest impact.

To analyze trends in the industry, Customer Equity and its drivers must be monitored over time. This shows which drivers are growing in importance, and the areas in which the firm is slipping, relative to the competition. Ideally all of this analysis would be performed by segment, as well as for the entire customer base, because different customer segments may have very different needs, and quite different perceptions. The next three chapters show how a particular kind of segmentation—segmentation by profitability—can be an important basis for strategy.

Customer Equity provides a coherent, customer-based framework for competitive strategy. In short, this approach to strategy enables the firm to analyze its competitive position and identify the most effective improvement efforts directly with respect to the drivers of Customer Equity, providing a financially accountable approach to growing the value of the firm.

Strategic Analysis	
KEY INSIGHTS	ACTION STEPS
1. Competitive strategy needs to be customer-centered rather than product-centered; providing utility to customers should drive strategy.	• Try to shift company thinking from internally defined concepts, such as differentiated products or core competencies, to Customer Equity concepts.
2. Customer Equity share is more important than market share.	• Calculate, store, report, and monitor the company's Customer Equity share, alongside market share.
3. Every firm should compare its performance on Customer Equity and its drivers against its competitors.	• Importance-performance analysis can be used to prioritize which Customer Equity drivers to focus on. • Build performance-importance graphs that show how the company is doing on Customer Equity and its drivers, compared to its major competitors.
4. The relative importance of Customer Equity drivers varies by industry.	• Based on customer data, determine which of the drivers of Customer Equity is most important in your industry.
5. Trends in the firm's Customer Equity and its drivers should be monitored over time.	• Implement systems to track Customer Equity and its drivers.

IV

MANAGING CUSTOMER EQUITY

Ultimately, a focus on Customer Equity implies a fully customer-focused approach to management. Because the focus of the business is on customer profitability, customer profitability tiers, and how to manage them, become focal issues. The quest to build customer profitability is greatly enhanced by customer networking technologies such as the Internet, which provide new capabilities for building the drivers of Customer Equity. The Customer Equity framework foreshadows the corporation of the future, one in which the management structure is aligned with the drivers of Customer Equity. When an entire company is focused on growing Customer Equity, that entire company is also focused on growing the overall value of the firm.

The Customer Pyramid

Customer Variation in Profitability

Service at Any Cost to Any Customer?

When service quality became the management mantra of the 1980s, many firms became known for their relentless pursuit to serve all customers as well as possible. Infamous stories about companies like Nordstrom's allowing customers to return automobile tires (when, of course, the company sold only apparel!) and L.L.Bean exchanging boots that were twenty years old fed the philosophy. These approaches might have been right for companies that sold to the top tier of customers, but when the strategies were implemented by a majority of firms, the fallacy of the thinking became apparent.

Innovative service companies today are beginning to recognize that not all customers are worth attracting and keeping. Federal Express Corporation, for example, has revolutionized its marketing philosophy by categorizing its customers internally as the good, the bad, and the ugly—based on their profitability. Rather than marketing to all customers in a similar manner, the company now puts its efforts into the good, tries to move the bad to the good, and tries to discourage the ugly.[1]

Similarly, the customer service center at First Union, the sixth-largest bank in the United States, codes customers by color squares on computer screens using a database technology known as "Einstein." Green customers are profitable and receive extra customer service support, and red customers lose money for the bank and are not granted special privileges such as waivers for bounced checks. This seeming departure from the every-customer-is-always-right service quality mantra of the 1980s is becoming an effective and profitable service strategy for firms such as FedEx, US West, First Union, GE Capital, Bank of America, and The Limited.[2]

These firms have discovered that they need not serve all customers equally well. Many customers are too costly to do business with and have little potential to become profitable, even in the long-term. While companies may want to treat all customers with superior service, they find it is neither practical nor profitable to meet (and certainly not to exceed) all customers' expectations. Further—and probably more objectionable to quality zealots—in most cases it is desirable for a firm to alienate or even "fire" at least some of its customers.[3] While quality advocates may be offended by the notion of serving any customer in less than the best possible way, in many situations both the company and its customers obtain better value.

In this book, we have urged that the true lifetime value of the customer be the focus of the profitability evaluations in a company. We have examined what constitutes Value Equity to customers, and how Brand and Retention Equity contribute to the creation of Customer Equity. What we have not yet explicitly examined is the fact that not all customers are desirable in terms of profitability, and that a firm can develop an approach to systematically categorize customers by profits.

In this chapter, we demonstrate that customers vary in profitability and that this fact has strong implications for companies. We also briefly review some convincing information about the relationship between service quality and profitability. Second, we demonstrate that in many firms there are differences in profitability of customers, particularly tiers of customers. Third, we describe a tool called the Customer Pyramid, which uses these differences to find, serve, and create profitable customers. Finally, we will show a real-world example of the Customer Pyramid as a valid tool for focusing service resources on the customers and issues that best drive profitability.

Are Service Quality and Profitability Related?

Prior to the 1990s, the general link between service quality and profitability had been questioned, but since the early 1990s has been persuasively established. The evidence to support the linkage came from a variety of sources, but is now convincing enough to lead executives to believe that a positive relationship does exist. Just knowing that it exists doesn't lead directly to an understanding of what strategies and tactics to use to achieve the desired ends, but it is a start. We will briefly overview the sources of evidence of the general relationship between service quality and profitability then turn to a discussion of strategies to increase the profitability of service by more precisely targeting groups of customers.

INDUSTRY EVIDENCE. One way the link between service quality and profitability has been established is through industry-wide, cross-industry, or cross-facility studies. The PIMS (Profit Impact of Market Strategy) project by Richard Buzzell and Bradley Gale demonstrated a correlation between quality and profits across both manufacturing companies and service companies.[4] In more recent studies, quality improvement has also been linked to stock price shifts, the market value of the firm, and overall corporate performance.

The most compelling evidence linking service quality or customer satisfaction to profitability has come from broad-based industry studies. Claes Fornell devised the Swedish customer satisfaction index, an extensive customer satisfaction study across many Swedish industries.[5] That effort and subsequent work in the United States have conclusively demonstrated a link between customer satisfaction and market share and profitability.

FIRM EVIDENCE. Because firms are managed at the individual level and not the industry level, executives still wonder whether improved service quality results in increased firm profitability. A growing number of studies bear this out. Many authors listed in the reference section to this chapter posit a chain of effects of the following form:

- A service improvement effort produces an increased level of customer satisfaction at the process or attribute level.[6]

- Increased customer satisfaction at the process or attribute level leads to increased overall customer satisfaction.[7]

- Higher overall service quality or customer satisfaction leads to increased behavioral intentions, such as greater repurchase intention, and intention to increase usage.[8]

- Increased behavioral intentions lead to behavioral impact, including repurchase or customer retention, positive word of mouth, and increased usage.[9]

- Behavioral impact then leads to improved profitability and other financial outcomes.[10]

The evidence is clear, at both the industry level and the firm level, that improving service quality can lead to increased profitability. But customer satisfaction measurement programs too often fail to recognize that some customers are more profitable than others are, and that different customer profitability segments may require different emphases and resources in the service extended to them. As progressive companies have discovered, they can become more profitable by acknowledging the difference in profit potential among customer segments, then developing tailored approaches to serving them.

Traditional Segmentation

Both goods firms and service firms have long practiced segmentation. The idea of identifying homogeneous groups of customers, assessing these segments, then more precisely creating offerings and marketing mixes to satisfy them is not new. Traditional bases for segmentation include demographic, geographic, and psychographic approaches. Among types of psychographic segmentation, usage rate, which divides the market into heavy users, medium users, light users, and nonusers, is one of the most fruitful forms. In some cases, particularly in industrial markets, a firm can identify heavy users by name and tailor individual offerings directly to them. In other cases, particularly for packaged goods, firms may not be able to identify individual consumers, but through marketing research can create profiles of them and their needs and then access them through appropriate media.

Segmentation by Profitability

To build and improve upon traditional segmentation, a small percentage of businesses can now identify segments or, more appropriately, tiers of customers, which differ in current and/or future profitability to a firm.[11] This approach goes beyond usage segmentation because it tracks costs and revenues for segments of customers, thereby capturing their financial worth to companies. After identifying profitability bands, the firm offers services and service levels in line with the identified segments. We are going to envision tiers of customers arranged in levels that correspond to their profitability, with the most profitable tier being at the top of what we will call the Customer Pyramid, and the least profitable tier being at the bottom.

Customer Tiers

While some may view the FedEx grouping of customers into the "good, bad and the ugly," as negative, it can be very useful internally to provide descriptive labels of the tiers. This is especially true if it helps the company keep track of which customers are profitable and which ones are not.

Different systems and labels can be useful. One possible four-tier system might be the following:

1. *The Platinum Tier* describes the company's most profitable customers, typically those who are heavy users of the product, are not overly price sensitive, are willing to invest in and try new offerings, and are committed customers of the firm.

2. *The Gold Tier* differs from the Platinum Tier in that profitability levels are not as high, perhaps because the customers want price discounts that limit margins or they are not as loyal. They may be heavy users who minimize risk by working with multiple vendors rather than just the focal company.

3. *The Iron Tier* contains essential customers who provide the volume needed to utilize the firm's capacity, but their spending levels, loyalty, and profitability are not substantial enough for special treatment.

4. *The Lead Tier* consists of customers who are costing the company money. They demand more attention than they are due given their spending and profitability and are sometimes problem customers, complaining about the firm to others and tying up the firm's resources.

Note that this classification, while superficially reminiscent of, is very different from usage segmentation done by airlines such as American Airlines. Two differences are obvious. First, in the Customer Pyramid, profitability rather than usage defines all levels. Second, the lower levels actually articulate classes of customers who require a different sort of attention. The firm must work either to change the customers' behavior—to make them more profitable through increases in revenue—or to change the firm's cost structure to make them more profitable through decreases in costs.

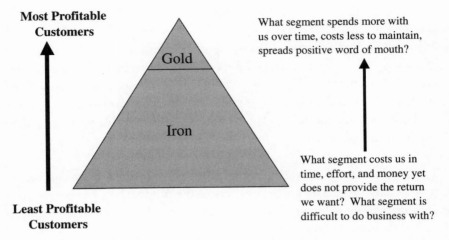

Figure 11-1. The "80/20" Customer Pyramid

The 80/20 Customer Pyramid

Virtually all firms are aware at some level that their customers differ in profitability, in particular that a minority of their customers accounts for the highest proportion of sales or profit. This has often been called the "80/20 rule"—20% of customers produce 80% of sales or profit. We will call this the "80/20 Customer Pyramid" (figure 11-1).

In this version of tiering, 20% of the customers constitute the Gold Tier, those who can be identified as the most profitable in the company. The rest are the Iron Tier, undistinguishable from each other but different from the Gold Tier in profitability. Most companies realize that there are differences among customers within this tier but do not possess the data or analytic capabilities to distinguish the distinctions. We will illustrate an empirical example of this pyramid in the next section.

The Extended Customer Pyramid

The 80/20 Customer Pyramid is a two-tier scheme that assumes that consumers within the two tiers are similar, just as conventional market segmentation schemes typically assume consumers within segments are similar. More than two tiers are likely, however, and can easily be employed if the available data provide sufficient information to analyze customer tiers more finely.

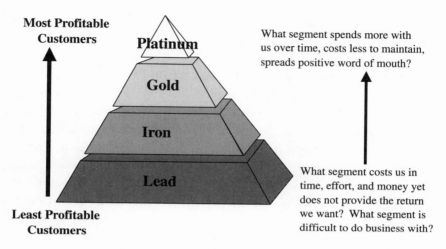

Most Profitable Customers

What segment spends more with us over time, costs less to maintain, spreads positive word of mouth?

What segment costs us in time, effort, and money yet does not provide the return we want? What segment is difficult to do business with?

Least Profitable Customers

Figure 11-2. The Expanded Customer Pyramid

Large databases are likely to reveal greater distinction among the tiers. Once a system has been established for categorizing customers, the multiple levels can be identified, motivated, served, and expected to deliver differential levels of profit. The number of tiers can be more numerous than four (as discussed above and shown in figure 11-2). At some point, however, too many tiers become cumbersome and make execution of the Pyramid less effective.

Illustration of the 80/20 Customer Pyramid

In this section we illustrate with an example how targeting specific tiers in the Customer Pyramid can lead to new insights and new managerial strategies. New insights and strategies make sense if four conditions are met:

1. if customers in different tiers have divergent profiles and characteristics;

2. if customers in different tiers view service quality in inconsistent ways;

3. if customers in different tiers have different drivers that lead to incidence and volume of new business;

4. if the profitability impact of improving service quality varies greatly in different customer tiers.

We'll discuss each of these conditions, then take a look at our example to see whether the conditions are met.

CONDITION 1: DIFFERENT TIERS HAVE DIFFERENT PROFILES AND CHARACTERISTICS.   Profitability differences in customer tiers are most useful when other variables can also define the tiers so that groups can be identified among customers. As is typical with customer segmentation, it is useful to find ways in which the customers in one tier are different from the customers in another tier, especially in terms of characteristics such as age, sex, or income. These descriptions can help us understand the tier's customers and can also help identify appropriate marketing activities. For example, a tier of customers who are primarily seniors will typically be managed in a very different way from a tier of customers who are primarily teenagers.

CONDITION 2: CUSTOMERS IN DIFFERENT TIERS VIEW SERVICE QUALITY IN INCONSISTENT WAYS.   In addition to having different descriptive characteristics, customers in different tiers can also have different needs, wants, and perceptions. Understanding the factors that affect the customer's decision to *purchase a new product or service* from an existing provider, as well as the factors that affect the decision to *increase the volume of purchases* from an existing provider, will be crucial for managing customers for profitability. Customers in different tiers may view service quality in different ways, which will have important managerial implications when a particular tier is targeted. Customers in each tier may not only have different needs, wants, and definitions of service quality, but also may have had different prior experiences with the firm. If they want different things and have had different experiences, different groups of attributes can be offered more efficiently than if the same bundle of attributes is offered to all customers.

CONDITION 3: CUSTOMERS IN DIFFERENT TIERS HAVE DIFFERENT DRIVERS THAT LEAD TO INCIDENCE AND VOLUME OF NEW BUSINESS.   Targeting customer tiers leads to particular marketing goals. A firm prefers to serve its most profitable customers better, because this strategy is likely to lead to more profit. Further, the firm desires to shift customers from lower tiers into higher tiers by attracting new business from them and increasing the volume of their purchases. Again, the differences in characteristics, needs, wants, and definitions of service quality seem likely to result in different drivers for the incidence and volume of new business.

CONDITION 4: THE PROFITABILITY IMPACT OF IMPROVING SERVICE QUALITY VARIES GREATLY IN DIFFERENT CUSTOMER TIERS. The most profitable customers should offer the greatest opportunity. Just as direct marketers routinely qualify lists to test for potential profitability, companies should routinely qualify their customer tiers for potential profitability. We have already stated that customer characteristics, needs, wants, and drivers of new and increased business should differ among tiers. If the Customer Pyramid is appropriate, the way customers respond to service and marketing should differ among tiers. Higher tiers should produce a much higher response to improvements in service quality. This response will be evident in increases in new business, volume of business, and average profit per customer.

Taken together, the disproportionately greater response to changes in service quality in each of these areas will result in an overall greater return on service quality improvements for the higher tiers of customers.

The sidebar describes a study we conducted to see if these conditions were met and, if met, what the implications were in terms of the Customer Pyramid.

Customer Pyramid Study

Customer Sample, Usage, and Demographic Data. We analyzed retail customer data provided by a division of a major U.S. bank that seeks to remain anonymous. The data included profitability information from an assortment of retail products organized by customer, as well as descriptive information about the customers, including sex, average account balance, average profit from account, average age, and income.

Customer Survey. These data were merged with responses to a service quality survey from the same set of customers. The survey asked many individual questions pertaining to particular aspects of service and an overall satisfaction question. A leading marketing research company in the second half of 1996 conducted the telephone surveys. Over 10,000 customers per month were sampled, and for ease of further data processing and analysis, a random sample of 796 of these respondents was drawn.

Data on Incidence and Volume of New Business. Eight months later, information regarding the amount of new business, including both the incidence of new business and the volume of new business (revenue from new accounts), was added to the data file by examining behavior following the survey. In this way, service quality measures could be used to predict future behavior utilizing a cross-sectional, time-series approach.

Analysis. First, we examined differences in customer descriptive statistics for the two tiers and conducted simple statistical tests where appropriate. To look at differences in service quality perceptions, we used a technique called "factor analysis" to group the service quality items into components, then examined the resulting factor structure to see the similarities and differences. We examined differences in the drivers of incidence of new business across tiers using a statistical approach called "logit analysis," and differences in drivers of volume of new business across tiers using a multiple "regression analysis." We used both logit analysis and regression analysis to project the increase in the percentage of customers who would open a new account, and the increase in the average account balance. Multiplying the projected average account balance by the average profit per account balance for each tier yielded an estimate for the projected increase in average profit per account. Multiplying that by the number of accounts yielded the total projected new profits from each tier. For more details on the specifics of the analysis and approach, please see the paper written by the three of us that is listed in the references to this chapter.

For simplicity of illustration in our study, we used the 80/20 Customer Pyramid. We divided the customer base into two customer tiers: the most profitable 20% (Gold Tier) and the least profitable 80% (Iron Tier). The results were as follows.

Customers in different tiers have different customer characteristics. We noted in particular that the Gold Tier had a higher percentage of women than the Iron Tier, an average account balance that is about five times as big, and average profit about *18 times* as much. The Gold Tier is older than the Iron Tier, has more upper-income customers, and has far fewer lower-income customers. However, there are a surprising number of lower-income customers in the Gold Tier (20.1%) and higher-income customers in the Iron Tier (7.1%). The Gold Tier produces more profit per volume of business, with an average profit per account balance of 2.53%, versus 0.71% for the Iron Tier. Finally, we note that the Gold Tier (the most profitable 20%) produces 82% of the bank's retail profits, an almost perfect confirmation of the 80/20 rule in this setting.

Customers in different tiers view quality differently. The Gold Tier viewed service quality in terms of three factors, which we call *attitude, reliability,* and *speed.* To these customers, *attitude* meant "treat you with respect," "eager to help you," and "values your business." *Reliability* meant, "right the first time," "keep promises," and "consistent service." Items that meant *speed* were "don't have to wait in line a long time," "time to get in and out," and "work quickly."

By contrast, the less profitable Iron Tier has a less sophisticated view of service quality, viewing service as only two factors that we label *attitude* and *speed.* These factors are very similar to the related factors from the most profitable tier. *Attitude* is described best by "eager to help you," "have your needs at heart," and "values your business." *Speed* is described by "don't have to wait in line a long time," and "time to get in and out." The reliability factor is not present for the Iron Tier.

What is compelling to note is that combining the survey scores for both groups would result in a muddied picture. If we looked at all customers together, it appears that all want the attitude and reliability factors, and that they mean the same thing to both groups. Looking at the groups as if they were the same muddles these factors together, resulting in a confusing and misleading picture of what service quality means to the customer base.

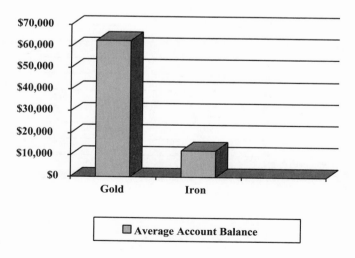

Table 11-1. Average Account Balances in Gold and Iron Tiers

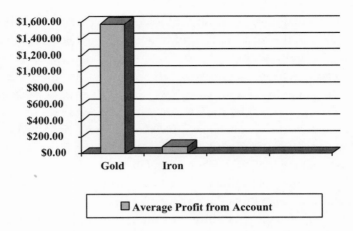

Table 11-2. *Average Profit from Accounts in Gold and Iron Tiers*

Different tiers have different drivers of incidence and volume of new business. Since we measured what customers did *after* they reported what was important to them, we captured something critical that is not usually obtained in surveys—what *actually* drove customers to make purchases, rather than what they *thought* would make them do so. For the Gold tier, *speed* was key to driving incidence of new business. The more profitable customer group was in a hurry and valued being able to get quick service. The

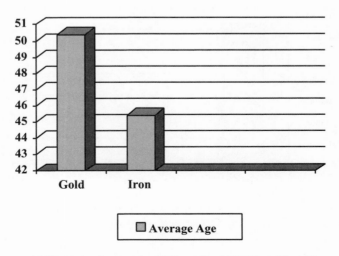

Table 11-3. *Average Age of Customers in Gold and Iron Tiers*

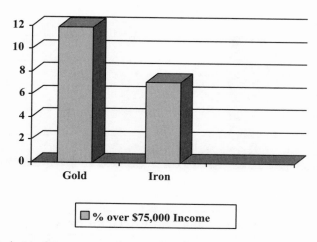

Table 11-4. % of Customers with More than $75,000 Income in Gold and Iron Tiers

Iron Tier required a different driver altogether. *Attitude* was the key driver for this tier; *speed* was not quite significant in a statistical sense.

Once again, we find that analyzing the entire customer base as a single group would be misleading. Both the combined *attitude/reliability* factor and the *speed* factor are key drivers for the group as a whole, but the combined analysis *would not reveal the fact that different strategies should be used for different profitability levels.*

Consistent with these results, different customer tiers have different drivers of new business. When it comes to increasing volume, the Gold Tier demands *speed* while the Iron Tier demands *attitude.*

The profitability impact of improving service quality varies greatly in different customer tiers. An across-the-board service quality improvement of the key drivers (approximated by a .1 increase in average satisfaction with each driver in each tier) resulted in a projected 3.65% increase in incidence of new accounts in the Gold Tier, but only a 2.00% increase in the Iron Tier. This result (shown in table 11-6) suggests that the Gold Tier was almost twice as responsive to the changes in service quality than the Iron Tier. When examining the projected increase in average account balance, the results were even more encouraging.

The projected increase in average account balance was $6.19 in the Gold Tier, but a meager $0.69 in the Iron Tier. Here, *the Gold Tier appeared to be almost ten times as responsive to changes in service quality.* Finally, the projected increase in average profit per customer was 15.7 cents in the Gold

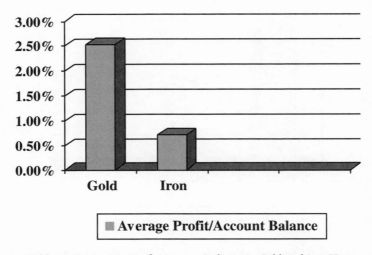

Table 11-5. Average Profit/Account Balance in Gold and Iron Tiers

Tier, but 0.5 cents in the Iron Tier. Again, the Gold Tier provided a substantially greater return on the service quality improvement. Of particular interest was that simultaneous improvement of the key drivers for both tiers produced a projected 89% of the new profits in the Gold Tier, but only 11% of the new profits could be attributed to the Iron Tier. This was an even higher percentage than the current percentage of profits.

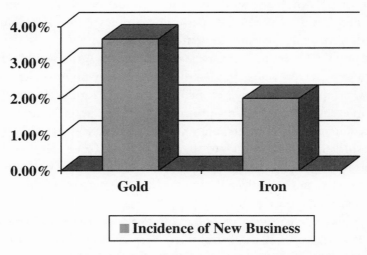

Table 11-6. Difference in Incidence of New Accounts Due to 1% Increase in Average Satisfaction with Each Driver in Each Tier

A Closing Note

As progressive firms have discovered, examining the profitability of customers and segmenting on that basis is a successful service strategy. In this chapter, we recommended a managerial methodology called the Customer Pyramid, which can be used to focus management resources on the customers who are likely to generate the greatest improvement in a firm's profitability. The framework provides a way to examine the extent to which customers in different profitability tiers weigh service quality attributes differently. More important, the Customer Pyramid provides a methodology with which firms can now examine the extent to which customers in different profitability tiers will respond to changes in service quality.

The Customer Pyramid results in many important implications for management, because it implies a new way of thinking about the relationship between customers and products. Using service tiers (such as "Platinum," "Gold," "Iron," and "Lead" as described previously) benefits the way service marketing is accomplished in multiple ways. First, tiers allow the company to allocate resources more efficiently. Rather than spending equal time with all customers, many of whom are a drain on the time, effort, and emotional energy of employees while returning little or nothing to the company, the company can isolate and expend resources more appro-

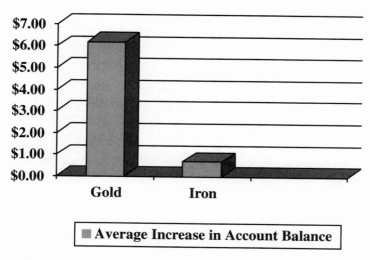

Table 11-7. Increase in Average Account Balance in Gold and Iron Tiers

priately. The evidence from our real-world example shows that expenditures on the upper tier yield far better returns than those on the lower tier. Second, by focusing on providing the very best service to leading customers, the firm's reputation is improved, creating word of mouth and a strengthening of competitive position. In essence, the firm becomes expert at those target groups they choose to serve. Third, because the goal of service tiers is to isolate and delineate each level, customer requirements can be understood more clearly. Finally, largely because of the clearer articulation of needs, better guidelines for development of new services for different tiers can be developed, providing more precisely targeted offerings with a greater chance for success in the marketplace.

The Customer Pyramid	
KEY INSIGHTS	ACTION STEPS
1. All customers are not equally valuable to the firm.	• Identify and classify customers using an approach such as the Customer Pyramid.
2. Customers in different tiers have different characteristics.	• Use segmentation analysis and other approaches to develop profiles of the different customer tiers.
3. Customers in different tiers view quality differently.	• Be sure to separate tiers when conducting research to understand what drives quality in the customer's view. • Adapt strategies according to the different views of quality, focusing most heavily on upper tiers.
4. Different tiers have different drivers of volume and incidence of new business.	• Identify the best prospects by matching them with current profiles of best customers.
5. The profitability impact of improving service quality varies greatly in different customer tiers.	• Allocate resources depending upon tiers.

12

Managing the Customer Pyramid

The Customer Pyramid in Action

The Customer Pyramid has been effectively used in a variety of industries, with financial services and retail firms leading the way, perhaps because of the vast amounts of data already existing in those firms. Below are just a few examples of the innovators in the field:

- In 1994, Bank One began to recognize that financial institutions were grossly overcharging their best customers to subsidize others who were not paying their keep. Determined to grow its top-profit customers, who were vulnerable because they were being underserved, the bank implemented a set of measures to focus resources on their most productive use. The company used the data resulting from the measures to identify the profit drivers in this top segment and stabilized their relationships with key customers.[1]

- FruitS is a segmentation approach used in the financial services sector that combines customer transactional data with market research on the same individuals. What results is a classification of adults according to their likely usage of financial services. Once classified, customers of the financial services company can be approached more efficiently with services that have a greater certainty to be accepted.

- Another bank, using a fictitious name to protect its competitive edge, started by using traditional segmentation on the basis of usage information, externally sourced demographic data, and life-cycle demographics. It then moved into profitability analysis with each segment, incorporating channel information to validate the value of each customer and to understand the differences in the top, average, and low performers. Once it knew the differences, it began to approach each segment in unique ways, maximizing the profit it was able to obtain from its customers. Among other things, it stopped offering high levels of service to low performers and found different ways to serve them that were more efficient.[2]

- First Commerce Corporation knew that customer segmentation could improve the effectiveness of all of its operations. After dividing clients into mutually exclusive groups of individuals based on demographics, the company then identified the reasons for profitability swings (including balances, product mix, and transaction behavior). The firm then defined three unique segments: the smart money segment, the small business segment, and the convenience segment. Tailoring its marketing efforts differentially to those segments made the company's programs far more effective.[3]

Now that we understand the concept of the Customer Pyramid—that there are tiers of customers that differ in characteristics, sensitivity to service, and, most important, profitability—the key is learning how to use it. When is the Customer Pyramid appropriate in a firm? When does it make sense to divide customers into tiers? For purposes of discussion, let's briefly review the four-tier Customer Pyramid we proposed as a possibility in the last chapter as a framework for this chapter. Those tiers included:

- *The Platinum Tier* describes the company's most profitable customers who are committed to the firm.

- *The Gold Tier* includes customers whose profitability levels are not as high because the customers want price discounts or are not as loyal to a single vendor.

- *The Iron Tier* contains essential customers who provide essential volume to use the firm's capacity but whose loyalty and profitability are not substantial enough for special treatment.

- *The Lead Tier* consists of customers who are costing the company money.

Under what conditions is the use of the Customer Pyramid most desirable? We will begin this chapter with this topic. We will also discuss the most important issues that arise in managing the Customer Pyramid. These include finding the most profitable customers and serving customers according to their tiers.

When Does the Customer Pyramid Work?

From the firm's point of view, the Customer Pyramid is desirable whenever the company has customers who differ in profitability, but the company is delivering the same levels of service to all customers. In these situations, the firm is using limited resources to stretch across a wide group of customers, possibly underserving its best customers. In each of the following conditions, it makes financial and practical sense to segment by profitability.

WHEN CUSTOMERS WANT DIFFERENT SERVICES OR LEVELS OF SER-VICE.   In many industries, particularly those with high technology or information technology offerings, customers have divergent requirements and aptitudes for service. One telephone company, for example, viewed its customers as being comprised of three groups. The first group's decision makers were sophisticated CIOs who wanted to configure their own systems and needed minimal service assistance from the vendor. The second group's decision makers were middle managers of large firms who wanted to purchase complex systems but needed considerable consulting to develop the best configuration. The third group consisted of CEOs of small firms who wanted sturdy, competent systems that were easy to understand and that included basic maintenance service. The three decision makers had completely different requirements; treating them with the same levels of service at the same high price would not only be inefficient but ineffective as well. A successful telecommunication firm would be one that recognized the different service requirements and matched service levels to requirements. If the CEOs were approached in the same way as the sophisticated CIOs, they would be confused and overwhelmed, unlikely to choose the firm's offerings. Similarly, the middle managers would not want to be left to configure their own systems and would probably pay far more to have that service performed for them. Serving these different customers involves widely different costs that are wasted if all customers are treated the same way. This is a situation where the Customer Pyramid, with its tiers of customers differing in characteristics, service sensitivity, and profitability, is ideal.

WHEN CUSTOMERS ARE WILLING TO PAY FOR DIFFERENT LEVELS OF SERVICE. Package delivery services such as Federal Express charge varying rates based on the type of delivery and the speed with which a package is delivered. The different types of delivery include express package service (under 150 pounds), express freight service (over 150 pounds), FedEx Letter, FedEx Pak, FedEx Box, and FedEx Tube, all of which have different prices associated with them. Speeds of delivery include FedEx Priority Overnight, FedEx Standard Overnight, and FedEx second-day, each with different prices. A customer can also purchase Saturday delivery and special handling—as expected—at additional cost. Customer sensitivity to these different services is high, leading to a willingness to pay considerably more or less depending on the desired delivery and speed. Customers clearly know in these situations when their packages must arrive, and they are willing to pay differential rates, making the Customer Pyramid not only appropriate but also easy to administer. Rather than having to use data to sort customers into the different tiers, the company need only offer different services at different rates and see what customers choose. The tiers are self-administering in these situations.

WHEN SERVICE RESOURCES, INCLUDING EMPLOYEE TIME, ARE LIMITED. One of the most important reasons for ascribing to the Customer Pyramid is to prevent the undesirable situation in which a company's best customers do not obtain the service they require because the company is expending too much time and effort on its least profitable customers. A restaurant would not want to fill up all its tables with students purchasing coffee with endless refills when customers who purchase soup-to-dessert dinners are kept waiting. Whenever any resource, such as employee time, is limited, a firm must identify the best use of the limited resource. This situation occurs frequently in professional services such as consulting, accounting, advertising, and architectural design. A firm has only so much professional time available, and its allocation must be done carefully so that the best customers are not kept waiting for their jobs while smaller and less profitable customers are served. One of the authors, who used to work in an advertising agency, found that inexperienced clients, typically those who just cleared the minimum dollar hurdle, were most demanding in terms of time and service. When the advertising firm's creative and managerial personnel acceded to the wishes of these small clients, redoing work and meeting unrealistic deadlines, the work of the agency's bread-and-butter clients was delayed and of lower quality.

When facing employee time and other resource constraints, the firm must identify customers to receive priority service. First, a system must be set up within the firm to determine which customers are in each tier, an approach that will be discussed later in this chapter. Next, employees must be trained to identify high tier customers. These mechanisms include structured programs, which allow customers to identify themselves at the beginning of the transaction with the firm (such as loyalty programs or levels of service), and a color-coding system such as the one used by First Union Bank on computer screens for individual customers. Without such mechanisms, firm resources may easily be focused on loud or demanding customers from lower levels of the Customer Pyramid while more profitable customers are kept waiting. A particularly compelling issue here is how to identify customers to receive special treatment without offending those who are in the lower tiers. Imagine how Federal Express customers would feel if they knew they were classified as one of the "uglies" in "the good, bad, and the ugly" internal classification system the firm now uses!

WHEN CUSTOMERS DEFINE VALUE IN DIFFERENT WAYS. As we described in chapter 5, customers define value in one of four ways: (1) value is low price; (2) value is whatever a customer wants in a product or service; (3) value is quality divided by price; and (4) value is all that a customer gets for all that she gives. In addition to monetary price, customers also consider nonmonetary prices such as time, effort, convenience, or psychic costs. When a service company has customers with all of these definitions of value, tiers of service can be designed to capture the best financial returns for the company depending on what the customer expects in terms of value. Perhaps the first value definition (value is low price) would cover the company's lowest level or Lead customers; this segment would be willing to accept less in exchange for paying less. Customers with the second value definition (value is whatever I want in a product or service) might be Platinum customers because they are not price sensitive. If their needs mesh with high-margin services the firm can provide, both buyers' and seller's needs are met. In between these two levels fall the Gold and Iron segments with value definitions that are both service and price sensitive, leading them to be more profitable than the Lead Tier but less profitable than the Platinum Tier.

WHEN CUSTOMERS CAN BE SEPARATED FROM EACH OTHER. Firms are and should be sensitive to the fact that customers in the lower tiers of the pyramid will be angry if they see other customers receiving better treatment than they receive. Unless the reason is readily apparent for service differentials (such as a 15% discount for seniors at a restaurant), the customers in different categories should not know that those in other tiers are viewed as different or are receiving different levels of service. As an example, telephone companies such as AT&T now have state-of-the-art customer service centers that can immediately identify which tier customers fit in when their call comes in to the customer service center. These automatic systems immediately route customer calls to different centers based on the value of the customer to the company. Once there, service standards, such as length of time spent on a customer call, differ depending on the tier of customer. For high-end customers, there is no time limit for the call, only the goal to satisfy the needs of the customer. For low-end customers, however, there is a goal to minimize the length of the call to reduce costs and keep the tier profitable. It is critical in a system such as this one—used by some catalog companies—that individual customers not realize that they are being hurried off the line. Training must be provided for the customer service representatives handling the low-end customers so that the perception of high quality service is still provided.

WHEN SERVICE DIFFERENTIALS CAN LEAD TO UPGRADING CUSTOMERS TO ANOTHER LEVEL. On the other hand, there are substantial benefits in some services for customers clearly seeing what other customers receive. For example, main cabin airline customers note that the services in the first-class cabin are better than what they receive, but the difference is substantiated by the obvious fact that those customers paid more for their seats. Another reason why customers are in first class is that they receive complimentary upgrades for being frequent travelers. Armed with this knowledge, otherwise nonloyal airline travelers may be motivated to consolidate their airline trips on a specific airline to be able to take advantage of these benefits.

Finding the Most Profitable Customers

Once a firm has decided that the Customer Pyramid is appropriate, the first and most difficult challenge in using the Pyramid is determining the profitability of individual (and/or segments of) customers.

Recent industry practice in using databases leans toward a technique called "data mining" for market segmentation where a computer program "looks through" customer data to see what kinds of hidden patterns can be found. Data mining is useful in several ways. First of all, it can summarize mountains of data, such as years of a bank's data on its customers. Second, because so much data exists, it can build models that help predict outcomes such as purchase or repurchase based on some of the customer characteristics and past behaviors in the database. Third, data mining can identify groups of individuals or households based on the information, using primarily geographic, demographic, or psychographic (lifestyle) bases. Finally, data mining can even assign customers to groups.[4]

The process of data mining, which is not typically used for identifying profitability segments, can be applied to the Customer Pyramid, but with important modifications. The following steps are recommended.

DETERMINE THE TOTAL MARKETING COSTS INVOLVED IN OBTAINING CUSTOMERS. This is by far the most difficult part of identifying profitability segments. While it is relatively easy to associate revenues with individual customers, figuring out the costs associated with serving different customers is not a simple task. In any firm that provides service, for example (and what firm doesn't provide service?), there are multiple customers being sought at any one time and multiple services being offered to these customers, so teasing out the costs of each is hard. However, it is possible to obtain cost estimates for salesperson visits, marketing materials, samples, and entertainment among other expenses.

DETERMINE THE COMPANY'S YIELD RATE ON MARKETING EXPENDITURES. The next step is to figure out how many times each marketing cost must be expended to obtain a customer. If only one customer out of twenty-five solicited by a salesperson becomes a customer, multiply the marketing cost by twenty-five and use that as the cost figure. If the company receives mail orders from just one customer in 100, multiply by 100 to represent the marketing costs of a customer.

FIND OUT WHAT CUSTOMERS SPEND ON THE COMPANY'S SERVICES.
This information is likely to be available for industrial or commercial clients
because the firms maintain sales histories. Understanding the actual purchase and usage behavior of their customers has become a key focus of many
service companies, especially financial service companies who currently are
engaging in data mining to seek usage and sales profiles of their customers.
Retailers are quickly becoming more sophisticated in this area as well, capturing cash, check, and credit card transactions in accessible and trackable
customer information files.

**CREATE CUSTOMER INFORMATION FILES TO TRACK INDIVIDUAL
CUSTOMER REVENUES.**   The Customer Pyramid has important implications for the information-related functions of the firm, especially accounting and information management. These functions must be designed to
align with the customer, rather than just the product. The first necessity is
to collect, store, and make accessible to managers the revenues associated
with each customer. This necessary shift is one that leading financial institutions have undertaken in the last ten years or so. Instead of data files being
organized by product, with customers listed several times if they buy several
products (e.g., a bank customer might be listed in a checking account file, a
savings account file, a home loan file, etc.), the data files are organized by
customer (see figure 12-1), with the products and affiliated revenues stored
by customer. Leading retail firms are also moving in this direction, developing and utilizing systems that organize purchases by customer as well as by
manufacturer, thereby allowing the data to be utilized by operations and
marketing to increase efficiencies.[5]

**RECORD AND STORE COSTS ASSOCIATED WITH EACH CUSTOMER IN
THE CUSTOMER INFORMATION FILES.**   The second necessity is to
understand, record, and store the costs associated with each customer in
these files, a much harder task. While such techniques as activity-based
costing (ABC) are useful in this regard, the truth is that in many cases the
allocation of cost to customers is arbitrary at best. Often the best approach
is to assign only variable costs, with the idea that the fixed costs will be allocated in a roughly constant manner across customers. Profit calculations
(more accurately, contribution calculations) conducted in this way should
lead to an ordering of customers that is very close to the ordering that might
result if all fixed costs were appropriately allocated.

Figure 12-1. Customer Information File for a Bank

Ultimately it is necessary that the information management include a summary profitability figure for each customer that can be easily accessed. This number is used to construct the tiers of the Customer Pyramid and will be a guide to managing the relationship with each customer.

DEVELOP PROFILES OF RESULTING TIERS. Analyses such as those described in chapter 11 would next be used to isolate homogeneous tiers of service customers. Recall that the approach used was to first try to identify customer characteristics that differentiated segments of customers. In an ideal scenario, the database will allow the firm to track changes in profitability by customer over time, such that each customer's movement up or down the Pyramid can be easily monitored by the firm.

DEVELOP MEASURES OF ATTRACTIVENESS FOR TIERS. Each tier that is isolated should not automatically be accepted as a target for the firm. Criteria for customer desirability must be designed by the firm. The most important of these will involve profits and profit potentials, but a firm need not limit the criteria to these. Another aspect that can be very important to firms is whether or not customers are innovators or early adopters of products or services. Innovators and early adopters are groups of customers who tend to try to buy offerings before the rest of the population and who then spread positive word of mouth to others about them. Identifying innovators and early adopters, then allocating them to the upper segments, is important because they are a critical source of potential profits that go beyond what they themselves spend. Another, this time nonfinancial, criterion is the amount a customer spends with a competing firm, and that could be converted to spending with the focal firm. Many other criteria, such as fit with the firm, could also be considered.

ELIMINATE FROM CONSIDERATION CUSTOMERS WHO ARE NOT PROFITABLE OR DESIRABLE FOR OTHER REASONS. Only those customers the firm believes can become profitable in terms of lifetime value should be continued as possible customers. The company must then end the relationships with nonprofitable customers, even if they have been the company's customers for some time. Alternatively, the company could work to convert unprofitable customers into more profitable customers, an approach we will discuss in the next chapter.

ARRAY SERVICE TIERS FROM PLATINUM (MOST PROFITABLE) THROUGH IRON (LEAST PROFITABLE BUT STILL DESIRABLE) TO LEAD (UNPROFITABLE AND UNDESIRABLE). Describe these customer profiles as completely as possible by adapting the criteria we presented at the beginning of this chapter to the company's own criteria. Verify that the tiers are different, especially in terms of profitability, using the types of analysis we described in chapter 11. Just as many marketers have learned using traditional segmentation, merely being able to group customers into segments is not effective. Segments must be substantially different in terms of characteristics, response to marketing, and profitability in order for the Customer Pyramid approach to be an improvement over treating all customers in a similar manner.

DETERMINE WAYS TO ACCESS THEM EITHER AS A GROUP OR INDIVIDUALLY. The step that follows isolation of tiers involves the traditional marketing strategies of product, price, promotion, and place. Now, however, instead of viewing the market as a uniform group of customers with similar potential, the firm views them as distinct groups with differing potential. At its best, this means developing different marketing strategies for each tier, especially different strategies for price and offering.

Steps for Implementing the Customer Pyramid

1. Determine the total marketing costs involved in obtaining customers.
2. Determine the company's yield rate on marketing expenditures.
3. Find out what customers spend on the company's services.
4. Create customer information files to track individual customer revenues.
5. Record and store costs associated with each customer in the customer information files.
6. Develop profiles of resulting tiers.
7. Develop measures of attractiveness for tiers.
8. Eliminate from consideration customers who are not profitable or desirable for other reasons.
9. Array service tiers from Platinum (most profitable) through Iron (least profitable but still desirable) to Lead (unprofitable and undesirable).
10. Determine ways to access them either as a group or individually.

Serving Customers According to Their Tiers

The Customer Pyramid implies that management strategy should be aligned with customer profitability, specifically that more attention should be paid to customers who will generate the firm's profits currently and in the future. We saw in the example in the previous chapter that this can mean paying more attention to the firm's profitable customers. It is also true that less profitable customers can be made more profitable through increasing the incidence and/or volume of purchase, a topic we will take up in the next chapter. For now, let's look at a few examples of companies, recognizing that they have different tiers and serve them in different ways.

- Historically, the IBM Corporation had a philosophy that, armed with its computers, virtually any client could become a large client. Prior to the introduction of the personal computer, it treated customers this way. Virtually all were handled using IBM's professional sales force, and all were granted the potential to become purchasers of the company's largest products, mainframe computers. It took IBM until the early 1990s to begin to realize that this approach was no longer valid. No longer did each customer merit a salesperson and the personal service attention that had been the company's hallmark. In a striking break with tradition, IBM created several telephone sales and service centers and channeled smaller customers to these centers. When they needed to purchase small orders for computers, customers called the company. When they needed service, they called the company and were handled by a different group of service repair people who often were able to fix their computers without coming to the customer location. IBM was able to vastly improve its profitability when it recognized that it was no longer sensible to try to serve all customers as if they were top customers.

- Many of the banks we described at the beginning of this chapter have identified the customer group that is on the bottom tier of the Customer Pyramid: college students. These customers have very little money of their own, cannot afford savings accounts, and often shop for and obtain free checking accounts. While banks realize that these customers may someday be good customers for them—and therefore do not want to alienate them—they also recognize that serving them is expensive. They therefore are developing strategies for dealing with these customers in inexpensive ways. For example, they encourage the students to bank by telephone or ATM, sometimes going so far as to require a fee if they visit tellers more than a couple of times a month. They require the students to have overdraft checking, a moneymaker for banks, to avoid the high cost and inconvenience (to the bank) of bounced checks. They charge high fees (one of the author's local banks charged her son a $30 late payment) when monthly payments are not on time. What is important here is that the banks are realizing that customers differ, have identified the differences, and have made changes in the way they market to obtain greater levels of profitability in the lower tiers of the Customer Pyramid.

Once the tiers have been established, various elements of service strategy can be adjusted to the tiers. For example, the need for customer information varies by tier. With Platinum and Gold customers, it is desirable to know individually what each customer wants, to develop a custom profile of each customer's history, preferences, usage, and expectations. For Iron customers, on the other hand, segment preferences and perceptions are usually adequate. Lead customers may be studied for different purposes altogether, such as to examine ways that they may be served more efficiently and with less cost.

The most important marketing task implied by the Customer Pyramid is to serve the most profitable customers in ways that extend and enrich their relationships with the company. A second important marketing task implied by the Customer Pyramid is to identify the company's most profitable *future* customers and serve these customers in ways that will move them to higher tiers as well. Careful consideration should be given to the product and service needs of these customers and to their value propositions. However, if the firm is to maintain profitability among these tiers, it must be careful not to focus on improving the value proposition by discounting and other price-related strategies. If the firm's Gold Tier customers want relationship value, and the "costs" they experience and want to reduce are nonmonetary rather than monetary, then discounting strategies will not be effective. If a company's Gold customers value speed over all else, time is a critical cost to them that could be addressed by the firm without lowering monetary prices. Lowering prices reduces the profitability of the segment, often unnecessarily, for monetary price may not be high on the list of requirements for this segment.

Managing the Customer Pyramid	
KEY INSIGHTS	ACTION STEPS
1. Different profitability tiers have different needs.	• Identify and address each customer tier differently. • Create customer information files to track individual customer profitability.
2. The factors that drive the satisfaction of the firm's best customers can be different from the factors that drive the satisfaction of most of the firm's customers.	• Carefully assess the needs of your firm's most profitable customers to maintain or increase their already high levels of profitability.
3. Efforts to serve the best customers are more profitable than efforts to serve lower-tiered customers.	• Serve the most profitable customers in ways that extend and enrich their relationships with the company.
4. Analyses that do not separate out the firm's most profitable customers can result in a misleading picture of what is required.	• Do separate analyses for each customer tier.

Customer Alchemy

Customer alchemy is the art of turning less profitable customers into more profitable customers. It can take place at any tier along the Customer Pyramid, but it is more difficult at some levels of the Pyramid than at others. For example, it is very difficult to move Lead customers up to higher tiers and is often necessary, as we will state in this chapter, to "get the Lead out" rather than try to move those customers up. If the decision is made to keep Lead customers, the strategies used are typically different than those used at other tiers. We will offer strategies for customer alchemy at each level in the Pyramid and, where they apply, for the three components of Customer Equity—Value Equity, Brand Equity, and Retention Equity.

Turning Gold into Platinum

The most important requirement for turning Gold customers into Platinum customers is to fully understand them and their needs. With an industrial or business-to-business firm and a dedicated sales force, this need is often already met. The salesperson knows the business well enough to stay constantly in touch with the client and to anticipate his or her needs. This customer intimacy, when done well, allows the company to move the customer to a higher tier because the company can develop offerings that satisfy the client's needs, can identify existing ways to serve the client better, and can communicate in the right way at the right times to clients.

When a company has a larger number of customers, the process of turning Gold into Platinum may seem more daunting but still involves the same basic foundation: building an information profile about customers that becomes the basis for becoming a full-service provider of whatever the firm can offer. Building this profile may involve collecting and consolidating existing information about the customer's history with the firm, including usage and customer satisfaction information. Alternatively, this may involve conducting very individualized customer research such as personal interviews or customer expectation sessions. Only when a company fully understands a Gold customer can it design strategies to turn that customer into a Platinum customer. Thorough knowledge of the customer is required to fully understand what is valued and thereby bring into play all three components of Value Equity, Brand Equity, and Retention Equity.

A simple example of building a customer information base to turn a Gold customer into a Platinum customer is illustrated by the strategy the Ritz-Carlton, the high-end luxury hotel chain, uses with its frequent travelers. Once a guest has stayed with the hotel a certain number of times, a computer profile is set up to catalog her likes, dislikes, and preferences. Employees at each Ritz-Carlton where she stays document what they learn and input it to the composite profile, which is then made available to any hotel where the guest registers. In this way, a Ritz-Carlton—even one where the guest has not stayed in the past—knows whether the guest likes feather pillows, king-size beds, requires meeting rooms, even whether room service is her preference. Such special treatment makes the guest want to spend all her travel time in a Ritz-Carlton rather than in a competing hotel, converting her from a Gold customer to a Platinum customer.

All three drivers of Customer Equity can be used to move customers from Gold to Platinum, as shown in figure 13-1 and as described below.

Increasing Value Equity

BECOME A FULL-SERVICE PROVIDER.   Home Depot, the U.S. hardware giant, has a strategy for making its good customers into great customers, thereby turning Gold customers into Platinum customers. The highly successful hardware superstore, which sells to virtually all levels in the Customer Pyramid, has a new strategy for the high end. In this strategy, it is focusing on two groups of target customers: those traditional customers who want to make major home renovations, and housing professionals,

STRATEGIES:
1. Develop multiple product lines with brand names.
2. Consolidate multiple brands and products to simplify.

STRATEGIES:
1. Become a full-service provider.
2. Provide outsourcing.

STRATEGIES:
1. Create service guarantees.
2. Create structural bonds.
3. Create learning relationships.

Figure 13-1. Customer Alchemy: From Gold to Platinum

such as managers of apartment and condominium complexes and hotel chains. Together, these groups spend about $216 billion every year, and Home Depot wants customers to spend all of it in its stores by increasing the Value Impact of its offerings. Its strategy is to become a full-service provider, offering everything these customers could possibly need to do their jobs.

The cornerstone of its strategy is the creation of Expo Design Centers. The design centers show off the expanded line of physical products the company offers but configure the products into finished and polished showrooms. Rather than just having row upon row of nails, hammers, and tile, the store is creating a showplace for upscale renovation as described by a *Fortune* magazine reporter in the following excerpt:

Upon entering the 88,000 square-foot store in Davie, Fla., last month, I didn't know which way to turn. Nearly 20 complete kitchens with fancy appliances were to my right, accented with exotic tiles, lighting, and stone floors. In front of me were dozens of finished baths with whirlpools and brass faucets, all so enticing I wanted to wrap up a couple of the rooms and take them home. A ceiling crowded with gleaming chandeliers was to my left in a room decorated with antiques (yes, they're for sale). Around the corner, I passed a $5,000 Sub-Zero refrigerator, a $7,500 Dacor range, $8,000 gas grills by Wolf and Viking, and an $8,500 Aquatic whirlpool bath. Honey, we're not in Home Depot anymore.[1]

Expo is a one-stop-shopping location for major renovations, which usually require homeowners to assemble a group of contractors and designers, then make separate trips to buy tiles, materials, drapes, appliances, and the like. All of these are now available at an Expo, making it unnecessary for a member of its target segments to buy from any other store to do her renovations. "Additionally, industry-certified designers and project managers oversee the entire project from beginning to end. Good-bye, general contractor."[2] Under these conditions, Gold customers become Platinum customers, getting everything they want from their full-service supplier Home Depot.

Another example of becoming a full-service provider comes from a service industry. The United States Automobile Association (USAA), one of the most profitable insurance companies in the United States, has what one would surely term a platinum relationship with its clients. Focused on a very targeted segment, U.S. military officers and their families, it supplies them with insurance and financial services to meet their lifelong needs. In fact, its goal is to "think about the events in the life of a career officer and then work out ways of helping him get through them."[3] One of the best examples of strengthening a relationship with its clients occurred during the Gulf War. The company encouraged members sent to the Persian Gulf to downgrade their automobile insurance to save themselves money. For instance, if their cars were just going to sit in garages while they were gone, they wouldn't need liability coverage. And when two-car families had one spouse in the Gulf, USAA gave them the rates for a single person with two cars. Actions such as these clearly indicate USAA's commitment to its members, adding Value Equity to move and keep them as Platinum members.[4]

PROVIDE OUTSOURCING. One of the best examples of increasing Value Equity, and thereby moving customers from Gold to Platinum levels, is through the technique of outsourcing. This technique, which is used most often in business-to-business situations, involves taking on an entire function that a customer firm used to perform for itself and providing it for them.

Examples of functions that are now outsourced include payroll, accounting, maintenance, information management, and even personnel. In each of these cases, the nonmonetary costs to the customer firm of engaging in these activities reduce its ability to perform its core competencies. The effort involved, for example, in staying abreast of new information technology, maintaining the systems, fixing hardware and software problems, and keeping qualified staff all become an interference with the firm's true purpose. In these and other cases of outsourcing, a supplier firm can perform these functions for a customer, increasing its Customer Equity and the profitability of the customer. The customer becomes tied to the organization and the business becomes predictable, making these customers extremely valuable to the company.

Increasing Brand Equity

Women's clothing is an area where few companies "own" customers in the sense that customers buy predominantly one brand and would therefore be called "Platinum" customers. Liz Claiborne, the world's largest women's apparel maker and marketer, however, has used Brand Equity to change that. First of all, the company established a strong brand reputation using most of the Brand Equity strategies we discussed in chapter 6, including establishing a customer fit with the brand, communicating with the customer about the brand, and creating a customer affinity for the brand. The company bonded with the female baby boom generation, being one of the first companies to target baby boomers and truly understand them and their needs. For example, it recognized that they were a fit generation that didn't want to get heavier and created clothing that made them continue to appear slim despite the few added pounds. It convinced its target group that it really knew them, thereby establishing a fit with them both literally and emotionally. Then the company very successfully extended its product lines: Liz Collection for professional clothing, Liz Wear for casual clothes, Elizabeth for large women. It soon became possible to dress completely in this one brand of clothing. The company was so successful in its Brand Equity strategy that it extended its lines into pocketbooks, shoes, belts, even perfume. The perception that Liz Claiborne was the brand for this group of women was so strongly held that many women buy virtually all of their clothing and accessories from this one manufacturer. The affinity is so strong that customers will forgo sales from other companies because they feel so loyal to the Liz brand they don't want to wear anything else.

Increasing Retention Equity

CREATE STRUCTURAL BONDS   Structural bonds (or learning relationships) are created by providing services to the client that are frequently designed right into the service delivery system for that client. Often structural bonds are created by providing customized services to the client that are technology based and serve to make the client more productive. Federal Express was a key example when it created PowerShip, a computer hardware and software system that was given to its best customers. The system allowed key customers to essentially have a FedEx branch in their companies, allowing them to create customer lists and shipping labels and track packages along the routes of delivery. The idea behind PowerShip and all structural bonds is that the customer company will find it so easy to deal with the provider that giving business to any competitor is not worth the time and effort. Although Power-Ship has been extended with Internet-based technology, the structural bond strategy remains. Its customers are tied strongly through this retention technique and become extremely loyal, as well as profitable, to FedEx.

Allegiance Healthcare Corporation, a spin-off of Baxter Healthcare, provides another example of structural bonds in a business-to-business context. The company has developed ways to improve hospital supply ordering, delivery, and billing that have greatly enhanced their value as a supplier. They created "hospital-specific pallet architecture" that means that all items arriving at a particular hospital are shrink-wrapped with labels visible for easy identification. Separate pallets are assembled to reflect the individual hospital's storage system, so that instead of miscellaneous supplies arriving in boxes sorted at the convenience of Allegiance's needs (the typical approach used by other hospital suppliers), they arrive on "client-friendly" pallets designed to suit the distribution needs of the individual hospital. By linking the hospital through its ValueLink service into a database ordering system and providing enhanced value in the actual delivery, Allegiance has structurally tied itself to its over 150 acute-care hospitals in the United States. In addition to the enhanced service ValueLink provides, Allegiance estimates that the system saves its customers an average of $500,000 or more each year.[5]

SERVICE GUARANTEES.   Research is clear that service problems and dissatisfaction lead to customer defections. For Platinum customers, therefore, it is essential that a company use the most powerful methods to find out when service problems occur and then to resolve them quickly and completely. Possibly the most effective strategy for accomplishing this is the service guarantee, whereby a company assures customers that they will be satisfied or else they receive some form of compensation commensurate with their problem. While many forms of service guarantees exist and cover different aspects of service (meeting deadlines, delivering a smile, achieving reliability), the type of service guarantee most relevant for the very best customers is a complete satisfaction guarantee. This, too, can take several forms, but the form that is best for the customer assures satisfaction and, lacking satisfaction, promises the customer that any problems that occur will be fixed immediately. Strategies exist for effective guarantees—they should, for example, be easy to invoke and have a clear payoff—and these should be followed to create the very best guarantee possible. That way, Gold customers will have no reason to leave and will want to stay and become Platinum customers.

Turning Iron into Gold

Customer alchemy can also change something ordinary (a less profitable Iron customer) into something valuable (a more profitable Gold customer). There are many ways to turn Iron customers into Gold customers. The foundation involves finding out what is most important to the Iron customers—not assuming that it is the same thing that is important to Gold customers—and then attending to the specific factors that drive the Iron customers' satisfaction and behavior. With this lower level of customers, often it is rarely necessary to find out what makes each individual customer satisfied. Instead, it is critical to find the key drivers of the relationships across the customers in the tiers. In our real-world example in chapter 11 we saw how improving the Iron Tier's key driver (attitude) could increase both incidence of new business and volume of new business, thereby turning some Iron customers into Gold. Once we identify these factors, we can use one of the three Customer Equity strategies to increase usage and profitability of those customers.

Increasing Value Equity

PROVIDE OUTSTANDING CUSTOMER SERVICE. One of the best ways to cement a relationship with customers is to provide outstanding service.

STRATEGIES:
1. Add brand names with meaning.
2. Create less expensive versions of prestige brand names.

STRATEGIES:
1. Provide outstanding service.
2. Reduce the nonmonetary costs of doing business.

STRATEGIES:
1. Develop frequency programs.
2. Create strong service recovery programs.

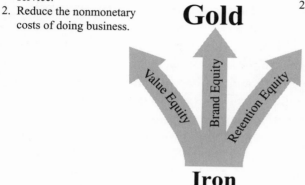

Figure 13-2. *Customer Alchemy: From Iron to Gold*

One company that is known for its "outrageous customer service," which has led to almost 100% customer retention, is PeopleSoft, a company that specializes in complex software for managing human resource functions, accounting, manufacturing processes, and other systems. While it competes with Oracle, Baan, and SAP, it has something very unique that has turned what could be Iron customers into solid Gold customers. It adds value both through outstanding service and reduction of effort, risk, and psychic costs. Its CEO empowers his employees to do anything it takes to satisfy and build customer relationships and spends considerable time himself learning about their needs. Every customer of the company has a customer advocate who represents him across all functions within the company. These advocates, called "Account Managers," are on salary and are rewarded not for sales revenues but for customer satisfaction. Based on what the company has learned about its customers, it also has reduced some important non-monetary costs that could occur with unsuccessful installation by bundling product installation, training, and maintenance support into the price of the software. Customers of PeopleSoft are so satisfied with its service and problem-free operation that they stay—and pay the price to be Gold customers.[6]

REDUCE THE NONMONETARY COSTS OF DOING BUSINESS.   Since the idea in Customer Equity is not to reduce price and thereby lower profit margins, a company should constantly be looking for ways to lower the nonmonetary costs of doing business with customers and thereby provide increased Value Equity. An excellent approach to this strategy involves reducing the hassle and search costs that customers associate with making purchases in many high-technology categories today. Small businesses, for example, have tremendous difficulty deciding what forms of communication technology to buy and from which suppliers. So many offerings and combinations of offerings exist, and a plethora of providers is constantly besieging customers with differences that are difficult for them to discern. Alltel, a full-service high-technology communications firm, offers an answer that works very well for small businesses and individuals. A customer can obtain all three components—paging, wireless, and long distance—from the company, have it all appear on the same bill, and deal with all service problems easily by having only one service department to deal with. In this package, the company has brilliantly also increased its business with the customer; it now obtains not just the customer's paging business or the long-distance business or the wireless business but all three. The costs of dealing with the customer are reduced as well, because handling a single customer with three services costs less internally than handling three different customers each with a single service. The customer is now a Gold customer rather than an Iron customer and is far more strongly linked into the firm because its associations cross service categories.

Increasing Brand Equity

ADD MEANINGFUL BRAND NAMES.   One of the most effective strategies that some discount retailers have used recently to turn Iron customers into more profitable Gold customers is to create a brand-within-a-brand image in their stores. Typically, this involves associating product lines in the stores with more favorable brand images than those of the store itself. For example, when Kmart was working to improve its image and profitability, it affiliated with Martha Stewart to manufacture and market an entire line of household soft goods such as sheets and towels. The line carried Martha Stewart's name and was priced considerably higher than other goods in the same category in Kmart. Rather than making small profit margins on these items, the company began to make much larger margins. It also generated loyalty and multiple purchases because the line of products was color-coordinated. Customers wanted to buy these products not because they were associated with Kmart but because they were affiliated with a very favorable and well-known person. By associating with this favorable brand, the store created a brand personality where none existed in the past and was able to improve the profitability of that product category in the store. As it became clear that the branding was successful, the company extended it beyond its original bounds to include other products.

CREATE LESS EXPENSIVE VERSIONS OF PRESTIGE BRAND NAMES. A Brand Equity strategy that can be useful to manufacturers is to extend a line of expensive products to a lower tier in the Customer Pyramid. Some high-end automobile manufacturers such as BMW were able to access an entirely different segment of customers by creating a less-expensive version of its very prestigious offering. While there is always some risk in using this strategy because it can erode the high prestige of associating the product only with the highest tier of the Customer Pyramid, it can be a very effective way to obtain the types of brand loyalty associated with these products.

Increasing Retention Equity

BECOME A CUSTOMER EXPERT.   Surely one of the best examples of adding Retention Equity and turning Iron customers into Gold customers involves the battery of strategies used by Amazon.com, the online bookstore. Initially, the company focused on being able to get virtually any book that the customer wanted. Once it established this ability, it recognized that developing profiles of individual customers was a winning strategy. Once a customer had purchased something from Amazon.com, the company started to build its information database about the customer's preferences. Whenever a customer ordered a book, the database produced a list of books from the same author and on similar topics that could expand the purchase. These suggestions were often very welcome to the customer, who was not aware of the other books. After multiple purchases, the database was designed to make suggestions as soon as the customer signed on, again increasing purchases. Before long, the company discovered that customers who bought books also bought CDs and movies, thereby expanding its product lines to satisfy other needs of the customer. To top the retention strategy off, the company asked customers if they wanted to receive information about products that were new and dealt with their interests. Using the customer's e-mail address, Amazon.com thereby created ongoing communication with customers about their personal interests, making it so easy to deal with the company that customers began spending all their book dollars—as well as CD and movie dollars—with it.

Retention Equity can also be built through social bonds with the company, either through a social network established with employees or with other customers. When built with employees, the firm sees customers as clients, not as nameless faces; they become individuals whose needs and wants the firm cares about. Services are customized to fit clients' individual needs, and employees find ways of staying in touch with their customers. For example, in a study of customer-firm relationships in the insurance industry, it was found that behaviors such as staying in touch with clients to assess their changing needs, providing personal touches like cards and gifts, and sharing personal information with clients all increased the likelihood that the client would stay with the firm.[7]

Caterpillar, the world's largest manufacturer of mining, construction, and agricultural heavy equipment, owes part of its superiority and success to its strong dealer network and product support services offered throughout the world. Knowledge of its local markets and close relationships with customers built up by Caterpillar's dealers are invaluable. "Our dealers tend to be prominent business leaders in their service territories who are deeply involved in community activities and who are committed to living in the area. Their reputations and long-term relationships are important because selling our products is a personal business."[8]

Social bonds are also possible and valuable between customers. At a local level, one can easily see the importance of other members of a country club to the loyalty and usage of its facilities. This same social network can be built into business-to-business relationships by having clients of a firm participate in golf tournaments, conventions, seminars, trips, and other social occasions to nurture their personal relationships with each other.

DEVELOP FREQUENCY PROGRAMS.   Chapter 7 discussed and gave examples of different types of frequency programs, all of which are extremely useful at this level in the Customer Pyramid. One recent example that illustrates the use of a frequency program shows how convenience-item retailers like VCR rental companies can effectively use frequency programs. Blockbuster has just developed a program called Blockbuster Rewards. For a one-time payment of

$9.95, a customer is able to get benefits that include: (1) rent five videos, get one free every month; (2) get two free video rentals a month just for joining; and (3) get one free video rental with each paid movie or game rental every Monday through Wednesday. Notice that it is not the one-time fee that makes the Blockbuster Rewards customer a Gold customer—it is the frequent use of the service. It is using capacity that the firm cannot otherwise sell, and making the customer turn to Blockbuster for all its video rental needs. Blockbuster doesn't drop the price on its video rentals, which would lower its profits. Instead, it increases the frequency of use.

CREATE STRONG SERVICE RECOVERY PROGRAMS. We cannot emphasize enough how important avoiding service problems is to keeping customers. We want not only to keep them but also to make them into better customers, and therefore a strong service recovery system—one that catches all possible service errors and corrects them promptly and appropriately—is critical. In fact, the recovery system should not be reactive but should be proactive. It should seek through all possible avenues to identify when customers are let down by a company's product or an interaction with someone from the company. Then it must have in place processes to rectify these situations, whether they involve billing, delivery, or any other important company function.

Getting the Lead Out

In some cases, allocating more effort to customers who are more valuable implies allocating *less* effort to customers who are *less* valuable. In particular, the firm's Lead customers only weigh the company down. Attempting to move customers from Lead to higher categories is not an easy task, as shown in our real-world example in chapter 11 and in the experience of many companies, and is not always recommended.

Lead customers are the ones who don't pay their bills. They are the college students who bounce checks. They are the telephone customers who run up large long-distance bills that require the company to pay agencies to collect. They are the industrial firms who make purchases, then in disputes over deliveries or quality, let their invoices go sixty or ninety days or longer.

Lead customers can also be those who buy so little that dealing with them costs more than they are worth. Marketing and personal selling

Figure 13-3. Strategies for Lead Customers

expenses may exceed the profit on small business accounts. Transaction costs for customers who place orders for one or two items in a year make them unprofitable. Or, as is sometimes the case, the smallest customers expect the most in terms of service, making the cost of handling them far higher than the profits received from them.

The best strategy with Lead customers is often for the company to try to free itself of them. The firm must do this carefully so that customers are not incensed to spread negative word of mouth that could deflect potentially profitable customers from choosing the firm. Alternatively, the firm could attempt to make these customers profitable. This can be accomplished in two basic ways: prices can be raised or costs to serve the customers can be reduced.

If, however, the future potential of a Lead customer is quite high (for example, the MBA student who is currently an unprofitable banking customer), then enduring a period of customer unprofitability may be justified.

Raise Prices

One effective approach is to increase prices to Lead customers by charging for services they have been receiving but not paying for. A software company that has been giving free technical help to Lead customers (who, by definition, typically abuse the privilege) can begin to charge for the service. True Lead customers will leave rather than pay; others may choose to stay and thereby join the Iron category because of the added revenue they are giving the firm.

An excellent example of this strategy is being used by a number of both large and small telephone companies with customers who don't pay their bills. Typically, this segment of customers owes one of the larger companies a considerable amount of money (greater than $300) in long-distance charges and has not made progress in paying it off. Their phone service has been canceled and they no longer can get even local service. Enter companies such as E-Z Tel of Dallas and Annox of Pleasant View, Tennessee, that offer prepaid local service. To get it, a customer has to go to her local pawnshop, plunk down $49 in cash plus $2 for a money order (compared to $17 for a regular customer). The customer then receives local phone and 911 service for the next month, despite her debt to a long-distance company. This niche market, consisting of about 6 million households that go unserved because of unpaid phone bills, generates considerable profit for the companies (who buy service from a local phone company at a 20% discount and resell it at a 300% premium). To use our Customer Equity Framework, the segment is receiving Value Equity in being able to get a service it could not in the past. To these customers, giving up more in terms of price is not the issue—having the telephone service is of most value to them. What is interesting about this approach is that some large companies are starting to offer the service to compete in this market because it is profitable. In most cases, they are changing the brand that they sell the service under to avoid undermining the Brand Equity that they currently have in the other tiers.[9]

Reduce Costs

The alternative to raising prices among Lead customers is to reduce costs and find ways to serve the segment more efficiently. Banks have accomplished this by reducing the number of full-service branches with tellers and staff and replacing them with ATMs that are able to service customers for far less money. Many industrial firms that previously served all customers with personal salespeople now handle only Platinum or Gold customers that way, serving Iron and Lead customers with inside salespeople.

IBM made a revolutionary switch from its historical way of dealing with customers when it realized in the early 1990s that it was highly inefficient to serve all small (many Lead) customers with the personal service that had characterized the firm in the past. Rather than have customer engineers personally fix old machines for unprofitable customers for free, the company started to charge for these repairs as well as develop ways to fix machines remotely, thereby saving money.

If either or both of these two approaches do not work, then the wisest solution may be to "get the Lead out," to stop serving unprofitable customers. It is critical that this be done in a manner that does not lead to negative word of mouth about the firm, so it must be accomplished carefully. Emphasis on not acquiring customers with this profile is wise.

The strategies that we have discussed in this chapter for Customer Alchemy or moving customers from lower levels of the Customer Pyramid to higher levels can be summarized in a table. As is evident in this table, the strategies for the upper levels are different from the strategies for the lower levels. In the lower level, which involves Lead customers, the basic decision is whether to keep the customers or not. It is very difficult to move most Lead customers from the low tier to a higher tier because they have characteristics that make them less desirable customers. They either don't pay their bills, don't have much money to spend, don't need what the company offers, or don't have the qualities that make them loyal to companies. If the company chooses to continue to serve them, it must do one of two things to make them profitable: either increase prices for what it offers or reduce costs so that they can be served more efficiently.

In the higher levels of the Customer Pyramid, on the other hand, customers can be moved up by finding out their needs and requirements and then better fulfilling them. In each case, there are strategies that are appropriate in terms of increasing Value Equity, Brand Equity, or Retention Equity.

Customer Alchemy			
KEY INSIGHTS	**ACTION STEPS**		
1. Customers can be moved using either Value Equity, Brand Equity, or Retention Equity strategies.	*Use the Following Value Equity Strategies* ↓	*Use the Following Brand Equity Strategies* ↓	*Use the Following Retention Equity Strategies* ↓
2. Moving customers from Gold to Platinum involves solidifying already strong relationships.	• Become a full-service provider. • Provide outsourcing.	• Develop multiple product lines with brand name. • Consolidate multiple brands and products to simplify.	• Create service guarantees. • Create structural bonds.
3. Moving customers from Iron to Gold involves building and strengthening relationships.	• Provide outstanding service. • Reduce the nonmonetary costs of doing business.	• Add brand names with meaning. • Create less expensive versions of prestige brand names.	• Become a customer expert. • Develop frequency programs. • Create strong service recovery programs.
4. It is difficult to move Lead customers to higher tiers.	• Raise prices or lower costs.		• Invest in the highest potential Lead customers for the future.

14

The Internet as the Ultimate Customer Equity Tool

The flexibility of the Internet allows a company to execute its Customer Equity strategy—focusing on Value Equity, Brand Equity, Retention Equity, or some combination of all three—in a way that supports or leads all its other marketing efforts. In this chapter, we will examine companies that have used the Internet effectively to increase Customer Equity using different drivers. In some cases, these are companies that did not exist prior to the Internet and have developed in the last few years to counter existing brick-and-mortar companies. As you might expect, one of the key differentiators of these companies is their access and therefore convenience. In most cases, however, these are companies that have conducted their business in traditional ways until the advent of the Internet, when they recognized the benefits in using the electronic medium to widen and deepen their influence with customers. While virtually all companies we selected use more than one driver of Customer Equity, we selected companies and their Web sites that are stellar—and thus particularly illustrative—in each driver.

Driving Value Equity with the Internet

In this section, we will discuss four key drivers of Value Equity—quality, service, price, and convenience—and show how Internet strategies highlight these drivers to supplement or lead a company's approach to Customer Equity.

Quality

The Internet offers a medium to showcase a company's products and services and provide as much information as consumers want. This is particularly beneficial for companies that sell durable goods (such as household appliances and automobiles), industrial products, and business-to-business services. Miele, a German manufacturer of household appliances, stands out in its ability to demonstrate the quality of its physical products, a main contributor to Value Equity.

MIELEUSA.COM.   Miele is a 100-year-old German manufacturer of household appliances renowned for its quality. Among the company's most critically acclaimed products is a European-style washing machine with a front-loading horizontal drum that is considerably more energy-efficient because it uses less water while getting clothes cleaner. Its Web site is an outstanding example of the use of the medium to demonstrate product quality. Connecting to the U.S. home page (*www.mieleusa.com*), one sees links to products, company, news, suppliers, centenary (this is the company's 100th year), and suppliers.

The product page showcases the company's unusually attractive appliances with full color, high-quality photographs, each of which links to details about the "legendary Miele quality" features of that product. For example, the front-loading washing machine page link stresses features such as fully electronic Novotronic controls, triple-A rating according to European energy labeling, 400–1600 rpm spin control, leakage protection system, and unbeatably quiet wash.

The company page shown in figure 14-1 features the corporate philosophy—"Forever Better"—and the imposing photographs of the two stalwart German founders Carl Miele and Reinhard Zinkann. One cannot read this page without recognizing the quality heritage of the company and believing in the care built into the products. As the centenary page states, "Reliability and durability combined with the use of advanced technology and superlative quality have built a foundation of trust which, in itself, explains why people who buy Miele products are so thoroughly satisfied."

Miele products cost 25 to 40% more than those of competitors, but builders and discriminating buyers are not hesitant to pay the premium. And the Internet site fully reflects the quality that drives Value Equity in this product.

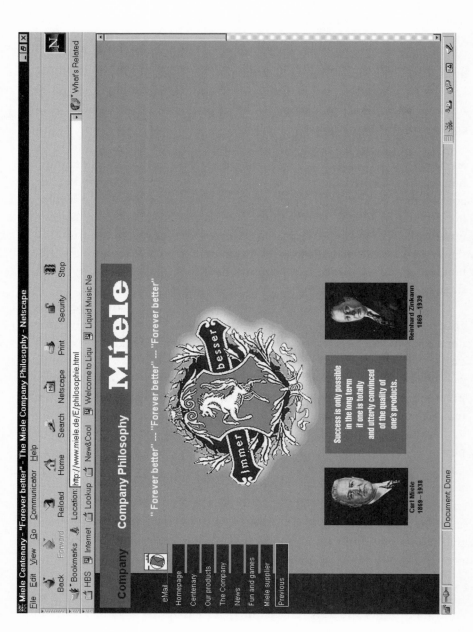

Figure 14-1. Miele Corporate Philosophy

Service

INTUIT.COM.   Intuit, the maker of Quicken and TurboTax financial software, has been so successful that the behemoth Microsoft tried (unsuccess-
fully because of government restrictions) to purchase the $300 million
company in 1995 for a whopping $2 billion. The company was founded in
1984 on three critical service-related principles: lifetime customer service,
customer-driven product development, and marketing research. Intuit
offered a lifetime guarantee on a piece of software that cost as little as $30
to $50, believing that the guarantee created two very important outcomes
for the company. First, it achieved a lifetime dialogue with its customers,
providing information about software problems, solutions, and changes in
customer tastes. Second, it created apostles, customers who were so satisfied with the company's service that they spread word of mouth so positive
that the company doesn't need advertising. The second principle of customer-driven product development means involving the customer every
step of the way in creating updates and new software. This principle is executed in part by its third principle of marketing research. The company
conducts and actively uses focus group interviews, customer surveys, new
product feature testing, and a unique "Follow Me Home" program where
company representatives go home with customers buying the products to
watch them install and use the software.

A look at Intuit's Web site (*www.intuit.com*) illustrates the company's
effective use of the Internet to fully implement the strategy. The site is
comprehensive, easy to use, and focuses more on customer service than
virtually all other software companies. The home page shows three main
categories (company, products/services, and support/updates) and also
features a link to a letter from the company's founder, Scott Cook. The
letter is entitled "Intuit—Exceeding Expectations" and claims "our goal is
not just customer satisfaction but to go beyond satisfaction and WOW
our customers." This is not an empty promise with Intuit. The letter continues with testimonials from more-than-satisfied apostles.

The service section, support, and updates are extensive but easy to use.
Five options are visible on the home page: support options, program
updates, product support, customer service, and user feedback. The page
for support options includes a surprisingly simple matrix with a list of thir-
teen service options (including phone support, KnowledgeBase Search and

Browse, online training, customer notices, Intuit Financial Professional Network, and fax-on-demand, etc.) and columns for the company's four product lines. Worthy of note is that fifty-three of fifty-four boxes in the matrix contain a "yes," meaning the service is available, and only three of the fifty-four contain a $, meaning that there is a charge for the service. The page for program updates lists all current versions and allows existing users of the products to locate patches, updates, and support news. The product support page shows links to technical support for each product offered by the company.

The customer service center page encourages customers to search for answers to any question, check online order status, contact the customer center (to change credit card, request replacement disks for products, cancel orders, receive refunds, or request changes to orders), download information about hot topics and frequently asked questions, and educate themselves about important current issues.

The page in the customer service section, user feedback, asks customers for information about their use of any product in multiple, reader-friendly ways. Customers can offer product suggestions, complete technical Web site surveys, and report bugs merely by filling out screens already prepared for the tasks.

Recently, Intuit has branched out into more comprehensive financial services and the site contains a link to Intuit's online banking, payment, investment tracking, credit card, and security services. Finally, Quicken.com is a one-stop personal finance center on the Web where customers can track their portfolio for free.

Although Intuit is a small company, its service is legendary and is the key driver of its Customer Equity strategy. As you may well imagine, customers have few reasons to leave the company once they buy a software product, because the company engages in so many different service efforts to keep them. The Internet strategy pursued by the software firm is well executed and carefully reviewed. After all, Intuit is a software firm and it has a lot to gain by doing information technology as well as possible.

Price

Many companies' Internet strategies use price as a driver of Value Equity, often because a company can position itself as the lowest-cost competitor when it has no bricks and mortar to finance. Virtually all of the new online trading companies such as E*Trade and Ameritrade have followed this strategy; unfortunately, some, like E*Trade, have suffered from system outages and customer support line busy signals that limit their effectiveness. In online trading, the most successful Internet story is Charles Schwab, the discount broker gone Internet savvy. While not the lowest-priced competitor, it still positions itself as a low-price provider that has not abandoned service. In the discussion that follows, we'll see that the company uses Internet technology as a way to provide and support personal service.

Another powerful way that companies can drive Value Equity through price is to link with one or more of the new pricing sites of which Priceline.com is probably the most famous. These sites take unsold inventory, particularly service inventory for airlines and hotels, and offer it out for bid to customers. The strategy gives customers a way to get a deal yet does not interfere with a company's traditional pricing policies because it sells only excess capacity. Some of these retail sites that handle merchandise, such as Buy.com, one of the largest, have developed reputations for hyping products that later prove to be on backorder for weeks or for reneging on superlow advertised prices. For this reason, companies selling on these sites need to be aware of the implications of these problems for their own reputations.

SCHWAB.COM.   Online trading has become one of the most successful examples of electronic service distribution, and the most effective company in implementing online trading is the discount broker Charles Schwab. Schwab was one of the first no-frills discount brokers who opted to target a market that didn't want service and advice as much as they wanted lower prices. Its path from face-to-face brokerage sales to Web sales is an excellent example of what companies face in deciding to use, and then harnessing, the power of the Web to sell their services.

Schwab's traditional marketing had been carried out in branch offices where customers met brokers in person or on the telephone, where Schwab was known for high-quality service in telephone representatives. Its investing Web site, *www.schwab.com,* however, is "arguably the most successful embrace of e-commerce by any major corporation outside the technology industry."[1] In just three years, Schwab went from zero to $4 billion worth of securities traded each week on its Web site, which represented more than half the company's total trading volume. Schwab is the number one Internet brokerage with 30% share of daily trading volume. More than a third of its customers invest on the Web, which now handles five times as many trades as the call centers.

The change has had powerful impact on the way the company markets, including its pricing. While the company averaged $80 commission per trade using traditional channels, it charges $29.95 per trade for most online transactions. That's a drop from the first online price of $39 and is still considerably more than its competitors rock-bottom commissions of $15 (E*Trade) and $8 (Ameritrade). While the company took a profit hit originally from this low price, it has been able to make up most of it through productivity gains and lower costs.

With the Internet, Schwab now can offer "personalized information to the customer in real time, at virtually no cost,"[2] allowing the company to gain Customer Equity despite the Value Equity positioning. On Schwab's site, customers can look up real-time quotes, news, historical financial data or use sophisticated software tools. They can also customize the home page to see their personal accounts when they log on, set up their own asset-allocation model, screen for the best-performing mutual funds that fit that model, and then buy the funds through Schwab. Among the improvements the company is now working on are screens to show investors the total returns on the securities in their portfolios, graphically rich e-mails that alert customers to events such as when their portfolios are not in balance with their asset-allocation models.

The company realized that its Internet strategy was going to work almost immediately. The service was introduced quietly with an announcement at the annual shareholders' meeting. Almost immediately, customers began using it. "We were totally unprepared. Customers began voting with their keyboards, and in two weeks we reached 25,000 Web accounts—our goal for the entire year."[3] By the end of 1997, online accounts had grown to 1.2 million. By the end of 1998, the number of accounts exceeded 2 million.[4]

PRICELINE.COM.   After the tyranny of airline pricing, consumers now have a refreshing way to buy a ticket. They go to *www.priceline.com* on the Web, name the day they want to travel and the price they want to pay, and press "search." The site then searches its database of most of the nine largest U.S. carriers or a major international airline to see if it can find a ticket for that price. If it does, the customer has a ticket within an hour at their price, usually a much lower price than they could get through a travel agent. Priceline.com had immediate success. In the week after its launch in April of 1998, the site had more than 1 million hits and sold over 10,000 tickets.[5] At the end of its first year, it had sold 1.9 million airline tickets even though it had not yet been profitable because it had to sell many tick-ets below cost.[6]

The consumer benefits of priceline.com are many, among them low prices and the ability to get tickets on short notice. Priceline.com is a revolu-tionary service for shoppers who can commit without knowing the full details of their purchases. So far, customers most likely to use the service are leisure travelers—students, senior citizens, consumers with relatives at a dis-tance, or others with flexible travel schedules. The service is free to cus-tomers, as is the service of competitors such as Bestfares.com, Biztravel.com, and Expedia.com.

The benefit to airlines, hotels, and other companies offering such Inter-net services is that providing cheap seats or rooms sells off their excess capacity that would go unfilled through traditional channels. Prices based on expected yield are the norm in these types of services. Because price com-petition hurts all players, airlines and hotels rarely offer truly rock-bottom prices up front because they know others will meet them. Priceline.com allows them to offer super-low prices but just on the inventory they could not sell anyway.

Of course, priceline.com is a company that is itself positioning on price and Value Equity. How does it make money? It keeps the margin between the bid and asking price, although during its start-up phase it sold many tickets below cost and therefore didn't pocket this money. It also makes rev-enues from fees collected from site-advertised credit-card issuers. The com-pany is very optimistic about its future as a service pricing revolutionary. Priceline.com has also added home mortgages, home refinancing, and home equity loans to its list of offerings.

Convenience

The Internet can add Value Equity to companies through convenience in two key ways. First, it can make many tasks involved in purchasing from traditional companies, such as ordering and finding the right size and item, much easier for customers. A customer who finds a pair of khakis in the local Gap store that are the right style but not the right size can easily go to the Gap's Internet site, make the purchase, and receive the goods at home. Second, many new online companies have been developed on the very platform of providing convenience to customers, particularly busy customers who no longer have the time and energy to shop. Online grocery delivery companies such as Peapod.com, Streamline.com, and HomeGrocer.com all developed to execute the chores normally associated with grocery store shopping. In this way, they provide convenience—at a price that, although high, customers are willing to pay—which drives Value Equity. Of benefit to the online company is that the up-front information gathered from customers about tastes and preferences provides high switching costs to customers. We demonstrate effective positioning on the components of convenience in our discussion of Amazon.com, the world's largest online company.

AMAZON.COM.   No company demonstrates the convenience components of location, ease of use, and availability that drive Value Equity as well as the leading Internet merchant Amazon.com. First conceived as an online bookstore, Amazon.com's mission is now to help people find almost anything they want to buy online, including 16 million items in categories such as books, CDs, videos, gifts, cards, drugstore items, and grocery items. Its location couldn't be more convenient physically (as close as any computer) and mentally (with the highest brand recognition of any online company, customers don't need to struggle to remember its name).

The ease of use of Amazon.com is the heart of its success, as anyone who has purchased from the company knows. The company's Web site is extremely user-friendly and customer-focused, thanks to innumerable hours spent tweaking its Web pages to remove every possible obstacle to purchasing. Amazon invented one-click ordering, which lets buyers store credit cards and addresses after the first purchase, and installed software that remembers and assesses what people have bought and suggests other purchases.[7] Because customers care about speed of delivery, the company built distribution centers around the world. In most geographies, a customer can obtain a purchase overnight and normally receives orders in two to three days.

Availability, the final cornerstone of convenience, is also a focus of Amazon.com. The company bills itself as "the earth's biggest selection." Whether it is books or CDs or videos, the company makes a practice of having a full range of products available. And when customers place orders, the screen provides them with accurate statements about exactly when they can be filled based on existing inventory. Because of its widespread distribution centers, the most in-demand merchandise is readily available. A special feature of the company is that it will search for hard-to-find merchandise, such as out-of-print books, locating them for customers for only a small charge.

No longer do customers have to travel from store to store to find what they want; they can trust that Amazon will have it or find it and get it to them quickly. Not incidentally, the company also charges approximately 30% less on any purchase than traditional bookstores, combining the convenience strategy with a low-price strategy.

What kind of Customer Equity does this strategy generate? On a customer base of 8.4 million, repeat purchasers account for 66% of sales.[8]

Driving Brand Equity with the Internet

Communications Programs

Brand Equity is driven by a variety of communications from the company, among them advertising, direct mail, sales promotions, publicity, and public relations. The Internet provides a compelling additional opportunity to deliver communications that positively affect Brand Equity. We will discuss one of Kraft Foods' Web sites that is particularly effective in using this strategy to reinforce Brand Equity.

In the future, companies must integrate the communications they send through all media—including the Internet—to create a unified brand image. While many companies today talk of engaging in integrated marketing communications, few do it as well as Mail Boxes, Etc., a company that targets small businesses. Its unique and highly successful integrated communications program, united through its Internet strategy, is profiled below.

KRAFTFOODS.COM.   Kraft Foods has several inviting Internet sites that feature its products in ways that encourage the customer to engage and communicate with the company. The most compelling is Kraft Interactive Kitchen (*www.kraftfoods.com*), which opens with the promise, "Let us help you bring your family together as only good food and good times can." Among the interactive aspects of the site, visible immediately on the home page, are the following:

- *Cookbook* and recipes for the meals a site visitor wants to make
- *Your Recipe Box,* to store favorites

- *Make It Now,* a particularly fun feature where a customer inputs three ingredients on hand and Kraft suggests recipes using the ingredients spiced up with Kraft brands
- *Recipes by E-mail,* a function by which the site stays in contact with the customer
- *What's for Dinner,* simple solutions for planning meals and tips for eating right
- *Recipe of the Day*
- *Calling All Moms,* a way by which customers share their thoughts and ideas about connecting their family at mealtime
- *July* (or current month) *in the Kitchen*

Each of these features is engaging and leads to repeated emphasis on the Kraft family of brands, which is highlighted in a link that leads to photographs of the brands themselves (shown in figure 14-2). The wealth of information available could lead a customer to spend hours on the site and to return frequently, even daily, to continue to gather information.

MAIL BOXES, ETC. The estimated 140 million people who annually watch the Super Bowl may have noticed in the past few years a somewhat unusual thirty-second commercial among the Budweiser lizards and the Toyota trucks. Rather than being for a mammoth global firm, these commercials feature the "little guys" of business—businesses, in fact, with fewer than twenty employees. Businesses like Jeremy's MicroBatch Ice Creams, a company run from the apartment of its twenty-two-year-old founder Jeremy Kraus. Or like tiny Pump Products that makes a handheld basketball-inflating pocket pump.

How can these small companies afford the roughly $1.6 million-per-commercial cost for such advertising? The answer lies in one of the most ingenious marketing communication campaigns of the last decade. The campaign was sponsored by the San Diego–based service franchise organization Mail Boxes, Etc., the world's largest nonfood franchise operation with over 4,000 centers in 58 countries. In addition to mail boxes, Mail Boxes, Etc. (MBE) offers all forms of mailing (FedEx, UPS, U.S. Postal Service), communication (voice mail, secretarial and answering services, fax, Internet, Western Union), packaging, and other office services (color copy-

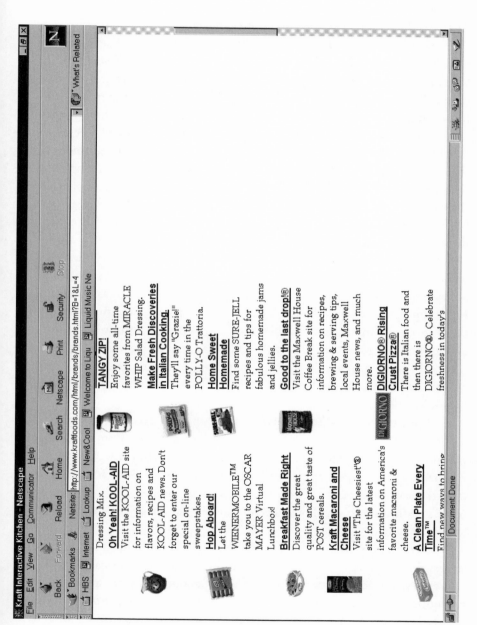

Figure 14-2. Kraft Family of Brands

ing, office supplies, design and printing of cards and stationery). The Super Bowl ad was part of MBE's overall program to reach, attract, and form a database of its primary target market: small businesses.

The company created the idea of a contest for a fifteen-second commercial slot inside MBE's thirty-second commercial on the Super Bowl to extend its investment in advertising by generating publicity and word of mouth. To be eligible for the contest, small businesses were required to submit both an application and an essay of 100 words or less about why they deserve to be featured. On-site mailings and promotions to franchisees built interest in the campaign. According to the agency handling the promotion, the contest "takes a commercial and turns it into an event," garnering publicity and extensive word of mouth.[9] A critical aspect of the contest was that the company was able to build an electronic database of its franchisees' customers from the entries, which then became the foundation for subsequent direct mailings and a database marketing strategy.

The contest began as part of MBE's $4 million "Making Business Easier Worldwide" campaign designed to emphasize the brand's ability to provide full-service solutions for small business. The initial mass-advertising campaign aired on television news, sports, prime-time network TV programming, and national cable. Radio advertising and point of purchase, including in-store materials and entry forms, were also disseminated. To further extend and coordinate the communication program, entries could be submitted on the Web, which contained more details and more advertising.[10]

In the first year of the campaign, the company received more than 3,500 entries. The total cost of the promotion was $3 million, including the Super Bowl commercial. An advertising critic from the trade paper *Advertising Age* pointed out that the contest and Super Bowl feature "not only taps vicarious excitement for the lucky entrepreneurs, it underscores MBE's dedication to small business." In his words, it was "the best idea on the Super Bowl."[11]

The company's Web site (*www.mbe.com*), shown in figure 14-3, encapsulates the integrated services communications approach: one can view the firm's television ad, open a franchise, find out about next year's Super Bowl promotion, read current publicity, send an e-mail to the customer service department, even find a job. To facilitate internal communications—another critical part of the marketing communications mix—MBE has

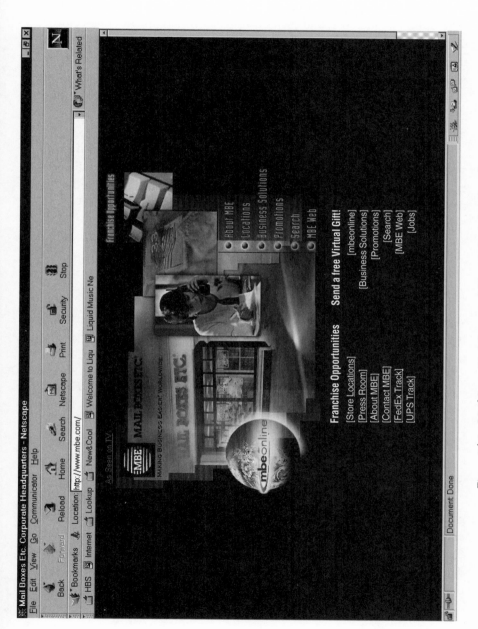

Figure 14-3. Mail Boxes, Etc.'s Integrated Communications Approach

established Internet communications within its system and for providing services to its franchisees and their customers. Among the internal communications implemented using the Internet are a "chat room" on the firm's Internet site that enables franchisees to discuss their problems and help one another; direct communications from corporate headquarters, including the monthly publication *Notes and News* with articles of interest to franchisees; and the capability to tailor an individual store's home page to show the special services it offers that other MBE franchisees do not.[12]

Mail Boxes, Etc. has used many elements of the marketing communications mix to drive Brand Equity effectively, particularly by coordinating external communication and by generating effective internal communication between the company and its franchisees and among franchisees.

Driving Retention Equity With the Internet

Loyalty Programs

WINE.COM. Wine.com, formerly Virtual Vineyards, is a unique membership company whose primary product line is specialty wines. Peter Granoff, "Proprietor and Master Sommelier," greets the visitor to the firm's Web site (*www.wine.com*) with a promise of a 10% discount on any twelve-bottle case of wine. But the wine discount isn't what creates loyalty so much as a monthly wine program that is tailored to the customer. Participation begins when customers input information about wine preferences (including category, variety, price, origin, and style), then sign on for a shipment of wines selected to "please [their] palate and expand [their] wine horizons." Gift subscriptions are also available, as are a wealth of "bang for the buck" values that are not so much inexpensive as they are good values for their price categories. The site also contains Peter's tasting chart, discussions about pairing food and wines, a feature called "Ask the Cork Dork," and educational links to wine magazines. An e-mail program delivers updates to customers and potential customers and creates a sense of loyalty to the site.

Affinity Programs

TY, INC. Ty, Inc. may not be a household name but its wildly successful products, Beanie Babies, are infamous and ubiquitous. Virtually anywhere a customer turns—Hallmark shop to flea market to Cracker Barrel restaurants along the highway—the miniature animals attract the most attention. Introduced in 1995, the collection of animals now contains over several hundred bears, bunnies, birds, monkeys, and pigs that customers crave. The product line features current offerings and "retired" items that cannot be purchased at current prices. New items introduced at a premium price (typically $12 for a four- to five-inch stuffed toy) often sell out in a day, leading customers to clamor to be the first to get the new items. And each item is carried for a limited time, leading customers who are true collectors to want to purchase soon enough to ensure that they get the item in their collection before it joins the ranks of retired offerings. A book showing the complete product line of the collectibles reveals that some of the earliest bears in the line are now worth as much as $400.

Ty's Beanie Babies Official Club Web site (*www.ty.com*), which boasts 2,955,187,589 visits, is a model for affinity programs. The site facilitates interaction among collectors through such mechanisms as Ty Talk Cyberboard, where visitors share their thoughts and ideas with collectors all over the world. Cyberboard contains the *Daily Tymes,* a newsletter with "news, rumors and gossip—hold nothing back . . . let it rip!" as well as sections called Bright Ideas (for ideas, criticism, and suggestions for Ty, its products, or Web site) and Grins & Gripes (for sharings on good, bad, and ugly shopping experiences). The Beanie Connection is Ty's official forum for communication, where customers register (in part so that Ty can properly monitor the site) and become official members.

One of the techniques used on the site to forge loyalty with young female collectors, the primary target audience, are diaries for each of the most successful Beanie Babies (such as Spangle, a bear, and Hippie, a rabbit). These diaries feature daily messages to collectors and encourage their letters back. Site visitors vote for their favorites who "win" popularity contests. Back files on each character's messages are retained so that new owners can catch up on the previous activities of the characters. All of these ingenious efforts make the characters real to their customers and strengthen their ties.

Beanie Babies have become so popular that imitations of them are almost as popular as Rolex watch imitations. The Web site's Guestbook feature includes warnings about where not to buy Beanie Babies because of the many unauthorized versions sold and traded. The Guestbook also allows members to identify collectors in all parts of the world who want to buy, sell, or trade their Beanies; hundreds of pages of such entries can be viewed on the page.

Community Programs

Ty's site also demonstrates the use of community programs to build Retention Equity as it explains the company's involvement in charities. It states:

> Ty is proud of the many contributions it makes throughout the year. Our involvement [is] in several charities, including the Maryville City of Youth, one of the nations largest residential child-care facilities for abused and neglected children; WGN-Radio Chicago Neediest Kids Fund, which provides support at holidays and throughout the year with an ongoing educational mentoring program to those in need; and in conjunction with Rosie O'Donnell, the national Toys for Tots program. In addition, we sponsor several local children's charities. As well, [we donate] profits from "Princess" to the DIANA, PRINCESS OF WALES MEMORIAL FUND. We encourage all our friends to participate in the joy of sharing with local charities![13]

Knowledge-Building Programs

FEDEX.COM. A company long known for its knowledge and information technology capabilities is Federal Express. In the late 1980s and early 1990s, the company pioneered PowerShip, an ingenious approach to creating loyal customers by actually incorporating them into the information infrastructure of the company. PowerShips were kits that FedEx gave to more than 26,500 of its best customers and involved both hardware and software that linked customers directly to its operations. The systems stored addresses and shipping data, printed mailing labels, and tracked the whereabouts of packages. They also offered prizes such as photocopiers and cellular phones to companies that boosted their usage with FedEx. After expanding the large systems to smaller users with a downscale version called FedEx ship, the company moved all of these operations to the Internet. Through its *www.fedex.com* site, all of these operations are available to regular customers. Customers are motivated to become loyal FedEx customers because all information that they would normally have to reenter (such as addresses and billing information) remains in the system.

FedEx benefits in more than the obvious ways of maintaining customers and increasing their loyalty. The Internet systems allow the company to track costs associated with individual customers, calculate their profitability, then sort them into tiers of profitability ("the good, the bad, and the ugly") as discussed in chapter 11. Thus the FedEx system illustrates a knowledge-building program for both the customer and the company.

Internet Strategies for Customer Equity

KEY INSIGHTS	ACTION STEPS
1. All Internet strategies are not the same—different drivers of Customer Equity require different Internet approaches.	• Use research to determine which drivers are most important to Customer Equity (see chapter 8). • Fit the Internet strategy to the positioning—focus rather than try to incorporate all drivers.
2. In virtually all cases, the Internet can provide information to support a company's quality strategy.	• When research reveals which quality dimensions and features are important, focus on these. • Feature full color photographs if possible. • Use testimonials from satisfied customers.
3. Convenience is a hallmark of the Internet. Regardless of what a company offers, the Internet can provide ways to increase convenience.	• Increase access to information by including more on the Web than is typically available in a store. • Assure ease-of-use of the Web site—tweak the site until it is free of impediments to customer use. • Increase availability by allowing customers to purchase all sizes, styles, and versions through the site or lead them to a conveniently located distributor.
4. While many companies attempt to use the Internet to drive Customer Equity, the ones who succeed provide reliable online service.	• Be sure the site can handle expected traffic. Customers are rarely forgiving if they face problems of reliability.
5. Great variability exists among the Web sites and Internet strategies in a given market.	• Get professional help in designing and implementing a Web site. • Examine all your competitors' sites before, during, and after implementation of your own.

15

The Customer Equity Corporation

In a rapidly changing technological environment, products come and go, but customers remain. The secret to success is maintaining relationships with customers that are profitable over the long-term, regardless of what products are involved, or how the products needed may change over time. Customer needs and customer preferences will change over time. The job of the modern company is to maintain the customer relationship, through valleys of recessions, over mountains of economic expansions, over changes in brand preferences, through life-stage changes. In general, the increasing emphasis on customers and relationship management coincides with a decreasing emphasis on products. It is not as though products are unimportant. It is just that they are secondary to growing Customer Equity.

The Truly Customer-Centered Corporation

When the effect of the inexorable shift to a service economy is combined with the firm's increased capability to capture and to analyze customer information, the result is a shift in emphasis from a product- or brand-centered corporation to a customer-centered corporation. The Customer Equity Framework, and the resulting Customer Equity Corporation, which we discuss in this chapter, are the culmination of this historic shift from product to service to customer, the culmination of a historic shift to a corporation built upon individual-centered customer information. The purpose of this chapter is to characterize the customer-centered corporation.

Figure 15-1. The Product-Centered Corporation

The Product-Centered Corporation

We first examine the product-centered corporation and contrast this traditional model with the hybrid corporation (product-centered, with customer-centered elements) and, finally, with the new Customer Equity Corporation. The product-focused organization (see figure 15-1) continues to be organized along traditional brand or product manager lines. Recall the logic of the product-centered corporation. If the unprofitable products are winnowed out, then they will cease to be a drain on the profitability of the firm. Only profitable products will remain, so the firm's resources will be focused where they yield the best return. Over time, the average profitability of the firm's products will become higher and higher, along with the overall profitability of the company. All of the major financial indicators of the firm (e.g., return on equity, return on assets, net profit, etc.) should increase as the company becomes increasingly successful.

It is hard to argue with this logic. However, what results is the Profitable Product Death Spiral, which involves the following inevitable outcomes:

- Company improves profitability by eliminating unprofitable products/services
- Elimination of unprofitable product produces diminished service
- Diminished service drives customers away and lowers profits

The main reason this happens is that companies are assessing *product* profitability rather than *customer* profitability. This error, combined with the failure to consider complementary customer choices, almost inevitably leads to the Profitable Product Death Spiral. The key marketing insight is that customers do not choose products in isolation. Rather, they choose *assortments* of products that fit together in a complementary manner.

What is the danger of focusing on product profitability at the expense of customer profitability? Decisions that seem to be increasing profitability actually alienate the customer by ignoring the effect of assortments of choices, eventually leading the firm to disaster. The implication is clear: to truly understand how to drive long-term profitability, it is essential to understand profitability from the customer side. It is the lifetime value of the customer that produces Customer Equity, and it is Customer Equity that has the greatest impact on the value of the firm. In the traditional organization, product or brand managers were charged with maximizing the revenue and/or profit of their individual brands or products. Often, such myopic vision hurts the overall organization.

The Hybrid

The hybrid corporation (see figure 15-2) represents the current state of the corporation. We see that many companies have begun to see the advantages of organizing the firm around the customer, but are often still stuck in traditional functional silos, or still focused on brands or products. In this case, although the organization is trying to serve the customer, each functional role continues to focus more narrowly on its particularities. For example, a certain segment of customers may be served most effectively if the firm were to change over to a new customer billing process. However, if this change requires substantial investment of firm resources (*finance's concern*) and substantial set-up and training resources (*operations' concern*), then these customers may not stick around long enough to ever see the new process come into being. Only by organizing the firm across functional areas, around the key drivers of long-term Customer Equity, will the true value of such changes be understood and embraced throughout the organization.

Alternative "hybridizations" of corporate structures can be seen by the myriad of organizations that have added customer satisfaction or customer loyalty "functions." These firms understand the value of keeping customers satisfied and retained in the long run, but still continue to make many decisions utilizing the traditional product-centered model.

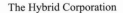
The Hybrid Corporation

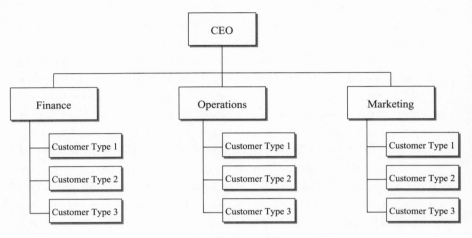

Figure 15-2. The Hybrid Corporation

Changes That Result from the Shift to
The Customer Equity Corporation

The Customer Equity Corporation succeeds (or fails) to the extent that it understands the drivers of Customer Equity for its business. The company no longer has a functional focus (e.g., finance, operations, marketing, and accounting). Rather, the organization and its resources are focused on the key drivers of Customer Equity (see figure 15-3). The role of understanding the flow of *information* in the business has been elevated to the highest level. The customers are the key stakeholders to whom the organization is accountable, with the organization focused in such a way as to facilitate such accountability.

In the new organization, the role of the customer manager is paramount. In a cross-equity matrix organization, the customer manager's goals are as follows:

1. to make sure that the actions chosen to drive Customer Equity (through Value, Brand, and Retention Equity) are consistent and synergistic whenever possible;

2. to understand the role of the customer's portfolio of purchase decisions (what links or connections do customers make with other prod-

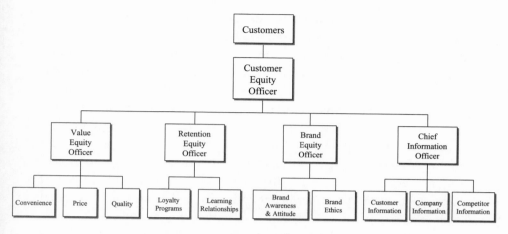

Figure 15-3. The Customer Equity Corporation

ucts or services, from this firm or others?), and to seize new opportunities to serve the customer;

3. to be the advocate for their customers as key constituents in the firm's growing Customer Equity.

The customer manager becomes the customer's champion in the firm. Growing a set of customers' "equity stakes" in the firm's overall Customer Equity will, in all probability, be the new fast track in the Customer Equity Corporation. Let's take a look at some of the specific changes that result from the shift to the Customer Equity Corporation.

Connecting Marketing with Finance

One of the most exciting opportunities in developing the Customer Equity Corporation is the possibility that marketing investments may finally be accountable, that marketing can finally be required to submit estimated return on investment for investments in Brand, Value, or Retention Equity. As we discussed in chapters 9 and 10, the Customer Equity Framework provides a methodology for understanding the return (in terms of changes in Customer Equity) for actionable drivers of Brand, Value, and Retention Equity. The Customer Equity Framework builds upon work by Srivastava, Shervani, and Fahey (1998), who pioneered the idea of "market-based assets."[1] They developed a conceptual model that suggests that market-based assets, such as customer relationships and channel partner relationships, are linked to market performance and, ultimately, to shareholder value. In their paper, they called for the "development of a theory that refines the concept of market-based assets, identifies the range and extent of such assets, and develops sets of indicators to measure their stock and flow."[2] The Customer Equity Framework is a move in this important direction.

In the new Customer Equity Corporation, there will finally be a home for number crunchers in marketing, and an overlapping (if not common) language between marketing and finance. The starting point for this détente, of course, is analyzing customer profitability. By understanding the current worth of a customer to the firm, we can begin to understand customer lifetime value and, eventually, Customer Equity. Gradually but inexorably, the things that business has traditionally concentrated on—current-period sales, profitability, and advertising effectiveness for each of its products—have been replaced in the savvy, modern corporation by such issues as future sales and profitability, customer satisfaction and retention, and relationship effectiveness for each of its customers or customer groups.

In order for the emerging corporation to accurately gauge the health of the organization, the company must consider the future performance of its customer relationships. Customers and customer groups must be evaluated according to their projected lifetime value to the firm—a task that requires cooperation from marketing and finance. The goal of any corporation is to grow the business, and to grow the value of the firm for the ultimate stakeholders, the shareholders. Whether private or public, mom-and-pop, or global enterprise, understanding the key drivers of firm value, with Customer Equity as a key component of that value, provides a solid platform from which to launch a new enterprise or build an existing enterprise.

Picture the new Customer Equity Corporation: the customer manager for gold-level mutual fund holders seeks to grow her Customer Equity. Through research and knowledge sharing with the key equity managers in her organization, she learns that the most important driver of Customer Equity for her set of customers is Value Equity, followed closely by Brand Equity. Surprisingly, Retention Equity is not that important, but upon further reflection this makes sense. Customers switch funds infrequently, so the key is getting them into the right funds when they have investable assets and making sure the funds perform well relative to their competitors. She creates a proposal outlining proposed investments in Value and Brand

Equity, focusing on key drivers for which her customers' funds lag behind key competitors in areas that are important to the customers. The investment proposal is reviewed by the Brand Equity Officer and by the Value Equity Officer. What do we see? Everyone is aligned in growing the firm's Customer Equity—finance fanatics, operations aficionados, marketing mavens, and product professionals alike. Everyone needs to understand the components of customer profitability, customer lifetime value, Customer Equity, and, at the end of the day, how to value the firm. At last, the key stakeholders' interests are fully aligned: what's good for the customer is good for the stockholder is good for the employees.

Realigning IT and Accounting

In the Customer Equity Corporation, we have elevated the role of information management to the highest level. To understand the genesis of this shift upward of the importance of information in the organization, let's take a look at how the use of information in an organization mirrors and even leads to the changes in the corporation that necessitate the shift to Customer Equity. We've seen the changing *purpose* of information: from managing products to managing customers. We've seen the changing *nature* of information: from product databases to customer databases. Finally, we've seen the changing *focus* of information: from product profitability to customer profitability. The shift from focus on product to focus on service, and the shift in power from the manufacturer to the customer are necessitated by, and are the result of, these shifts in the purpose, nature, and focus of information available to the organization. To successfully implement the Customer Equity Framework in an organization, capturing and managing the right types of information is critical. We do not delve into the details of how to develop and manage customer information systems in this book, but other resources are available that provide detailed information on these topics. (See, for example: *The One-to-One Fieldbook,* by Peppers and Rogers; *The New Rules of Marketing,* by Fred Newell; and *Customer Connections,* by Robert Wayland and Paul Cole.)

If a firm does not elevate the role of information management to the highest level, it will be left behind. Competitors will understand the key role of information management. Three changes are key in shifting the role of information management in the Customer Equity Corporation. First, the *purpose* of the entire IT (information technology) system must be shifted to a CIS system (customer information system). As noted in figure 15-3, the CIO's group is charged with capturing and analyzing customer, company, and competitor information, but it must be remembered that company and competitor information is gathered to see how they fit in as *(a)* drivers of Customer Equity, or *(b)* benchmarks for drivers or sub-drivers of Customer Equity.

Second, the *nature* of the data must shift, from a product focus to a customer focus. Currently, many Customer Information Databases are really Product Information Databases with customer information attached. They were designed to monitor the flow of goods and services through a firm or through a channel, and the customer information appeared as an add-on that firms finally figured out had value. The information systems must be designed to capture and analyze customer information, at the individual customer level. Clearly, such sytems will also capture product information as well, but this should be a secondary focus. In the next twenty to thirty years, the products that a firm sells its customers will be less important than the relationship that the firm has with its customers. By designing CIS systems that focus on the customer, firms will be able to spot customers' changing needs earlier and respond to them with ever-changing products and services as never before.

Third, the *focus* of the data must shift, from product profitability to customer profitability. Developing and managing individual customer level databases will be easier for some firms (particularly in the business-to-business sector) than others (particularly for firms such as consumer products companies who have millions of customers). But understanding the individual profitability and potential of each existing customer is key to the Customer Equity Framework and profitable customer management (as outlined in chapters 11 and 12). In addition, individual customer profitability and customer lifetime value are important in determining the types of new customers to attract to the firm. Why not figure out what attributes are shared by all "Gold" customers in the firm's Customer Pyramid and seek to attract additional "Gold potentials" to the firm?

Financial Accountability

Who can argue with offering customers better value, or retaining them more effectively, or building stronger Brand Equity? But not all efforts to improve Customer Equity are profitable. For *best* performance, the company must differentiate between improvement efforts that are profitable, and those that are not.

Modern thinking in accounting and finance suggests that short-term benefits demand short-term investments, and long-term benefits demand long-term investments. For example, it is inappropriate to incur long-term debt to pay for short-term, current obligations. However, it is entirely appropriate to make long-term investments that will generate a long-term return.

Because Customer Equity is a long-term financial concept, it is more appropriate to consider the role of long-term investments versus short-term spending. In essence, it is important to match the customer relationship orientation to the financial orientation. If the customer relationship orientation is short-term and transaction-oriented, then long-term investments in Customer Equity are wasted.

On the other hand, if the customer relationship orientation is relationship-based, then long-term investments can be the right thing. For example, a credit card company typically wishes to maintain long-term relationships with its customers. In this situation, it may be entirely appropriate to make long-term investments in Value Equity, Retention Equity, and Brand Equity.

Management initiatives that improve Customer Equity are best viewed as investments, because of the long-term nature of Customer Equity. Viewing improvement efforts as investments means that those initiatives need to be financially accountable and yield an acceptable financial return.

The firm's most important asset is its customers. In the new Customer Equity Corporation, the Customer Pyramid will serve to focus resources on the customers who are likely to generate the greatest improvement in a firm's profitability. The Pyramid provides a common language for accounting, marketing, and CIS (customer information systems). In addition, the Customer Pyramid provides a methodology with which firms can now examine the extent to which customers in different profitability tiers will respond to changes in drivers of Value, Brand, and Retention Equity.

The needs of the firm's most profitable customers must be assessed carefully to assure that everything is being done to maintain—and increase, if possible—their already high levels of profitability. Implementation and management of the Customer Pyramid will have significant implications for the traditional roles of marketing, accounting, and information management. Only by working together to understand the profitability of each cus-

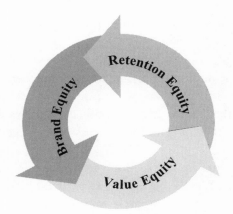

Figure 15-4. The Components of Customer Equity

tomer tier, the equity drivers of each customer tier, and the growth potential of each customer tier can the Customer Equity Corporation achieve its full potential.

Connecting to the Customer: Organizing Around the Sources of Customer Equity

The Value Equity Sphere

Value Equity represents the customer's perception of the quality received from the firm (in the form of goods and services) and the price paid for such goods and services. In addition, the value connection encompasses the importance the customer attaches to the value received from the firm. Specifically, this input to Customer Equity represents what the firm brings to the firm/customer relationship: how well the firm delivers on its promises. Quality, price, and convenience drive Value Equity. This chain of effects permits us to evaluate the Return on Quality (the return on investment from improvements in quality or customer satisfaction), Return on Price (considering the long-term impact on Customer Equity), and the Return on Convenience (including such elements as adding new retail locations or increasing distribution). Therefore, the Value Equity Sphere is responsible for managing the drivers of Value Equity and relating these drivers to the drivers of Retention and Brand Equity.

The Brand Equity Sphere

Brand Equity represents the effect of the strength of the brand connection on Customer Equity. The brand connection represents the strength of the perceptual relationship between the firm and the customer, built up on both sides over time: by the firm through its marketing strategies and tactics, and by the customer through life experiences and connections. The brand connection expresses the customer's emotional tie to the firm. Advertising typically increases Brand Equity. By employing the Customer Equity chain of effects, the Return on Advertising can be quantified and evaluated. Therefore, the Brand Equity Sphere is responsible for managing the drivers of Brand Equity and relating these drivers to the drivers of Retention and Value Equity.

The Retention Equity Sphere

Retention Equity is the effect of the strength of the retention connection on Customer Equity. The retention connection represents the importance the customer associates with the company's retention programs and relationship building, and the extent to which the company excels in these areas. Retention Equity is typically increased by the use of retention (loyalty) programs. The Customer Equity Framework permits objective, quantifiable evaluation of the profitability of those programs. The Retention Equity Sphere is responsible for managing the drivers of Retention Equity and relating these drivers to the drivers of Value and Brand Equity.

The Customer Equity Officer (CEO)

In the Customer Equity Corporation, the CEO is the true steward of Customer Equity. The CEO should be evaluated on the basis of his or her ability to grow the firm's Customer Equity. The CEO must not only consider the individual drivers of Value, Retention, and Brand Equity, but will be faced with decisions in which he or she must consider the effects of a change in one equity or another. The successful CEO will be able to achieve growth in Customer Equity through the identification of key drivers of Value, Retention, and Brand Equity, but will be able to identify and capitalize on synergies among the equities (see figure 15-4). In considering the effect of this organizational change on the market, and on the typical large corporation's current focus on short-term strategies, this should bring good news to firms and to the market. By focusing on growing Customer Equity, rather than on growing short-term market share or short-term bottom-line profitability, the interests of the CEO will finally be fully aligned with the interests of the market—long-term, sustainable growth in Customer Equity, which will result in long-term sustainable growth in earnings.

Customer-Based Strategy

The time has come to replace product-based strategy with a competitive strategy approach based on how the firm addresses the specific drivers and sub-drivers of Customer Equity. Such an approach to strategy is the natural implication of the economy's shift from a goods economy to a service economy, combined with modern database and information system technology.

Business must pay less attention to market share, which reflects only current performance, and more attention to Customer Equity share, which reflects both current and future business. Customer Equity share can be thought of as being the best leading indicator of future market share, because it compares the firm's total customer lifetime value against competition.

Driving Customer Equity share is the firm's relative standing on the drivers of Customer Equity—Value Equity, Retention Equity, and Brand Equity. It is essential that the firm identify its industry's success factors, paying more attention to the Customer Equity drivers that drive customer choice, and perhaps paying less attention to the ones that don't. By identifying drivers (and sub-drivers) for which there is great importance, and on which the firm is performing relatively poorly, the firm can isolate the areas in which improvement resources are likely to have the greatest impact.

This results in a customer-centered (yet competitor-cognizant) approach to strategy, enabling the firm to analyze its competitive position and identify the most effective improvement efforts directly with respect to the drivers of Customer Equity—Value Equity (quality, price, and convenience), Brand Equity (advertising and marketing communications), and Retention Equity (retention programs, loyalty programs, and relationship programs).

Initiatives proposed by the Value, Brand, or Retention Equity groups to build Customer Equity (e.g., quality initiatives, customer satisfaction programs, distribution efforts, retention/loyalty programs, advertising expenditures) can be objectively and quantifiably evaluated within the same framework, and by the same criterion—return on investment. This enables management to make intelligent determinations as to the effectiveness of alternative strategies to grow Customer Equity.

The Customer Equity Corporation: Dominant, Dynamic, and Driving the Future

Firms that choose to become Customer Equity Corporations will represent a keen departure from the corporations of today. They will fully realize the implications of making customers the heart of the organization. The new CEC will be *dominant* because it will base its strategy and tactics on what is important to the customer, taking actions that will truly build Value, Retention, and Brand Equity. The new CEC will see customer-based actions, based upon customer input, leading to substantial growth in Customer Equity.

The new Customer Equity Corporation will be *dynamic*. In this age of the potential of one-to-one marketing, the CEC can achieve an understanding of the drivers of Customer Equity for each and every customer. More important, the CEC will be able to measure, manage, and grow Customer Equity over time, monitoring changes in the drivers of Customer Equity as customer relationships with the firm grow and mature. In addition, the CEC can anticipate changes in key drivers of Customer Equity (for the firm, or for the entire industry), using customer defections or small changes in Customer Equity as potential "leading indicators" of such change.

Finally, the Customer Equity Corporation will *drive the future*. The potency of the Customer Equity Framework lies in its ability to direct resources where they will have the most impact. By choosing investments that maximize return from investments in Customer Equity, the new CEC will improve efficiency and effectiveness in achieving Value, Retention, and Brand Equity. These firms will leapfrog their traditional competitors in the marketplace.

The Customer Equity Corporation will focus its key resources on the key asset that separates one firm in an industry from another—its customers. This new organization will be fully aligned with its key stakeholders: growing Customer Equity will grow the value of the firm. In the new Customer Equity Corporation, the voice of the customer will finally be heard. And the organization will respond to the voice of the customer with confidence, taking quick, decisive action that will *drive* Customer Equity.

Obtaining the Lifetime Value

Once we have the brand's projected share of wallet, for this customer, plus the inputs listed in chapter 3, it is straightforward to estimate the lifetime value of the customer. If LV_i is the lifetime value of customer i, t indicates time period, T is the length of the planning horizon, d is the discount factor, F_{it} is the expected frequency of customer i's purchases in the product category per time period t, S_{it} is the expected share of customer i's wallet for this brand in time t, and π_{it} is the average contribution from a purchase by individual i in time t, we can estimate the lifetime value as:

$$\text{Lifetime value} = \sum_{t=0}^{T} [(1 + d)^{-t}\, F_{it} S_{it} \pi_{it}]$$

Alternatively, we might instead have information about revenue per period (R_{it}), and contribution margin (M_{it}). In that case, the lifetime value expression can be computed as:

$$\text{Lifetime value} = \sum_{t=0}^{T} [(1 + d)^{-t}\, R_{it} S_{it} M_{it}]$$

APPENDIX
8.1

Example of Customer Survey

Here are some examples of survey items that might be used to measure Customer Equity and its drivers. This survey is based on the survey we used to analyze the airline market.

Market Share and Transition Probabilities
(the headings in this Appendix are for explanatory purposes and would not be read to the respondent)

1. Which of the following airlines did you most recently fly (please check one)?

American Airlines   _____
Delta Airlines   _____
Southwest Airlines   _____
United Airlines   _____

2. The next time you fly a commercial airline, what is the probability that you will fly each of these airlines?

Airline   *Probability (please provide a percentage for each airline and have the percentages add up to 100%)*

American Airlines   _____
Delta Airlines   _____
Southwest Airlines   _____
United Airlines   _____

Size and Frequency of Purchase

3. When you fly, how much on average does the airline ticket cost?

_____less than $300
_____between $300 and $599
_____between $600 and $899
_____between $900 and $1199
_____between $1200 and $1499
_____between $1500 and $1799
_____between $1800 and $2099
_____$2100 or more

4. On average, how often do you fly on a commercial airline?

_____once a week or more
_____once every two weeks
_____once a month
_____3–4 times per year
_____once a year
_____once every two years, or less

Value Equity Drivers

5. How would you rate the overall quality of the following airlines?

Airline	Very High Quality				Very Low Quality
American Airlines	5	4	3	2	1
Delta Airlines	5	4	3	2	1
Southwest Airlines	5	4	3	2	1
United Airlines	5	4	3	2	1

6. To what extent is the quality of the following airlines worth the price paid?

Airline	Worth Much More				Worth Much Less
American Airlines	5	4	3	2	1
Delta Airlines	5	4	3	2	1
Southwest Airlines	5	4	3	2	1
United Airlines	5	4	3	2	1

7. How would you rate the competitiveness of the prices of each of these airlines?

Airline	Very Competitive				Not at All Competitive
American Airlines	5	4	3	2	1
Delta Airlines	5	4	3	2	1
Southwest Airlines	5	4	3	2	1
United Airlines	5	4	3	2	1

8. The airline flies when and where I need to go.

Airline	Strongly Agree				Strongly Disagree
American Airlines	5	4	3	2	1
Delta Airlines	5	4	3	2	1
Southwest Airlines	5	4	3	2	1
United Airlines	5	4	3	2	1

9. It is easy to make reservations with the airline.

Airline	Strongly Agree				Strongly Disagree
American Airlines	5	4	3	2	1
Delta Airlines	5	4	3	2	1
Southwest Airlines	5	4	3	2	1
United Airlines	5	4	3	2	1

10. Please rate the "everyday" or regular prices charged by each of these airlines, compared to other airlines.

Airline	Much Lower than Other Airlines				Much Higher than Other Airlines
American Airlines	5	4	3	2	1
Delta Airlines	5	4	3	2	1
Southwest Airlines	5	4	3	2	1
United Airlines	5	4	3	2	1

11. Please rate the discounted prices offered by each of these airlines.

Airline	Much Lower than Other Airlines				Much Higher than Other Airlines
American Airlines	5	4	3	2	1
Delta Airlines	5	4	3	2	1

Southwest Airlines	5	4	3	2	1
United Airlines	5	4	3	2	1

Brand Equity Drivers

12. My attitude toward the airline is extremely favorable.

Airline	Strongly Agree				Strongly Disagree
American Airlines	5	4	3	2	1
Delta Airlines	5	4	3	2	1
Southwest Airlines	5	4	3	2	1
United Airlines	5	4	3	2	1

13. I often notice and pay attention to the airline's media advertising.

Airline	Strongly Agree				Strongly Disagree
American Airlines	5	4	3	2	1
Delta Airlines	5	4	3	2	1
Southwest Airlines	5	4	3	2	1
United Airlines	5	4	3	2	1

14. I often notice and pay attention to information the airline sends to me.

Airline	Strongly Agree				Strongly Disagree
American Airlines	5	4	3	2	1
Delta Airlines	5	4	3	2	1
Southwest Airlines	5	4	3	2	1
United Airlines	5	4	3	2	1

15. The airline is well known as a good corporate citizen.

Airline	Strongly Agree				Strongly Disagree
American Airlines	5	4	3	2	1
Delta Airlines	5	4	3	2	1
Southwest Airlines	5	4	3	2	1
United Airlines	5	4	3	2	1

16. The airline is an active sponsor of community events.

Airline	Strongly Agree				Strongly Disagree
American Airlines	5	4	3	2	1

Delta Airlines	5	4	3	2	1
Southwest Airlines	5	4	3	2	1
United Airlines	5	4	3	2	1

17. The airline has high ethical standards with respect to its customers and employees.

Airline	Strongly Agree				Strongly Disagree
American Airlines	5	4	3	2	1
Delta Airlines	5	4	3	2	1
Southwest Airlines	5	4	3	2	1
United Airlines	5	4	3	2	1

18. The image of this airline fits my personality well.

Airline	Strongly Agree				Strongly Disagree
American Airlines	5	4	3	2	1
Delta Airlines	5	4	3	2	1
Southwest Airlines	5	4	3	2	1
United Airlines	5	4	3	2	1

19. I have positive feelings toward the airline.

Airline	Strongly Agree				Strongly Disagree
American Airlines	5	4	3	2	1
Delta Airlines	5	4	3	2	1
Southwest Airlines	5	4	3	2	1
United Airlines	5	4	3	2	1

Retention Equity Drivers (asked only for the airline most frequently flown)

20. I have a big investment in the airline's loyalty (frequent flyer) program.

Strongly Agree   *Strongly Disagree*

    5   4   3   2   1

21. The preferential treatment I get from this airline's loyalty program is important to me.

Strongly Agree   *Strongly Disagree*

    5   4   3   2   1

22. I know this airline's procedures well.

Strongly Agree   *Strongly Disagree*

  5   4   3   2   1

23. The airline knows a lot of information about me.

Strongly Agree   *Strongly Disagree*

  5   4   3   2   1

24. This airline recognizes me as being special.

Strongly Agree   *Strongly Disagree*

  5   4   3   2   1

25. I feel a sense of community with other passengers of this airline.

Strongly Agree   *Strongly Disagree*

  5   4   3   2   1

APPENDIX
10.1

Calculating the Importance of Customer Equity Drivers

The relative importance of Value Equity, Brand Equity, and Retention Equity within an industry can be calculated according to the following formula (using Value Equity as an example):

$$\text{Importance of Value Equity} = \sum_{k} [CE(VE_{\text{best}} - CE(VE_k)] / TOT$$

where CE denotes Customer Equity, VE_{best} denotes the best Value Equity in the industry, VE_k denotes the Value Equity of firm k, and TOT is the sum of the numerators for the Value Equity, Retention Equity, and Brand Equity calculations.

NOTES

Chapter 1

1. Robert C. Blattberg and John Deighton, "Manage Marketing by the Customer Equity Test," *Harvard Business Review,* 74 (July–August 1996), 136–144.
2. Todd Godbout, "Employment Change and Sectoral Distribution in 10 Countries, 1970–90," *Monthly Labor Review* (October 1993), p. 8.
3. Stephen M. Shugan, "Explanations for the Growth of Services," in *Service Quality: New Directions in Theory and Practice,* Roland T. Rust and Richard L. Oliver, eds. (Newbury Park, CA: Sage Publications, 1993).
4. Todd Godbout, "Employment Change and Sectoral Distribution in 10 Countries, 1970–90," *Monthly Labor Review* (October 1993), p. 8.
5. Wagner A. Kamakura and Gary J. Russell, "Measuring Perceptions of Brand Quality with Scanner Data: Implications for Brand Equity" (Cambridge, MA: *Marketing Science Institute Report 91–122,* 1991).

Chapter 2

1. Will Pinkston, "Is Something Wrong at Opryland Hotel?" *The Tennessean,* (September 20, 1998), 1E–2E.
2. Gaylord ultimately announced plans to replace the theme park with a shopping mall.
3. Pinkston, op. cit.

Chapter 3

1. See P. D. Berger and N. I. Nasr, "Customer Lifetime Value: Marketing Models and Applications," *Journal of Interactive Marketing,* 12 (1), 1998, 17–30, for an excellent discussion of the lifetime value of the customer.
2. Frederick F. Reichheld and W. Earl Sasser, Jr., "Zero Defections: Quality Comes to Services," *Harvard Business Review* (September–October 1990), 105–111.
3. Grahame R. Dowling and Mark Uncles, "Do Customer Loyalty Programs Really Work?" *Sloan Management Review* (Summer 1997), 71–82.

4. Frank M. Bass, "The Theory of Stochastic Preference and Brand Switching," *Journal of Marketing Research,* 11 (February 1974), 1–20.
5. Andrew S. C. Ehrenberg, *Repeat-Buying: Facts, Theory, and Applications,* (London: Charles Griffin and Co., 1988).

Chapter 4
1. Michael Valenti, "Double Wrapped," *Mechanical Engineering,* (Jan. 1999), 52–56.
2. Craig Stedman, "Data Mining Despite the Dangers," *Computerworld* (Dec. 29, 1997), pp. 61–62.
3. Barb Cole-Gomolski, "Chase Uses New Apps to ID Best Customers," *Computerworld* (Sept. 1, 1997) 49–50.
4. Allan J. Magrath, "Where It's at in Branding," *Ivey Business Quarterly* (Spring 1997), 65–70.
5. Geoffrey Brewer, "Hewlett-Packard," *Sales and Marketing Management* (Oct. 1997), p. 58.

Chapter Five
1. John Updike, *Toward the End of Time* (New York: Alfred Knopf, 1997).
2. Roland T. Rust, Anthony J. Zahorik, and Timothy L. Keiningham, *Service Marketing* (New York: HarperCollins 1996).
3. W. Edwards Deming, *Out of the Crisis* (Boston: Massachusetts Institute of Technology, 1982.)
4. Valarie A. Zeithaml, A. Parasuraman, and Leonard L. Berry, *Delivering Quality Service* (Free Press, 1990).
5. Noriaki Kano, Nobuhiko Seraku, Fumio Takahashi, and Shinichi Tsuji, "Attractive Quality and Must-Be Quality," *Quality: The Journal of the Japanese Society for Quality Control,* 14 (April 1984), 39–48. See also Joseph M. Juran, *Juran's Quality Control Handbook,* 4th Ed. (New York: McGraw-Hill, 1988).
6. Richard L. Oliver, Roland T. Rust, and Sajeev Varki, "Customer Delight: Foundations, Findings, and Managerial Insight," *Journal of Retailing,* 73 (Fall 1997), 311–336, and Roland T. Rust, Anthony J. Zahorik, and Timothy L. Keiningham, *Return on Quality: Measuring the Financial Impact of Your Company's Quest for Quality* (Burr Ridge, IL: Irwin, 1994).

Chapter 6
1. Kevin Lane Keller, *Strategic Brand Management: Building, Measuring and Managing Brand Equity* (New Jersey: Prentice Hall, 1998).
2. Interbrand Group, *World's Greatest Brands: An International Review* (New York: John Wiley, 1992).
3. Patricia Sellers, "Inside the First e-Christmas," *Fortune* (Feb. 1, 1999) 70–73; Joshua Macht, "Toy Seller Plays Internet Hardball," *Inc.* (Oct. 1998), 17–18; Seth A. Fineberg, "eToys Takes On Toy Giants," *Venture Capital Journal* (Aug. 1, 1998) p.1.
4. Susan Fournier, "Consumers and their Brands: Developing Relationship Theory in Consumer Research," *Journal of Consumer Research,* 24 (March 1998), 343–373.

5. Nikhil Deogun, "Pepsi's New Advertising Effort, Scraps 'Generation Next' Campaign," *Wall Street Journal* (Mar. 5, 1999), B5.

6. This notion of "fit" captures the differentiation and relevance dimensions in the Young and Rubicam BrandAsset Valuator™ Model described above, as well as David Aaker's notion of "brand-as-person, and Keller's Brand Associations). See also: David A. Aaker (1991), *Managing Brand Equity* (New York: Free Press, 1991); David A. Aaker (1995), *Building Strong Brands* (New York: Free Press, 1995).

7. Chris Reidy, "In Marketplace, They're No Longer Such a Great Fit," *The Boston Globe* (Tuesday, February 23, 1999), A1.

8. For more information on brand associations, see Gerald Zaltman and Robin Higie, "Seeing the Voice of the Customer: The Zaltman Metaphor Elicitation Technique," Marketing Science Institute Report Number 93–114, and Geraldine R. Henderson, Dawn Iacobucci, and Bobby J. Calder, "Brand Diagnostics: The Use of Consumer Associative Networks for the Brand Manager," working paper, Fuqua School of Business, Duke University, 1998.

9. Don E. Schultz, Stanley I. Tannenbaum, Robert F. Lauterborn, *Integrated Marketing Communications* (New York: NTC Publishing Group, 1994).

10. Mark A. Freidman and Marni Shapiro, *Gap Inc.: Industry Leader Increasing Market Share* (New York: Merrill Lynch, Global Securities Research and Economics Group, 1999).

11. Nina Munk, "Gap Gets It," *Fortune,* 138, (August 3, 1998), 68–82.

12. David A. Aaker and Kevin Lane Keller, "Consumer Evaluations of Brand Extensions," *Journal of Marketing* (January 1990), 27–41.

13. Grant McCracken, "Who is the Celebrity Endorser? Cultural Foundations of the Endorsement Process," *Journal of Consumer Research* (December 1989), 310–321.

14. The Ethics driver of Brand Equity is evidence of Aaker's notion of the brand-as-organization, 1995.

15. Charles A. Garfield, "Do Profits and Social Responsibility Mix?" *Executive Excellence* (Mar. 1, 1992), 5.

16. Deborah Gunthorpe, "Business Ethics: A Quantitative Analysis of the Impact of Unethical Behavior by Publicly Traded Companies," *Journal of Business Ethics* (Apr. 1997), 537–43.

Chapter 7

1. Maria Holmlund, *Perceived Quality in Business Relationships* (Helsinki: Swedish School of Economics and Business Administration, 1997).

2. George Anders, "High-Tech Rivals Are Battling to Make Their Web Sites 'Sticky,'" *Wall Street Journal* (Feb. 11, 1999), B1, *URL:http://interactive.wsj.com/archive/retrieve.cgi?id=SB918682602435312000.djm.*

3. Adrienne Mand, "Online Retailer Bluefly has High Hopes for Web Sales," *Brandweek* (August 10, 1998) p. 37.

4. Meeting with First USA's CEO, Randy Christianson (April 8, 1999).

5. Clare Conley, "Loyalty Cards Are Missing the Point," *Marketing Week London,* 21 (16, June 18, 1998), 21–22.

6. Alan Mitchell, "Critical Mass Is the Key to Loyalty Card Survival," *Marketing Week,* London, 21 (11, May 14, 1998), 24–25.

7. Lynn Weinstein, "Packaged Programs: The Ties that Bind," *Bank Marketing,* 30 (4, April 1998), 13–14.

8. Ibid.

9. Newell/Seklemian's New Rules of Marketing Conference, Duke University (Durham, N.C., 1996).

10. Kurt Johnson, "Choosing the Right Program," *Direct Marketing,* 61(2, June 1998), 36–38.

11. See, for example, www.streamline.com, www.peapod.com, or www.netgrocer.com.

Chapter 8

1. Meetings with cofounders of Netcentives, Inc., cofounders Elliot Ng and Eric Tilenius, and CEO West Shell, March 6, 1999.

2. Gerald Zaltman and Robin Higie, "Seeing the Voice of the Customer: The Zaltman Metaphor Elicitation Technique," Marketing Science Institute Report Number 93–114.

3. In practice this analysis is accomplished by special types of regression analysis that control for the high degree of "multicollinearity" that typically exists in survey data of this sort. Variables (such as the process quality ratings or brand attitude ratings) are multicollinear when respondents tend to rate all (or most) of them high or all (or most) of them low at the same time. This causes a problem because the estimated regression weights will be unstable. Special types of regression analysis have been devised for addressing multicollinearity. The three approaches that have been used the most in customer satisfaction survey data are (1) *ridge regression* (see, for example, A. E. Hoerl and R. W. Kennard (1970), "Ridge Regression: Biased Estimation for Non-Orthogonal Problems," *Technometrics,* 12, 55–67); (2) *the equity estimator* (see, for example, Lakshman Krishnamurthi and Arvind Rangaswamy (1987), "The Equity Estimator for Marketing Research," *Marketing Science,* 6 (Fall), 336–357); and (3) *PLS* (see H. Wold (1974), "Causal Flows with Latent Variables," *European Economic Review,* 5, 67–86); all do a reasonably good job of controlling for multicollinearity, and perform much better than ordinary least squares regression analysis.

4. Bradley Gale, *Managing Customer Value* (New York: The Free Press, 1994).

5. Raymond E. Kordupleski, Roland T. Rust, and Anthony J. Zahorik, "Why Improving Quality Doesn't Improve Quality," *California Management Review* 35 (Spring 1993), 82–95.

6. Bradley Gale, op cit.

7. Roland T. Rust, Peter J. Danaher, and Sajeev Varki, "Comparative Service Quality and Competitive Marketing Decisions," Center for Service Marketing Working Paper, Vanderbilt University, 1999.

Chapter 9

1. Rajendra K. Srivastava, Tasadduq A. Shervani, and Liam Fahey, "Market-Based Assets and Shareholder Value: A Framework for Analysis," *Journal of Marketing,* 62 (January 1998), 2–18.

2. Al Ehrbar, *EVA: The Real Key to Creating Wealth* (New York: John Wiley & Sons, 1998).

3. Tom Copeland, Tim Koller, and Jack Murrin, *Valuation: Measuring and Managing the Value of Companies* (New York: John Wiley & Sons, 1996).

4. Mark Ivey and John Carey, "The Ecstasy and the Agony," *Business Week* (October 21, 1991), p. 40.

5. L. M. Sixel, "Quality-Award Winner Files for Chapter 11," *The Houston Chronicle* (January 30, 1992), Business Section, p. 1.

6. W. Earl Sasser, Jr., Christopher W. L. Hart, and James L. Heskett, *The Service Management Course: Cases and Readings* (New York: The Free Press, 1991), pp. 427–444.

7. L. M. Sixel, "The Quality Question: Have the Means Become an End for Many Firms?" *The Houston Chronicle* (October 20, 1991), Business Section, p. 1.

8. Robert Chapman Wood, "A Hero Without a Company," *Forbes* (March 18, 1991), pp. 112–114.

9. William W. Arnold and Jeanne M. Plas, *The Human Touch: Today's Most Unusual Program for Productivity and Profit* (New York: John Wiley & Sons, 1993).

10. David A. Fox, "Centennial Medical Center Names a New President," *The Tennessean* (May 30, 1993), p. E1.

11. Report by the Council on Financial Competition (1996).

12. Andrew J. Parsons, "Focus and Squeeze: Consumer Marketing in the 90's," *Marketing Management,* 1 (1), 1992, 51–55.

13. Peter J. Danaher and Roland T. Rust, "Determining the Optimal Level of Media Spending," *Journal of Advertising Research,* 34 (January/February 1994), 28–34.

14. John Phillip Jones, *How Much is Enough?: Getting the Most From Your Advertising Dollar* (New York: Lexington Books, 1992).

15. Evert Gummeson, *Total Relationship Marketing* (Oxford: Butterworth-Heinemann, 1999).

16. Roland T. Rust, Anthony J. Zahorik, and Timothy L. Keiningham, "Return on Quality (ROQ): Making Service Quality Financially Accountable," *Journal of Marketing,* 59 (April 1995), 58–70; and Roland T. Rust, Anthony J. Zahorik, and Timothy L. Keiningham, *Return on Quality: Measuring the Financial Impact of Your Company's Quest for Quality* (Burr Ridge, IL: Irwin, 1994).

17. A related framework is known as the "service profit chain." For more details on the service profit chain and its validation, see James L. Heskett, Thomas O. Jones, Gary W. Loveman, and W. Earl Sasser, Jr., "Putting the Service Profit Chain to Work," *Harvard Business Review,* 72 (March–April 1994), 164–174; and Gary W. Loveman, "Employee Satisfaction, Customer Loyalty, and Financial Performance: An Empirical Examination of the Service Profit Chain in Retail Banking," *Journal of Service Research,* 1 (August 1998), 18–31.

18. See Chapter 8.

19. Roland T. Rust, Timothy Keiningham, Stephen Clemens, and Anthony Zahorik, "Return on Quality at Chase Manhattan Bank," *Interfaces,* 2 (March–April 1999), 62–72.

20. Duncan I. Simester, John R. Hauser, Birger Wernerfelt, and Roland T. Rust, "Implementing Quality Improvement Programs Designed to Enhance Customer Satisfac-

tion: Quasi-Experiments in the U.S. and Spain," *Journal of Marketing Research,* forthcoming (1999).

21. Frederick F. Reichheld and W. Earl Sasser, "Zero Defections: Quality Comes to Service," *Harvard Business Review* (September/October 1990), 105–111.

22. Grahame R. Dowling and Mark Uncles, "Do Customer Loyalty Programs Really Work?" *Sloan Management Review* (Summer 1997), 71–82.

Chapter 10

1. C. K. Prahalad and Gary Hamel, "The Core Competence of the Corporation," *Harvard Business Review,* 68 (3) (1990), 79–91.

2. Michael E. Porter, *Competitive Advantage: Creating and Sustaining Superior Performance* (New York: The Free Press, 1985).

3. Kenichi Ohmae, "Getting Back to Strategy," *Harvard Business Review,* (November–December 1988).

4. Adrian J. Slywotzky, *Value Migration: How to Think Several Moves Ahead of the Competition* (Boston: Harvard Business School Press, 1996).

Chapter 11

1. Rick Brooks, "Alienating Customers Isn't Always a Bad Idea, Many Firms Discover," *Wall Street Journal* (January 7, 1999), A1 and A12.

2. Ibid.

3. Michael Schrange, "Fire Your Customers," *Wall Street Journal* (March 16, 1992), A8.

4. Richard Buzzell and Bradley Gale, *The PIMS Principles: Linking Strategy to Performance* (New York: The Free Press, 1987).

5. Claes Fornell, "A National Customer Satisfaction Barometer: The Swedish Experience," *Journal of Marketing,* 56 (January 1992), 6–21.

6. Ruth N. Bolton and James Drew, "A Longitudinal Analysis of the Impact of Service Changes on Customer Attitudes," *Journal of Marketing,* 55 (January 1991a), 1–9.

7. Roland T. Rust, Anthony J. Zahorik, and Timothy L. Keiningham, *Return on Quality: Measuring the Financial Impact of Your Company's Quest for Quality* (Burr Ridge, IL: Irwin, 1994). See also Roland Rust, Anthony J. Zahorik, and Timothy L. Keiningham, "Return on Quality (ROQ): Making Service Quality Financially Accountable," *Journal of Marketing,* 59 (April 1995), 58–70.

8. Valarie A. Zeithaml, Leonard L. Berry, and A. Parasuraman, "The Behavioral Consequences of Service Quality," *Journal of Marketing,* 60 (April 1996), 31–46.

9. Ruth N. Bolton, "A Dynamic Model of the Duration of the Customer's Relationship with a Continuous Service Provider: The Role of Satisfaction," *Marketing Science,* 17 (1), (1998) 45–65.

10. Anthony J. Zahorik and Roland T. Rust, "Modeling the Impact of Service Quality on Profitability: A Review," in Terri Swartz et al., eds., *Advances in Services Marketing and Management* (Greenwich, CT: JAI Press, 1992), 247–276.

11. See Debra Connelly, "First Commerce Segments Customers by Behavior, Enhancing Profitability" (1997); Guenther Hartfeil, "Bank One Measures Profitability of Cus-

tomers, Not Just Products," *Journal of Retail Banking Services* (1996), 18, 2, 24–31; and Carla McEachern "New Ways to Build Loyalty and Profitability," *Bank Marketing* (1997), 29, 9, 24.

Chapter 12

1. Guenther Hartfeil "Bank One Measures Profitability of Customers, Not Just Products," *Journal of Retail Banking Services* (1996), 18, 2, 24–31.
2. Carla McEachern "New Ways to Build Loyalty and Profitability," *Bank Marketing* (1997), 29, 9, 24.
3. Debra Connelly "First Commerce Segments Customers by Behavior, Enhancing Profitability," *Journal of Retail Banking Services* (1997), 19, 1, 23–27.
4. Peter R. Peacock "Data Mining in Marketing: Part 1," *Marketing Management,* 6, 4 (Winter 1998), 9–18.
5. Frederick Newell, *The New Rules of Marketing: How to Use One-on-One Relationship Marketing to Be the Leader in Your Industry* (New York: McGraw-Hill, 1997).

Chapter 13

1. Joy S. Johnson, "Home Depot Renovates," *Fortune,* November 23, 1998, 200–204+.
2. Ibid., 202.
3. Thomas Teal, "Service Comes First: An Interview with USAA's Robert F. McDermott," *Harvard Business Review,* September–October 1991, pp. 117–127.
4. Valarie A. Zeithaml and Mary Jo Bitner, *Services Marketing* (New York: McGraw-Hill, 1996).
5. Arthur Anderson, *Best Practices—Building Your Business with Customer-Focused Solutions* (New York: Simon and Schuster, 1998), pp. 125–27. Discussed in Valarie A. Zeithaml and Mary Jo Bitner, *Services Marketing and Management* (New York: McGraw-Hill, 2000).
6. Eryn Brown, "PeopleSoft: Tech's Latest Publicly Traded Cult," *Fortune* (May 25, 1998), 155–56. Also "PeopleSoft Corporation: Delivering Outrageous Customer Service," a Best Practice Case published by Information Technology Services Marketing Association (ITSMA) (Boston, 1996).
7. Lawrence A. Crosby, Kenneth R. Evans, and Deborah Cowles, "Relationship Quality in Services Selling: An Interpersonal Influence Perspective," *Journal of Marketing* (July 1990), pp. 68–81.
8. Donald F. Fites, "Make Your Dealers Your Partners," *Harvard Business Review* (March–April 1996), pp. 84–95.
9. Karin Schill, "Dial-a-Deal," *The News and Observer* (January 31, 1999), p. E1–3.

Chapter 14

1. Erick Schonfeld, "Schwab Puts It All Online," *Fortune* (December 7, 1998), pp. 94–100.
2. Ibid., p. 95.
3. Ibid., p. 96.

4. Ibid., p. 100.
5. David Leonhardt, "Make a Bid, But Don't Pack Your Bags," *Business Week* (June 1, 1998), p. 164.
6. Lauren Rublin, "Offerings in the Offing: Beam Me Up Scotty," Barron's (March 8, 1999), pp. 33+.
7. Robert Hof and Linda Himelstein, "eBay vs. Amazon.com: The Fight You Never Thought You'd See," *Business Week* (May 31, 1999,) pp. 129–140.
8. Ibid., page 131.
9. Alice Z. Cuneo, "Promotion Prize: Super Bowl Ad," *Advertising Age* (September 1, 1997), p. 29.
10. Cuneo, p. 29.
11. Bob Garfield, "Bud Lizards Electrify Super Bowl Ads," *Advertising Age* (January 26, 1998), p. 1 and 53.
12. Thomas Love, "High Tech Meets Franchising," *Nation's Business* (June 1998), p. 77–82.
13. TY Beanie Babies Official Club Web page (www.ty.com).

Chapter 15
1. Rajendra K. Srivastava, Tasadduq A. Shervani, Liam Fahey, "Market-based Assets and Shareholder Value: A Framework for Analysis," *Journal of Marketing*, 62 (January 1998), 2–18.
2. Ibid.

INDEX

ABOUT THE AUTHORS

ROLAND T. RUST is one of the world's leading experts on service and its financial impact. He is the Madison S. Wigginton Professor of Management and Director of the Center for Service Marketing at the Owen Graduate School of Management, Vanderbilt University. A prolific researcher, his articles in the areas of service marketing, customer satisfaction, advertising, and return on quality have won four best article awards. He has won career achievement awards from the American Statistical Association, the American Academy of Advertising, and the University of North Carolina at Chapel Hill. He has consulted with many leading companies worldwide, including Allstate Insurance, American Airlines, AT&T, Chase Manhattan Bank, Dow Chemical, DuPont, Federal Express, NCR, Northern Telecom, Pacific Bell, Procter & Gamble, Unilever, USAA, and many others. He serves on several corporate and non-profit boards. His six books include *Return on Quality: Measuring the Financial Impact of Your Company's Quest for Quality*, and *Service Marketing*. He is the founding editor of the *Journal of Service Research*.

VALARIE A. ZEITHAML is an eminent authority in the areas of service quality and customer value. She is Professor, Marketing Area Chair, and Sarah Graham Kenan Distinguished Scholar at the Kenan-Flagler Business School of the University of North Carolina at Chapel Hill. She devoted the last eighteen years to researching and teaching the topics of service quality and services management, for which she has received six best article awards and three teaching awards. She has conducted research in more than forty industries including banking, health care, insurance, finance, education, and information technology. She has consulted with many product and service companies including IBM, Kaiser Permanente, U.S. Steel, General Electric, John Hancock Financial Services, Aetna, AT&T, Campbell Soup, Sears, Metropolitan Life Insurance, Chase Manhattan Bank, U.S. West, Procter and Gamble, and BellSouth. She is co-author of The Free Press book, *Delivering Quality Service: Balancing Customer Perceptions and Expectations,* and a textbook, *Services Marketing,* now in its second edition.

KATHERINE N. LEMON is a recognized expert in the area of customer retention. She is on the faculty of the Harvard Business School. Professor Lemon teaches courses focusing on Dynamic Customer Relationship Management and Database Marketing and has presented her research at conferences around the world. She has conducted research in a myriad of industries, including telecommunications, interactive television, computing, retailing, the Internet, consumer products and banking. Prior to receiving her Ph.D., she held positions as Vice President of Marketing for a new high technology venture in Silicon Valley, and Senior Field Director of Marketing for a health care concern. She lectures and consults globally on the art of customer relationship management. She has consulted with and taught executives at many leading global companies, including Deloitte Consulting, Siemens Corporation, Citigroup, SkyMall Corporation, Hewlett-Packard, IBM, and Marketing 1to1/Peppers and Rogers Group. She will be joining the marketing faculty of the Wallace E. Carroll School of Management at Boston College in the fall, where she will be teaching Marketing Principles and Service Marketing.